T0244571

North to Boston

North to Boston

Life Histories from the Black Great Migration in New England

BLAKE GUMPRECHT

OXFORD
UNIVERSITY PRESS

OXFORD
UNIVERSITY PRESS

Oxford University Press is a department of the University of Oxford. It furthers
the University's objective of excellence in research, scholarship, and education
by publishing worldwide. Oxford is a registered trade mark of Oxford University
Press in the UK and certain other countries.

Published in the United States of America by Oxford University Press
198 Madison Avenue, New York, NY 10016, United States of America.

© Blake Gumprecht 2023

Library of Congress Cataloging-in-Publication Data
Names: Gumprecht, Blake, author.
Title: North to Boston : life histories from the black Great Migration in
New England / Blake Gumprecht.
Other titles: Life histories from the black Great Migration in New England
Description: New York, NY : Oxford University Press, [2023] |
Includes bibliographical references and index.
Identifiers: LCCN 2022039018 (print) | LCCN 2022039019 (ebook) |
ISBN 9780197614440 (hardback) | ISBN 9780197614464 (epub)
Subjects: LCSH: African Americans—Massachusetts—Boston—Social
conditions—20th century. | African Americans—Massachusetts—Boston—
Biography. | Migration, Internal—New England—History—20th century. |
Great Migration, ca. 1914-ca. 1970. | Charles Street African Methodist
Episcopal Church (Boston, Mass.)—Biography. | Boston (Mass.)—
Race relations—History—20th century.
Classification: LCC F73.9.B53 .G867 2023 (print) | LCC F73.9.B53 (ebook) |
DDC 305.896/073074461—dc23/eng/20220823
LC record available at https://lccn.loc.gov/2022039018
LC ebook record available at https://lccn.loc.gov/2022039019

DOI: 10.1093/oso/9780197614440.001.0001

Printed by Sheridan Books, Inc., United States of America

Contents

Preface

I began collecting the life histories featured in these pages while I was a geography professor at the University of New Hampshire and working on a book entitled "The Peopling of New England." I had been working on that project for several years. Its purpose was to tell the story of migration to New England over the last twelve thousand years. It was meant to correct the common misconception that most New Englanders are White, Anglo-Saxon, and Protestant, descendants of the earliest English settlers. In truth, New England has long been one of the most diverse regions in the United States.

That project was colossal in scope, probably too large, I now realize. I decided to leave academe in 2017 to return to my first love, journalism, and put that work aside. When I left New Hampshire, I left most of my files for that research with a friend, just in case I decided to return to it later. However, I brought one set of files with me—those about Black people in New England. Let me explain why.

I discovered while working on that book that remarkably little had been written about Black people who migrated to New England from the American South as part of what is called the Great Migration, one of the most important migration events in American history. When I realized that virtually no research had been published about Blacks who migrated to Boston from the South, I set out to find a few people to interview who made that move. Most Black southern migrants came between World War II and 1980. By the time I embarked on my research, those who were still living were quite old. I feared that if someone didn't record some of their stories before long, they would be lost forever.

I contacted a variety of people in Boston's Black community in search of people to interview—community leaders, ministers, scholars, and editors— but struggled to make any useful connections. Some of the people I contacted questioned the idea that Boston received many migrants from the South, even after I provided them statistics proving that was true.

One day, I contacted the Reverend Gregory Groover, minister of Charles Street African Methodist Episcopal Church in Roxbury. Groover's family migrated from South Carolina to New York City, so he knew all about the

Great Migration and appreciated its significance. He has been pastor of Charles Street since 1994. He knew that many of his parishioners had migrated from the South and offered to help identify a few of them who would be willing to speak to me for my project. Ultimately, he identified ten migrants who I eventually interviewed. I interviewed eight of those people in person in the Boston area. I interviewed two more people by telephone after I left New England.

I continued to try to elicit the help of people in Boston's Black community in hopes of diversifying my interview subjects, but those efforts never produced a single person to interview. Rev. Groover, however, has continued to help me. When I resumed this project after putting it aside for three years, he helped me reconnect with some of the people I interviewed originally and found a few more people who had migrated who were willing to speak with me. He also helped connect me with family and friends of some of my subjects so that I could learn more about their lives. He even took a few photos for me.

This book would not exist without the help of Rev. Groover. I owe him a significant debt. Thank you, Greg. Thank you.

When I began conducting interviews in 2015, I was immediately inspired by the lives of the migrants I met and realized the value of what I was doing. That microscale examination of one element of New England's migration history appealed to me more than the macroscale focus of the larger planned book. I prefer working at smaller scales because that makes it possible to examine a subject in greater depth. I also like to learn about individual lives, particularly those of ordinary people about whom too little is written. I brought my Great Migration interviews with me when I left New Hampshire, along with all my research files about Black people in New England. I thought perhaps I could write a separate book based on those interviews in my spare time or when I retired. It seemed like a much more manageable project than the larger book for which the interviews were originally conducted.

An unexpected opportunity to do that came in 2020 when the coronavirus pandemic hit. I had recently moved to a small town in Texas to buy a weekly newspaper business, but had a change of heart. I was looking for work when the world shut down because of the virus. I was frozen in place. Newspapers, like many companies, stopped hiring. I couldn't do anything or go anywhere.

I was living in a town where I knew nobody and where there is little to do. I tried to figure out a way to occupy my time and remembered my Great

Migration interviews. I decided the time was ideal to turn those interviews into this book. I ended up doing considerable new research. I interviewed two additional people about their lives. I conducted follow-up interviews with most of the people featured in the book to understand their stories more completely. Work on this book gave me something to do and helped me retain my sanity during a difficult time.

I am proud to present these stories and to be able to preserve them for the future. I think they help us understand an important but largely unknown aspect of New England's history. I am deeply grateful to the ten individuals featured in this book who were willing to share their lives with me. Thank you Charles, Thomas, and Lucy. Thanks Ollie, Elizabeth, Willie, and Geraldine. Thank you Barbra, Al, and Elta. I enjoyed getting to know each one of you and greatly appreciate your help.

Thanks also to my editor at Oxford University Press, Nancy Toff, who more than anyone recognized the worth of my project and provided many helpful suggestions for making it better. Thanks to Dave McBride, also at Oxford, an old publishing ally, who told Nancy about my manuscript. Thanks to Zara Cannon-Mohammed and Leslie Johnson, who shepherded my project through production, and Richard Isomaki for copyediting.

Thanks to family members and friends of the individuals featured for their assistance, especially Danné Davis, Marquis Davis, Laniel Pittman, Stephanie Denise Castro, Alfreda Harris, Karl Hobbs, and Jason Murray.

Thanks to Brian Halley of University of Massachusetts Press, Debbie Gershenowitz of the University of North Carolina Press, and Gayatri Patnaik of Beacon Press for their interest and help. Thanks also to four anonymous reviews at Oxford and UMass for their support and recommendations, which helped me improve the book.

Thanks for other assistance to Alison Barnet, Marta Crilly, Susan Dominus, Earnest Green, James N. Gregory, Robert C. Hayden, Michael Haynes, Mary Hoffschwelle, James Jennings, Andrew Lichtenstein, Al Martin, Jean McGuire, Omar M. McRoberts, Jason Murray, Jim Peterson, Leslie Picca, Jenna Savage, Debra Thomas, Richard Vacca, Kathleen van Wormer, Jason Morgan Ward, Skippy White, Rudy Winston, and Robert H. Woodrum.

Thanks to all the authors whose work informed mine, and Open Library, an invaluable resource for a writer when you are living far from a research library, particularly during a pandemic. If bricks and mortar libraries are allowed to exist, Open Library should be permitted to continue doing what it does.

1

The Great Migration in New England

They came from places like Morven, North Carolina; Birmingham, Alabama; Quitman, Mississippi; and Sun, Louisiana. They left cities, small towns, and rural areas. They traveled by train, bus, and automobile. They fled racism, limited opportunity, and hopelessness. They moved north in pursuit of better jobs, equal treatment, and the promise of greater freedom.

One sought to escape the memory of being raped by her employer. Another was tired of harassment by police. A third refused to work as a domestic. One feared he would have died a violent death if he had remained in the land of his birth. Others moved for comparatively mundane reasons: like migrants throughout history, they sought to improve their lives.

Most came alone. Some came as part of married couples. A few brought children. They knew not what they would find. They hoped only that it would be better than what they left behind.

They were but a few of tens of thousands of Black people who migrated to Boston from the American South in the twentieth century. They were part of the Great Migration, which transformed urban areas nationwide, including Boston and other cities in New England.

Between World War I and 1980, more than six million Black people left the South and moved to urban areas in the North and West.[1] The Black population of northern cities grew tremendously as a result. Detroit's Black population increased 1,300 percent, New York City added 1.7 million Black residents, and Black people came to make up nearly 40 percent of Chicago's population.[2] The Black exodus from the South dramatically altered the geography of Black America. In 1910, nearly nine out of every ten Black people lived in the rural South, a legacy of slavery and emancipation, which gave them their freedom but little else. By 1980, nearly half of Black people in the United States lived outside the South, most of them in cities.[3]

Much has been written about the Great Migration and its impact on cities such as Chicago and Detroit, but almost nothing has been written about its history in Boston and New England. Books and articles about the Great Migration rarely mention Boston or cities such as Hartford that also saw

North to Boston. Blake Gumprecht, Oxford University Press. © Blake Gumprecht 2023.
DOI: 10.1093/oso/9780197614440.003.0001

significant Black migration from the South. Contemporary authors writing about New England have largely ignored the subject.[4] A few scholars have written about the migration of Black southerners to Connecticut, but most of their work has been published in journals and books with limited reach.[5] Research about Black Boston rarely mentions the Great Migration, except in passing, and underplays its significance.

New England has likely received less attention than other areas because fewer Black southerners moved to the region than elsewhere, but the volume of Black migration from the South was still sizable and its impact was great. Significant Black migration to New England from the South began earlier than elsewhere. The Black population in the region nearly doubled between the end of the Civil War and 1900. New England added another 750,000 Black people in the twentieth century. Not all that growth was the result of migration from the South—the region has also attracted many Black migrants from the Caribbean and Africa—but it was the most important factor.[6]

By 1980, when Black southern migration slowed, one-third of US-born Black people living in New England had been born in the South. The number of southern-born Black people increased from fewer than 5,000 before the Civil War to more than 144,000.[7] An even greater number of Black people living in New England today are the children or grandchildren of southern migrants, so statistics on the number of Black people born in the South understate the impact of the Great Migration. The descendants of migrants carry forward the culture and lifestyles their parents and grandparents brought from the South, magnifying their influence on Black life in the region.

Black migration from the South was greatest during and after World War II, just as it was nationally. Many historians divide the Great Migration into two parts, separated by the Great Depression of the 1930s, which discouraged people from moving because conditions were bad everywhere. World War II inspired Black people once again to leave the South. The war created job opportunities as northern industries expanded production to supply the war effort. The war also caused labor shortages, because many US workers joined the military, and fighting overseas largely halted immigration from Europe.

The number of southern-born Black people in New England increased 72 percent during the 1940s, more than in any other decade of the twentieth century. The volume of migration grew after the war, as earlier migrants encouraged family members and friends to join them. Between 1950 and 1980, the number of southern-born Black people living in the region nearly tripled.[8] Nearly every major city in southern New England was transformed by Black migration. Between 1860 and 1980, Boston's Black population grew by nearly 125,000 people. Hartford in 1910 was home to fewer than 2,000 Black residents, but the Connecticut capital added 44,000 Black people by the end of the Great Migration. Black residents now make up at least one-quarter of the population in five large New England cities—Boston, Bridgeport, Hartford, New Haven, and Springfield.[9]

Migration and the growth of Black populations changed the region's cities in a variety of ways. Black neighborhoods expanded to meet the newcomers' housing needs. Black-owned businesses proliferated. Black churches increased in number and variety. Black culture flourished and Black social organizations were established. Black people fought to gain greater political clout and Black issues became central to political debates.

Why did urban areas in New England receive fewer Black migrants from the South than other northern cities? Some have suggested that White New Englanders actively worked to keep Black people out, but the true reason probably has more to do with geography.[10] In 1940, the sociologist Albert Stouffer proposed a theory of "intervening opportunities" to help explain why migrants choose one destination over others. Stouffer argued that migrants are less likely to move to a place if they encounter an intervening opportunity on the way to that place. In other words, most migrants will stop at the first destination that provides whatever they are seeking.[11] New England urban areas were at a disadvantage in attracting southern migrants because Black people traveling north along the Atlantic Seaboard encountered several large cities—Washington, then Baltimore, Philadelphia, and New York—before they would reach New England. Many migrants chose to stop in one of those urban areas rather than continuing northward.

More Black southern migrants moved to Connecticut than any other New England state, which demonstrates the validity of Stouffer's theory. By 1980, there were more than 76,000 southern-born Black residents in Connecticut. Relatively few Black southerners migrated to the largest cities in the three northernmost New England states.[12] Within New England, Boston was somewhat of an exception to that pattern because it is the largest urban area in the region and thus provides greater opportunities than smaller cities. Its pull was stronger than midsize cities such as Hartford or New Haven farther south.

This book focuses on Black migration to the city of Boston because it is the largest urban area in New England, because it contains the greatest concentration of Black residents and attracted more Black migrants than any other city in the region, and because little has been written about the twentieth-century migration of Black southerners to the city. Other cities in the Boston area, such as Cambridge, also received many Black migrants, but they won't be examined here.

Following a short history of Black migration to Boston from the South, this book will take an unconventional approach. I will tell the story of the Great Migration through the life histories of ten people who came to Boston from the South between 1943 and 1969 (the dates in the chapter titles are the years of their migration). Each of those individuals will be the subject of one chapter. The chapters are written as short biographies that tell the story of each person from birth to the present.

Some may ask whether these ten people are representative of the many Black southerners who moved to Boston. In statistical terms, they probably are not. All did reasonably well. They were employed as teachers, factory workers, welders, security guards, salespeople, and civil servants. None achieved fame or fortune. They are regular folk, who have lived largely private lives, experiencing triumphs but also difficulties. They came from six southern states. Most followed family members to Boston. They share one characteristic other than their southern roots: they have all belonged to the same church, Charles Street African Methodist Episcopal Church in Roxbury. That reflects the way connections were made. The individuals featured were not chosen in any strategic way based on a desired set of characteristics. I did not want to manipulate the book's message in that way.

Charles Street AME is the one of the oldest Black churches in Boston. Originally named the First African Methodist Episcopal Church, it was organized on the north slope of Beacon Hill in 1818. Its first permanent home was on Anderson Street, a short walk from the Massachusetts State House. In the lead-up to the Civil War, the church was the frequent site for abolitionist meetings and rallies led by antislavery activists such as William Lloyd Garrison, Frederick Douglass, and Sojourner Truth. It led local opposition to the 1850 Fugitive Slave Law and was a stop on the Underground Railroad. After the war, the church grew too large for its original building and in 1876 relocated a few blocks away to Charles Street, adopting its present name. It remained there until 1939, when it moved to its current home on Warren Street in Roxbury. By then, Boston's Black population had shifted away from

Beacon Hill and few of its members still lived in the area. It was the last Black institution to leave Beacon Hill.[13]

Although the people featured in these pages have belonged to one church, their stories are illustrative of the experiences of Black people everywhere who left the South. We learn what their lives were like before they moved north. We discover the factors that motivated them to migrate to Boston and come to appreciate how important family connections were in influencing their decisions. We follow their lives after they arrived in Boston, became settled, had families, and moved from short-term jobs into long-term careers. We learn why most chose to remain in Boston's Black community even when they had the means to live elsewhere. We hear about their encounters with racism in Boston, conditions they hoped they'd left behind in the South. We see the adjustments they have made, whether their hopes were fulfilled, and how their lives were changed by their moves. Their stories are invaluable for understanding the Great Migration.

The life histories in this book are based primarily on my interviews with the people who are featured. I interviewed most of my subjects three or more times between 2015 and 2021. Because none have been public figures, there are few other sources for reconstructing their lives, though I have occasionally talked to family and friends. I chose to rely on the migrants themselves because they know their lives better than anyone else. I recognize that memory can be faulty, particularly when it extends over seven or eight decades. In addition, we all shape the stories we tell about ourselves to present the view that we prefer and sometimes leave out details that are contrary to that perspective. Nevertheless, I believe that the people featured were honest in telling me about their lives.

The story of migration is the story of people—individuals who risk everything in hopes of finding a better life. The best way to tell that story, in my view, is through the lives of the migrants themselves. I have chosen to let those stories stand alone because they showcase how the Great Migration affected ordinary people. Devoting each chapter to one person enables us to more clearly hear the voices of the people featured than would be possible if their stories were integrated with others in a more conventional narrative. Seeing their lives whole also enables us to better appreciate the long-term impacts of migration.

The written record favors those who have led unusual and extraordinary lives. Ordinary people are rarely written about and seldom document their own experiences, so that our body of knowledge is incomplete and one-sided, and presents a distorted view of reality. Everybody's life is different. Everyone has a story to tell. Each of those stories is worth telling because they help us better understand the human experience. The stories of individual lives, even if unexceptional, are compelling if told creatively.

This is the first book, or serious research of any kind, about the Great Migration's impacts on Boston. It expands our knowledge of the subject beyond the cities that have been the focus of previous research. It reveals a hidden aspect of the city's history and shines a spotlight on a singularly important event in the making of Black Boston, yet one that is unknown to many of the city's residents, or underappreciated. It also amplifies the voices of ordinary Black Bostonians, whose voices are seldom heard in the public sphere.

Although most historians date the beginning of the Great Migration to the years of World War I, substantial movement of Black people to Boston from the South began earlier than that, likely owing to the city's reputation as a center for the abolitionist movement and its history as a sanctuary for people who fled slavery.

The first Black people in Boston were brought there as slaves during the colonial era, perhaps as early as 1624, but certainly by 1638. It was not until 1783 that slavery was abolished in Massachusetts, when the state Supreme Court ruled in favor of an enslaved person who sued for his freedom. Boston did not attract many Black people before the Civil War, probably because it was not a major stop on the Underground Railroad and offered a limited range of jobs for them. The city's Black population grew slowly in the first part of the nineteenth century. Boston had fewer than twenty-three hundred Black residents in 1860, not counting escaped slaves who avoided census takers.[14]

Before the Civil War, most Black people in Boston were employed as servants and lived on the north side of Beacon Hill, then considered part of the West End, near the homes of the wealthy White families where they worked. White people called the area "Nigger Hill." This grew to be the largest area of Black settlement because it was also convenient to the food markets of Faneuil Hall and nearby docks, where many Black laborers worked. Black residences were concentrated near Joy and Phillips Streets. Many Black people lived in ramshackle wooden houses, which were described as "the most miserable huts in the city." Cambridge Street on Beacon Hill was lined with businesses catering to the Black population. Even after Black residents began leaving the area, a Boston newspaper in 1904 observed that the street "looks most like a business thoroughfare in a southern city. Out of every ten people you pass . . . about eight of them are Black."[15]

The movement of Black people to Boston increased dramatically after the emancipation of slaves and the end of the Civil War. The number of Black people living in Boston more than doubled from 1860 to 1880, and doubled again by 1900. Most of that growth was due to migration from the South. Writing in 1914, the sociologist and settlement house worker John Daniels observed that Boston experienced "a veritable tidal wave" of migration by Black southerners following the war. The city added nearly ten thousand Black residents in the last four decades of the nineteenth century. That number may not seem large, but it was relative to the size of the Black population before the war. As migration grew, the share of Black residents who had born in the South rose dramatically, from 29 percent in 1860 to 59 percent in 1900.[16]

Some of those migrants came as part of organized efforts to resettle ex-slaves in the North. The Freedmen's Bureau, a federal government agency, transported 1,083 ex-slaves from the South to the Boston area in two years. During one two-week period in 1870, a Boston employer of cooks, maids, and other servants brought 250 Black people from Richmond, Virginia, to the city.[17]

Most Black people who migrated to Boston came initially from the upper South, traveling to New England on coastal ships or later by train on the Seaboard Air Line and railroads that formed the Atlantic Coast Line. In 1900, 50 percent of Black southerners in Boston had been born in Virginia; 23 percent were born in North Carolina. Most Black southern migrants to Boston came not from farms and rural areas, but from cities. The historian Elizabeth Hafkin Pleck found that two-thirds of Black Virginians who married in Boston in the 1890s came from Richmond and other cities in that state.[18]

Boston was far ahead of the South and most other cities in its treatment of Black people. Massachusetts in 1783 granted taxpaying Black men the right to vote, and in 1839 it repealed laws against interracial marriage, legalizing a process already practiced. In 1855, Boston abolished its segregated schools after a long boycott by Black families. A decade later Massachusetts outlawed discrimination against Black people in public places. A year after that, two Black men from Boston were elected to the Massachusetts legislature, among the first Black people elected to any state legislature. In the 1870s, a Black physician was elected to the Boston School Committee and a Black barber won a seat on the Boston Common Council. Boston hired its first Black schoolteacher in 1890.[19]

The *Boston Sunday Herald* called the city "a paradise for Negroes" in a 1904 article that took up one full page in the newspaper. Such an article might be easily dismissed as local boosterism and was almost certainly penned by a White writer. But one of the first American magazines devoted to Black culture, the *Colored American Magazine*, founded in Boston in 1900, reprinted the article and disseminated its message to a national audience. William H. Lewis, who migrated to Massachusetts from Virginia for college, later graduated from Harvard Law School, and became the first Black US assistant attorney general, told the article's author, "Here in Boston the Negro enjoys without a doubt greater liberty than anywhere else in the country."[20]

As migration from the South intensified, Black residents began to leave Beacon Hill, pushed out by deteriorating housing and rising rents. Most of the southern migrants who arrived after the Civil War settled initially in the South End, which was convenient to the railroads and hotels where many of them worked. Three Black churches developed in the area, two of them moving there from Beacon Hill. Ebenezer Baptist, founded in 1871 by formerly enslaved people from Virginia, became the only church composed almost exclusively of Black southern migrants. By 1880, two-thirds of all southern-born Black people in Boston lived in the South End. The Black population on Beacon Hill gradually disappeared.[21]

Black southern migrants then spread into adjacent lower Roxbury, the flow increasing dramatically after the turn of the century. By 1910, more than five thousand Black people lived in one ward in lower Roxbury, nearly 40 percent of all Black people in the city. The South End and lower Roxbury were diverse neighborhoods at the time. Both had long been receiving areas for immigrants, and about one-third of residents were foreign born. Irish immigrants and their children were most numerous, followed by English-speaking Canadians and Russian Jews. Black residents lived on the same streets and often in the same buildings with White residents. Black children attended integrated schools. At the turn of the century, the Franklin School in the South End had 200 Irish, 170 "American," 121 Jewish, and 61 "colored" students, plus 124 of other nationalities.[22]

Tremont Street in lower Roxbury became the hub of Black business activity in the early 1900s. In one three-block stretch, there was a Black hotel, a Black bank, a Black undertaker, a Black-owned pharmacy, a Black beauty school,

Thomas Lucas, a Black migrant from Virginia, operated the Southern Dining Room restaurant on Tremont Street in lower Roxbury in the early 1900s. The street became a hub of Black business activity. Reproduced from National Negro Business League convention program, 1915.

a Black-run print shop, and other businesses catering to Black people. The Melbourne Hotel was one of three Black hotels in the city. The Eureka Co-Operative Bank, started in 1910, advertised that it was "the only bank in the East owned and operated by Colored People." The Southern Dining Room, operated by Thomas Lucas, a Black migrant from Virginia, promoted itself as "cool, clean, commodious." The B. F. Stark grocery sold "Southern Products."[23]

The rapid increase of Boston's Black population nurtured Black community development. By 1900, there were 197 Black-owned businesses in the city. Black churches increased in number and size. Southern migrants made up more than half the membership at four Black churches. One Black church, Calvary Baptist, tripled its membership in seven years. Six Black women formed the Harriet Tubman House in the South End to "assist working girls" from the South. In 1901, William Monroe Trotter launched the *Boston Guardian*, which became an influential Black weekly newspaper.[24]

Such information suggests that life for Boston's Black residents was better than it was. The *Herald* article said that the city offered Black people "the same political, civil and educational privileges which it offers to the White man," but that was an overstatement.[25] Black people in Boston were not treated equally by most measures. Furthermore, as the abolitionist spirit in Boston faded and Jim Crow swept over the country, the treatment of Black people in the city deteriorated. Boston's largest immigrant group, the Irish, resented the Black migrants because they competed directly with them for jobs. Irish contempt for Black people has bedeviled race relations in Boston to the present day, though certainly not all Irish are racist and not all racists in the city are Irish.[26]

Black workers in the late nineteenth and early twentieth centuries were shut out of better-paying occupations, most worked in menial jobs, and they showed little improvement in economic status for decades. They were often paid less than White laborers for the same work. Few Black residents were able to buy their own homes and they were largely restricted to a few neighborhoods by housing discrimination. The areas where most Black people lived were unhealthy slums. In 1900, Black children were nearly twice as likely as those of Irish immigrants to die before they reached their first birthday.[27]

White people in positions of power, meanwhile, sought to reduce the political influence of the growing Black population. In 1895, the city of Boston redrew its election districts, dividing the Black population and making it more difficult for Black people to be elected. Fewer Black candidates won election to city positions as a result, and not a single Black person was elected to the Boston City Council between 1908 and 1949. Black people also stopped winning election to the Massachusetts legislature. Between 1902 and 1947, not a single Black candidate was elected to the state senate or house of representatives.[28]

"The North is not all it was supposed to be," wrote the sociologist John Daniels.[29] Scholars agree that prejudice against Black people in Boston grew beginning in the late nineteenth century. There was a dramatic increase in residential segregation. The rate of interracial marriage, which had once been comparatively high in the city, declined significantly. Hotels, restaurants, and candy stores stopped serving Black customers, though they came up with false reasons for doing that. Even churches stopped welcoming Black worshipers. The most serious discrimination came in employment, and one observer suggested that better jobs were open to Black workers in the South than in Boston. Remarkably, some Black business owners refused to hire Black workers for fear of losing their White customers. "The color line is drawn in Boston—silently and courteously," wrote *Zion's Herald*, "but positively and rigorously."[30]

Some blamed the southern migrants for altering White attitudes. The newcomers were different from northern-born Black people, some of whom had lived in Boston for decades. They lived differently. They acted differently. They talked differently. Whites reacted negatively to those differences. "Most of them were utterly uneducated," Daniels wrote. "Nearly all of them were more or less uncouth, many were ragged and dirty, and a large proportion were crude, dull, and indeed brutish in appearance." Faced with the "black horde," he said, White residents "recoiled." Daniels was a White sociologist, paternalistic and racist, but the Black minister J. M. Henderson, pastor of Charles Street AME, also decried the negative impact of the migrants on Boston's Black community. Describing southern migrants as "the lower type," he said they were causing trouble by "making noise" about discrimination in the city. "Had no colored people from the outside come to New England," he said, "there would be no disquietude here."[31]

As Henderson's comments suggest, the movement of Black southerners to Boston also created divisions within the city's Black community. Those divides have persisted to the present. Northern-born Black residents, some of whom traced their New England roots to the colonial era, often looked down on the migrants. The most successful among them were nicknamed the Black Brahmins, after Boston's wealthy English elite. Northern-born Black residents lived apart from southern migrants. They were better educated. They dressed differently and had a different demeanor. Many had relatively light skin. They mimicked White behavior and often attended White churches. They spoke like New Englanders.

W. E. B. Du Bois, the leading Black intellectual of the era, was born and raised in Great Barrington, Massachusetts, in the western part of the state, and became the first Black person to earn a doctorate at Harvard University. He wrote that in northern cities there were "two classes of people, the descendants of Northern free negroes and the freed immigrants from the South." He called southern migrants "largely ignorant and unused to city life" and said they posed the "gravest" danger to Black society in northern cities. He wrote that the "influx of low characters" in Boston "made the problem of home life among the better class of negroes . . . difficult."[32]

The migration of Black southerners to Boston slowed after 1900, even though conditions for Black people worsened across the South after Reconstruction collapsed, Black voters were disenfranchised, Jim Crow laws were enacted throughout the region, and violence against Black people increased. World War I stimulated an unprecedented wave of Black migration from the South, which is why most historians designate that time as the beginning of the Great Migration. But the new surge largely bypassed Boston.

Nearly a half million Black people fled the South for northern cities during the 1910s. Multiple factors created labor shortages in northern industries during the war years and inspired employers to send recruiters to the South to entice Black people to come north. Expanded wartime production created new jobs, many White workers had joined the military, and the war halted immigration.[33] The Black population of many northern cities grew rapidly during the war years. Detroit's Black community grew the fastest: from 1910 to 1920, the number of southern-born Black people in the city grew tenfold. Chicago's Black population more than doubled, and New York City gained more than sixty thousand Black residents.[34]

Boston's Black population, in contrast, grew modestly in the first two decades of the twentieth century, the city adding fewer than five thousand Black residents. From 1910 to 1920, the number of southern-born Black people living in Boston actually declined. Some of the Black newcomers were immigrants who came from islands in the English-speaking Caribbean, especially Barbados, Jamaica, and Montserrat, adding a third element to Boston's Black community. Although Boston had a small West Indian community dating to the late nineteenth century, West Indian immigration grew on the eve World War I, when the Boston-based United Fruit Co. began offering passenger service on ships from islands where it owned or managed fruit plantations.[35]

Boston's declining number of Black southerners does not mean, however, that migration to the city from the South stopped. A more likely explanation is that the city had fewer southern-born Black residents because earlier migrants had died, and some migrants had left the city. The loss of Black migrants was likely greater than the number of new arrivals.

There is no precise way to measure the volume of Black southern migration because the US government does not keep statistics about internal migrants in the same way that it counts immigrants. One way to measure Black migration is to calculate the difference between the number of Black people born in the South, as measured in the decennial census, from one census year to the next. But such a calculation undercounts actual migration because in any decade some earlier migrants die, while others leave. Migration experts have devised methods to approximate migration flows using data on all three subjects, but they are imperfect measures.[36]

Unlike Boston, other New England cities experienced significant Black migration from the South during World War I. Hartford's Black population more than doubled from 1910 to 1920. Many Black people who moved to Connecticut came initially to work on tobacco farms near Hartford, and then relocated to the city when they grew dissatisfied with farm work. Connecticut tobacco growers joined with the National Urban League to recruit Black college students in the South to work temporarily in tobacco fields during summer months. They included future civil rights leader Martin Luther King Jr. But tobacco farmers also sent recruiters to the South to obtain permanent workers. More than three thousand Black southerners came to the Hartford area in a single year. Most of the new migrants were from Georgia.[37]

Why didn't Boston attract many Black migrants during World War I? Writing in 1920, Emmett Scott said that the city "has not . . . at any time afforded any great variety of occupations for the peasant class of negro." He observed that, while there were industries in Boston that added workers during the war, "barriers prevented negroes in large numbers from entering them." He didn't explain what those barriers were.[38] Perhaps word had spread that Boston was not as tolerant as its image suggested, which may have discouraged Black people from migrating to the city. Studying census returns from 1880 and 1900, the historian Pleck found that few southern-born Black males who lived in Boston in 1880 remained in the city twenty years later. Four out of five had either left Boston or died, which suggests that many may have been disheartened by what they found in the city.[39]

Black southern migration to Boston remained modest during the 1920s. The city added fewer than two hundred Black southerners during the decade. Migration slowed considerably across the country during the Great Depression. The volume of migrants, as estimated by the historian James Gregory, dropped by half. Boston gained about a thousand southern-born Black residents during the thirties.[40]

World War II changed everything. Demand for workers in cities in the North and West drove Black migration to unprecedented levels. The reasons were the same as they had been during World War I. Industries suffered labor shortages because they lost workers to the military, immigration from Europe largely stopped, and factories accelerated production to aid the war effort. Black workers who left the South helped satisfy those labor needs.[41] Cities in the North and West, including Boston, experienced their greatest surge in

Black worker at the Boston Naval Shipyard, 1946. The shipyard added more than forty-six thousand workers during World War II, many of them minorities. Millions of Black migrants came north during the war years, drawn by the availability of industrial jobs. First Naval District, US Navy.

Black migration during the war years. Nearly 1.5 million Black people fled the South during the 1940s, three times as many as moved in the previous decade. Boston's Black population and the number of southern-born Black people living in the city nearly doubled in ten years. The city gained nine thousand southern-born Black residents. In 1950, people born in the South made up 42 percent of Black residents in the city.[42]

Defense industries increased production, and other companies retooled to help in the war effort. The Boston Naval Shipyard produced dozens of ships for the military and added more than forty-six thousand workers during the war, hiring many minorities and women. Gillette, the Boston-based razor-blade manufacturer, began making parts for military aircraft and was ordered by the US government to reserve all its razors and blades for soldiers.[43]

"Factories were pleading for manpower," the *Boston Globe* reported. "There were plenty of good jobs available."[44]

World War II also helped boost Black migration after the war. Many Black men first experienced life outside the segregated South while they were serving in the military. What they saw inspired some of them to leave the region permanently once they were discharged. Many Black soldiers passed through Fort Devens, an army base in the Boston suburbs, which had sixty-five thousand soldiers in uniform at peak activity. The military was still segregated at the time, but an all-Black unit, the 366th Infantry Regiment, was based there. Countless Black soldiers who served in Massachusetts chose to return to Boston to live after the war.[45]

The rising Black population stimulated growth in all areas of Boston's Black community. The Black residential district expanded outward from the South End and lower Roxbury to upper Roxbury and beyond. By 1950, there were more than fifty Black churches in Boston. Some, such as Charles Street AME, relocated to be nearer to the new centers of the Black population. Black people formed social service organizations, such as Roxbury's Freedom House. Black-oriented businesses spread along Tremont and Washington Streets in the South End and Roxbury. Black diners ate barbecue at Slade's and southern cooking at Estelle's. They listened to jazz at the Hi-Hat Club and Pioneer Club, a private after-hours club where Duke Ellington and Louis Armstrong once jammed until 6:00 a.m.[46]

Boston's expanding Black community made a powerful impression on a young Malcolm Little, who later became the radical civil rights leader Malcolm X. Little moved to Boston from Michigan in 1940 to live with his half-sister, Ella Little-Collins, who had migrated to the city from Georgia. He was fourteen years old and had dropped out of school after the eighth grade. He lived in Boston for seven years (and later returned to help found the city's first Nation of Islam temple). Little and his sister resided in the Sugar Hill section of upper Roxbury, an area that was home to many of Boston's northern-born Black elites. But lower Roxbury, where most southern Blacks lived and socialized, was the part of Boston that opened the eyes of the young Malcolm X.

"No physical move in my life has been more pivotal or profound in its repercussions," Malcolm X wrote in his autobiography. "I didn't know the world contained as many negroes as I saw thronging downtown Roxbury at night. Neon lights, nightclubs, pool halls, bars, the cars they drove! Restaurants made the streets smell—rich, greasy, down-home Black cooking!

Jukeboxes blared Erskine Hawkins, Duke Ellington, Cootie Williams, dozens of others. I saw for the first time occasional White-Black couples strolling around arm in arm. I saw churches for Black people such as I had never seen."[47]

The Black social environment in Boston may have been blossoming, but Black people still struggled to gain political influence in the city, and White political leaders took actions that assured they would not. In 1949, Boston revised its charter to change how city council members were elected. Previously, councilors were elected to represent geographically defined wards, but after the revision, all councilors were elected "at large" to represent the entire city. In 1950, Black people made up only 5 percent of the city's population, making it difficult for them to win citywide elections. After the charter revision, no Black candidate was able to win election to the city council for nearly twenty years.[48] "Everything was being done to keep Blacks out of office," Michael Haynes, a prominent Black minister, pastor of Twelfth Baptist Church, later said.[49]

Boston's economy, which had been stagnant for three decades, expanded greatly after World War II as the city and region developed into a high-tech center, partly based on research begun under wartime military contracts. Route 128, the ring road that encircles Boston, became known as "The Technology Highway." Waltham-based Raytheon became one of the largest aerospace and defense companies in the world. Computer companies Digital Equipment Corp. and Wang Laboratories employed more than thirty-five thousand workers. MIT professors started dozens of companies to market their innovations. The presence of world-class hospitals and university researchers stimulated the emergence of a biotechnology sector and enlargement of the healthcare industry. Regional growth created demand for workers in all sectors of the economy, which encouraged the continued migration of Black southerners to the city.[50]

Between 1950 and 1980, the city's Black population tripled, and its number of southern-born Black people doubled. The Black population in the metropolitan area, including the suburbs, quadrupled to more than 160,000. Not all the Black population growth could be attributed to migration from the South. The city also saw increasing Black immigration from the Caribbean and Africa, especially Barbados, Jamaica, and the Cape Verde islands.[51]

The source areas for Black migrants from the South changed as transportation evolved. As cars, buses, and airplanes replaced railroads and ships as

An unidentified band performs at the Hi-Hat Club on Columbus Avenue in the South End, circa 1950. The South End and lower Roxbury became the focus of Black social activity as Boston's Black population grew due to migration from the South. Photograph by Winifred Irish Hall; used with permission, Northeastern University Archives and Special Collections.

the principal means of travel, migrants came from further away and from a greater variety of places than before. By 1980, nearly one-fifth of southern-born Black people living in Boston had been born in Georgia, which provided more than any other state. But nearly as many came from Alabama, North Carolina, and South Carolina. Virginia was no longer one of the top suppliers. Significant numbers of migrants came from as far away as Mississippi, Louisiana, and Texas.[52]

The Black southern migrants who arrived after World War II needed housing for themselves and their families. The Black district expanded southward across Roxbury, then to Dorchester, and eventually to Mattapan and Hyde Park. By 1980, four out of every five Black residents of Boston lived in those four neighborhoods. The South End's Black population declined, as lower-income residents were pushed out by urban renewal and gentrification.[53]

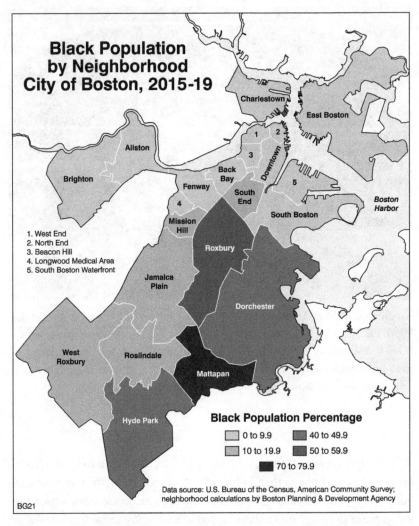

Black Population by Neighborhood City of Boston, 2015-19

Charlestown
East Boston
Allston
Brighton
Back Bay
Fenway
South End
South Boston
Boston Harbor
Mission Hill
Roxbury
Jamaica Plain
Dorchester
West Roxbury
Roslindale
Mattapan
Hyde Park

1. West End
2. North End
3. Beacon Hill
4. Longwood Medical Area
5. South Boston Waterfront

Black Population Percentage

- 0 to 9.9
- 10 to 19.9
- 40 to 49.9
- 50 to 59.9
- 70 to 79.9

Data source: U.S. Bureau of the Census, American Community Survey; neighborhood calculations by Boston Planning & Development Agency

BG21

Black migration from the South transformed Boston's racial and ethnic geography. By 1980, four-fifths of Black residents lived in just four neighborhoods—Roxbury, Dorchester, Mattapan, and Hyde Park. That is still true today. Map by Blake Gumprecht.

As Black residents left the South End and Black migrants from the South arrived in the city, Roxbury and Dorchester became the heart of Black Boston. In 1950, Roxbury was still three-quarters White, but over the next three decades the racial makeup of the neighborhood reversed. By 1980,

Black residents made up 80 percent of the population. Urban renewal and slum clearance in Roxbury during the 1960s reduced the housing supply there, forcing Black people to move further south to Dorchester. The Black population continued to grow, causing residents to seek new areas to live. Black people began moving to Mattapan in large numbers in the seventies and Hyde Park in the eighties.

Before Black people began moving to the four neighborhoods where most live today, residents of those areas were primarily Jewish and Irish Catholic. Most areas where Black people settled initially had been Jewish districts, but Black residents eventually displaced Irish Catholics from many areas, too. A few Catholic areas were able to resist racial turnover. The historian and political scientist Gerald Gamm has convincingly argued that Jewish people experiencing racial change in their neighborhoods were more likely to leave those areas than Catholics because their chief institutions, synagogues, are movable. Catholic parishes are not. They are territorially defined institutions and Catholics living in them are anchored to those neighborhoods by their churches. They were less willing to leave and more likely to stay and fight.[54]

Dorchester added thirty-five thousand Black residents during the 1960s as Black settlement spread south along Blue Hill Avenue, once the main thoroughfare of Jewish Boston. Block after block, Black people moved in and Jewish and other White residents moved out. "The process of change was relentless," Gamm observed. From Dorchester, Black settlement moved south along Blue Hill to predominantly Jewish Mattapan. More than ten thousand Black residents moved to Mattapan in the 1970s, changing it to a majority-Black neighborhood. That process was aided by a city-organized program to increase lending to minority homebuyers, the Boston Banks Urban Renewal Group program. Mattapan became home to middle-class Black people who could afford to buy homes, while incomes in Roxbury and Dorchester were lower, poverty was more prevalent, and most residents rented.

Upper Roxbury and the north Dorchester were already declining neighborhoods when Black people started moving to them in large numbers. Some of the housing was a hundred years old. Most of it had been built between 1870 and 1900, as streetcar lines were extended outward from the city center. Many of the houses had already filtered down from the Boston businessmen who were the original owners to the Jewish middle class and then to working-class Jews, who did not have enough money to maintain or restore the aging structures. By the 1950s, when Jewish people were leaving these areas for good, much of the housing was rundown and in need of repair. Some areas were on their way to becoming slums. In 1960, 41 percent of housing units in Roxbury and 18 percent in north Dorchester were classified as "dilapidated" or "deteriorated."[55]

As Roxbury, Dorchester, and Mattapan became Black neighborhoods, Blue Hill Avenue evolved into the commercial spine of the Black community. For decades, it had been the main street of Jewish Boston, nicknamed "Jew Hill Avenue." Stretching four miles from Roxbury south to the Boston city limits, it had been lined with kosher butchers, fish markets, delicatessens, bakeries making challah and other Jewish specialties, and Jewish wedding halls. Gradually, Jewish merchants followed their customers to the suburbs and were replaced by businesses and institutions catering to Black residents—barbecue and soul food restaurants, Black barbershops and beauty salons, record stores selling R & B and jazz, and storefront churches. It also became home to several Black civil rights organizations. The Black Panthers took over a former dry-cleaning shop. "Once, it was a world peopled with the Yiddish and their offspring," Alan Lupo wrote in the Boston Globe in 1969. "Today, it is more Mississippi than Minsk."[56]

The expansion of Black Boston gave rise to racial conflicts within the city. As often happens when racial transition is sudden, long-term residents reacted angrily to the changes. That was especially true in Catholic parts of Roxbury and Dorchester. Black residents were attacked or harassed when they moved into those areas. Violence was most common after a federal judge in 1974 required Boston to implement busing to desegregate its schools, which inflamed racial tensions throughout the city. White youths threw stones at the cars of Black families looking for homes. Arsonists burned the garage and car of a Black man who bought a house in Mattapan. Some Black people responded to the hostility by attacking Whites and their institutions. Black teens mugged elderly Jews on Blue Hill Avenue. Two Black men threw acid in the face of a Mattapan rabbi; his synagogue was sold a month later. Other synagogues and Catholic churches were set on fire.[57]

Most White residents responded to the Black influx not with violence, but by relocating to the suburbs. As late as 1960, Dorchester and Mattapan were still almost completely White, but they were transformed over the next two decades. Dorchester lost nearly one hundred thousand White residents in twenty years, while Mattapan's White population declined by three-quarters. More than fifty thousand Jewish residents left upper Roxbury and Dorchester from 1950 to 1970, and they continued to exit. Catholics remained in the area longer, but their population declined by more than half between 1960 and

1980. There are still strong Irish Catholic pockets in southeastern Dorchester. White flight to the suburbs caused Boston's White population to fall by 365,000 people between 1950 and 1980, the prime period of Black southern migration. In the process, Boston became one of the most segregated cities in the United States—more segregated than southern cities such as Atlanta, New Orleans, and Birmingham.[58]

As Boston's Black population grew, Black people organized to demand equal rights. They protested racial discrimination in public housing and lending by banks for home mortgages. The city of Boston in response created the Boston Banks Urban Renewal Group program, an agreement with local banks intended to increase lending to minority homebuyers. Because B-BURG loans were restricted by geography to Roxbury, Dorchester, and adjacent areas, the program contributed to residential segregation and ensured that the Black population would remain concentrated in one part of the city. The B-BURG program has also been blamed for driving Jews out of Mattapan.[59]

Activists also organized to demand that Boston businesses increase their hiring of Black workers. They convinced the city to adopt rules requiring construction projects to hire more Black laborers. An organization led by Black mothers, meanwhile, protested their treatment by the city's welfare department and, in 1967, seized control of a welfare office in the Grove Hall section of Roxbury to draw attention to their demands. When they were forcibly removed by police, Black people rioted up and down Blue Hill Avenue for three days, causing millions of dollars in property damage.[60]

The economic status of Black workers in Boston gradually improved, as federal and state governments sought to eliminate employment discrimination. The proportion of Black people who worked as unskilled laborers fell by half from 1940 to 1970, while the share who worked in white-collar occupations, as factory workers, and skilled laborers rose significantly. Despite those gains, the income gap between Black and White workers actually grew. Black males in 1949 earned 72 percent as much as White males, but by 1979 they earned 64 percent as much. That suggests that while Black workers had gained entry into preferred careers, they were still relegated to lower-paying jobs within those occupations. Poverty also remained widespread in the Black community. In 1979, one-quarter of Black families had incomes below the federal government's poverty level. Boston's Black unemployment rate was near double that of Whites.[61]

Because school assignments were based on residential location, school segregation in Boston grew as Black residents came to make up an increasing share of the population in the neighborhoods where they

Black students arrive at South Boston High School as police stand guard on the first day of court-ordered busing in Boston in September 1974. Used with permission, Bettman Archive, Getty Images.

lived. Most Black children attended schools that had few White students. Parents complained that schools in Black neighborhoods were old, run-down, and inferior in quality to those in White parts of the city. There were few Black teachers in the schools. Boston may have been more progressive than Birmingham, but northern Whites practiced their own forms of racism.

Black people waged their most sustained battles over the schools. They demanded the city address persistent inequities. Schools in Black neighborhoods in the early 1960s received 65 percent as much funding per pupil as schools in White sections, comparable to racial disparities that existed in the South during the Jim Crow era. In 1965, after all efforts to reform Boston schools failed, the Boston chapter of the National Association for the Advancement of Colored People sued the city, demanding an end to school segregation.

Eventually, in 1974, a federal judge ordered Boston to implement busing to integrate its schools, which stimulated a violent and sustained resistance by White Bostonians. Busing opponents staged protests all year long, many of them openly and shockingly racist. Protestors threw rocks at school buses carrying Black children, breaking windows. They shouted racial epithets at Black youngsters. Many White parents kept their children at home rather than send them to school with Black children, while other White families enrolled their kids in private schools. The racist attitudes expressed by White people during the busing crisis, especially in traditional Irish neighborhoods such as South Boston and Charlestown, focused unfavorable attention on Boston nationally. South Boston was compared to Selma, Alabama, as a symbol of bigotry.[62]

The proportion of Black people in Boston who were born in the South diminished over time. By 1980, there were about thirty-six thousand southern-born Black people living in the city, 28 percent of its Black residents. But those numbers are deceiving and do not accurately convey the impact of the Great Migration on Boston because they exclude the children and grandchildren of migrants, who would not likely have been in the city had their kin not moved north. There is no precise way to measure the number of people who are the children or grandchildren of Black southern migrants, because such data are not collected. However, it is possible to calculate estimates of the number of migrant children, which helps us better appreciate how important the Great Migration has been to the making of Black Boston.

If Black women in Boston who were born in the South had children at the same rates as Black women in Massachusetts in 1980, they would have had about twenty-five thousand children. That suggests that nearly half of Black people in Boston in that year were born in the South or were the children of mothers born in the South. While some of the children may have been migrants themselves, so counted twice, that estimate still undercounts the children of southern migrants because it does not include the children of Black males whose partners were nonsoutherners. Moreover, it does not include the grandchildren of Black southern migrants, and they would likely have been numerous by 1980. In truth, the number of Black people in Boston with southern roots was likely considerably larger. It seems safe to assume that at least half of Black residents of Boston in 1980 were born in the South or were the descendants of people who were.[63]

Black migration from the South slowed considerably in the 1970s and a return migration developed, especially among Black people who missed the land and culture of their youth. The South has changed. Discrimination and overt racism have diminished. Opportunities for Black people have improved, particularly in booming cities such as

Atlanta and Houston. Some Black people who left the South chose to re-turn home. Others who were born in the North but felt an ancestral pull to the South joined them.[64]

As migration northward diminished, the share of Black Bostonians born in the South continued to decline, so that by 2019 barely one in ten Black residents of the city were southern born, though a much higher percentage had southern roots.[65] Yet for more than a century, Black people born in the South made up anywhere from one-third to three-fifths of native-born Blacks in the city. They strongly influenced the development of Boston's Black community.

Black migration from the South transformed the Black popula-tion in Boston from a small minority community into the largest non-White group in the city and helped make Boston the majority-minority city that it is today. Non-Hispanic White residents make up an ever-shrinking portion of the city's population, declining from 97 percent in 1940 to 44 percent in 2018. During the same period, the Black popula-tion share grew from 3 to 23 percent. Boston's Black population share is even higher, 29 percent in 2019, if people who claimed to be multiracial are counted.[66]

Has the Great Migration been worth it? In an essay in the *Boston Globe Magazine*, Kim McLarin questioned whether it was. A novelist and professor at Emerson College in Boston, she is hardly the typical Black migrant from the South. She came to New England from Memphis at age fifteen to attend Phillips Exeter Academy, an elite prep school in New Hampshire. She wrote that she had never heard the word "nigger" applied to her until she lived in Exeter.

Noting that Black unemployment rates are no better in the North than in most southern states and that Black youth in Boston graduate from high school at "virtually the same low rate" as Black people in Mississippi, she wondered whether Black incarceration rates, homeownership rates, and the wealth gap were any better in Boston than in the South. Reflecting on Isabel Wilkerson's award-winning book about the Great Migration, *The Warmth of Other Suns*, McLarin wrote, "If you transplant but the transplant doesn't take, where does that leave you? Still better off than in the rocky soil you left behind? Or dry and withering in the sun?" She asked, "Had we stayed 'home' and, as Booker T. [Washington] suggested, acquired land, built more institutions, and worked collectively, would we, as a people, be better off?"[67]

None of the Black southern migrants featured in this book enjoy the comparatively luxury of McLarin, a tenured professor and award-winning author. None seem to have spent much time reflecting on whether their moves were worth it. But none expressed any serious regrets about moving to Boston. All stayed and rejected suggestions that they return to the land of their birth. Assessing whether the Great Migration was worth it is more complicated than McLarin suggests. It cannot be evaluated using statistical indicators alone. There are countless other factors that must also be considered. The life histories that follow help us better understand that.

2

Charles Gordon

Baton Rouge, Louisiana, 1943

Charles Gordon does not remember his life in Louisiana.

Born in 1939 in New Orleans to Maurice and Ethel Gordon, he lived for his first few years in Louisiana's capital and second largest city, Baton Rouge. His father ran a dry-cleaning business there. But his family moved to Boston during World War II, when he was still a young boy.[1] He heard stories when he was growing up about life in the South from his parents and their friends, and the way Black people like him were treated there. Because of what they told him, he never had any desire to return to the region. One story stuck with him.

His father attended Southern University in Baton Rouge and was a member of the marching band. The band traveled all over the South to accompany the school's football team when it played games against other Black colleges. Once, in the 1930s, the football team and band traveled to Mississippi. It was a rainy Saturday. The roads, some unpaved, had become muddy and occasionally difficult to pass. The buses came upon a sheriff whose patrol car was stuck in the mud. The sheriff and his deputy, who were White, flagged down the buses to stop. The bus drivers complied. Gordon's father figured a few of the stronger football players would get off the buses and push the sheriff's vehicle so that the officers could get back on the road.

The sheriff, soaked to the skin through his uniform and seething with anger, according to Gordon, had other ideas. He ordered everybody to get off the buses and stand in the rain until his vehicle was pushed from the mud. Some of the Southern football players and band members resisted. They didn't want to stand in the rain. Some were so upset that their thoughts turned violent.

"My father said he's never been so scared in his life because they were going to kill the sheriff," he said.

Eventually, a few students who managed to remain calm convinced the others that, given the way Black people were treated in Mississippi in the 1930s, where perceived Black misdeeds were sometimes punished violently, if anything happened to the sheriff, the consequences for them would be far

North to Boston. Blake Gumprecht, Oxford University Press. © Blake Gumprecht 2023.
DOI: 10.1093/oso/9780197614440.003.0002

Charles Gordon at Charles Street African Methodist Episcopal Church in
Roxbury, 2015. Photograph by Blake Gumprecht.

worse. So the students stood in the rain until the sheriff was back on the road and then resumed their trip to the football game.

"That's when my father decided, 'I will not raise my family here,'" Gordon said.

Maurice Gordon had tried previously to leave the South. After graduating high school, he headed west to California, a common destination for Black migrants from Louisiana, and enrolled at Los Angeles City College. But that move did not stick. He returned to Baton Rouge and entered Southern University, but he never finished college. His family set him up in business. Soon he got married. Then he and his wife had their first child, Charles.

World War II created labor shortages in northern industries because many companies increased production to help in the war effort, but had lost workers who joined the military. That created opportunities for Black southerners, just as it had during World War I. Northern factories sent recruiters to the South looking for workers. When the war broke out, Gordon's father was rejected for military service. Charles does not know exactly why. "Maybe a heart murmur," he said. But he was able to get a job at the Boston Naval Shipyard and the family moved north about 1943. The shipyard added tens of thousands of workers during the war, including many Black workers, as it increased production of ships for the military. He secured the job before they left Louisiana, according to Charles.[2]

Gordon's father had become interested in Boston because he listened to a jazz radio show that broadcast performances by Black musicians from a nightclub in the city. Gordon said it was broadcast from the Hi-Hat Club on Columbus Avenue, one of the city's best-known jazz venues. But Richard Vacca, who wrote a book about Boston's jazz history, said that the Hi-Hat did not integrate and start booking Black artists until 1948. He said that other Boston jazz venues, such as the Southland Café, did book Black artists during World War II and their shows were broadcasts on the radio. Gordon was too young to remember that time, and perhaps his father was confused when he later told him about the club where the broadcasts originated.[3]

Unlike most migrants profiled for this project, the Gordons knew nobody in Boston when they arrived. They didn't follow other family members who migrated there. They had no friends in the city. "It was the radio show that made him interested in moving to Boston," Gordon said. "He had no knowledge of anybody in Boston."

The family moved into an apartment on Warwick Street in Roxbury. Later, they moved to another apartment on the same street, where they lived for about

The Sherwin School in Roxbury, where Charles Gordon attended junior high school. Used with permission, Boston City Archives.

a decade. Warwick Street in 1950 was inhabited entirely by Black people and many of the residents were migrants from the South, along with a few Caribbean immigrants and New England natives. Most of the Black southerners came from states on the Atlantic coast nearest to New England—Virginia, North Carolina, South Carolina, and Georgia. But migrants came from virtually every southern state, including Alabama, Mississippi, and Arkansas, even as far west as Texas. The street was a microcosm of the Black South.[4]

After World War II, Gordon's father worked as a dining car waiter for the Boston and Albany Railroad, then as a shoe repairer. Gordon's parents had two other children. Gordon's father never made much money. They struggled economically. Eventually, they moved into public housing on Washington Street in the South End, which was still nearly one-third Black. "We were what you would call poor," Charles said, "but we always ate."

Charles attended elementary and junior high school in Roxbury. Nearly all students in those schools were Black, while most of the teachers were

White. He began to realize in junior high school at the Sherwin School in Roxbury that Black students were treated differently, and that the quality of education he was receiving was inferior to that received by White students. Those issues came to forefront in the 1960s, when Black people began to protest segregation and inequities in Boston schools. Many schools in Black neighborhoods were old and dilapidated. In the early 1960s, schools in Black areas received about two-thirds as much money per pupil as schools in White neighborhoods.

The Sherwin School, which was more than 90 percent Black, was considered one of the worst. Built in 1870, it was frequently singled out as one of the schools most in need of rehabilitation or replacement, and was the site of a demonstration about conditions in 1963. It was destroyed by fire later that year, prompting a Black Roxbury legislator, Alfred Brothers, to say, "Thank God it was burned down."[5]

As late as 1963, only 1 percent of teachers in Boston's schools were Black.[6] Gordon said that some of his teachers at the Sherwin School were young White males who had fought in the Korean War, then went to college on the GI Bill, and had little choice in their first teaching assignments. "We had some of the worst teachers in the world and some of the best teachers in the world," he said. "We had people come into class and tell us straight out, 'Look, I went to war with you folks, I had to be with you folks. I didn't like being with you folks. Here's what we're going to do. If you're quiet and listen while I do my work, that's what I'm going to grade you on.' They said read the first three chapters. Next day, read another three chapters. As long as you were quiet and didn't do anything . . ."

Nevertheless, Gordon was a good student. Many of his relatives in Louisiana had been teachers, one of the few careers open to educated Black people in the South at the time. Near the end of junior high, he took a citywide admissions test for placement in one of Boston's elite public high schools. He scored high enough to be placed in Boston English, considered a step below Boston Latin, the city's top public high school. He entered Boston English in 1954.

Gordon hoped to play football for Boston English, but racism eliminated that desire. He loved football and played in youth leagues for many years while growing up. A running back, he tried out for the Boston English team. But he said the school had a quota on how many Black students could play on its varsity and he was placed on the junior varsity instead. "I could play!" he said. "I did everything. There was no question about me making the [varsity] team. Everybody knew I'd make the team. I didn't expect to go to the junior varsity. So the coach called me in. They told me straight out, there's a kid, White Irish, that they were pushing for a [college] scholarship. They said, 'You play the same position he plays, and you'd come out there and get all the attention.'"

Because of that, Gordon chose not to play football for Boston English, but instead played for several adult teams in the city's Park League. He continued to play for Park League teams after high school. But he also faced hostility because of his race while playing for those teams. Gordon's teams were composed almost entirely of Black men who lived in Roxbury, the South End, and other Black neighborhoods. It played against teams from other parts of the metro area, whose players were mostly White.

If there was one section of Boston that Blacks of Gordon's generation avoided because of a fear for their safety, it was South Boston, which had long been home to the city's largest and most proud Irish community. Residents of South Boston violently opposed court-ordered busing when it was implemented in 1974. Residents there threw rocks and bottles at buses carrying Black students to South Boston High School. They attacked a Black Haitian man driving through South Boston to pick up his wife from work.[7] Almost every person profiled for this project said they avoided going to South Boston because of its reputation for racism. The neighborhood has experienced gentrification in recent years because of its proximity to downtown and the ocean, and it is not so thoroughly Irish or White today. The Black population has grown. But in 1960, South Boston had only seventy Black residents out of a population of more than forty-two thousand.[8]

When Gordon's football team played games in South Boston, he said, the team's vehicles required a police escort. South Boston residents had a similar fear of the city's Black neighborhoods, so the South Boston team also had a police escort when it played in Roxbury. Players "got along fine," he said, and there were never any fights or other problems during games.

Students at Boston English were predominantly White, so Gordon experienced for the first time what it was like to be a minority and learned first-hand what some White people thought of Black people like him. He recalls a conversation he had with a White classmate about integration that inspired an angry response from him. "One of the Irish kids says to me, 'I don't want integration, I don't like integration, because I don't want you to marry my sister, date my sister,'" Gordon recalled. "Well, he's a fat kid. I says, 'Who the

Charles Gordon as a senior in
high school at Boston English
High School. Reproduced from
Boston English yearbook, 1957; used
with permission, Boston City Archives.

hell wants to date your sister? I wouldn't date your sister in a million years.'
I let him know in no uncertain terms: this is not about dating your sister.
Period."

Gordon also faced discrimination during high school in other ways.
Male students at Boston English trained in military drills and participated
in an annual Boston Schoolboy Cadets parade. Traditionally, students on
the honor roll at Boston English were made platoon leaders in the Cadets,
he said. He struggled initially at Boston English because it had higher
standards than his elementary and junior high schools. But he improved
his grades by the time he was a junior and consistently placed on the
honor roll. Gordon marched one year in the parade, but never again because he was denied a position as a platoon leader despite being on the
honor roll.

"There were no Black platoon leaders because [school leaders] just didn't
want to do it," he said. "One day, they said all those [who are on] the honor

roll who want to be platoon leaders, step forward. I stepped forward and Captain Fisher told me to get back. I said, 'Why?' He said, 'I don't need you.' [I said,] 'I'm on the honor roll. What is the [problem]?' [He had] all kinds of excuses."

Boston could be a difficult place for Black people in the 1950s, but it still was preferable to the South.

While in high school, Gordon got a glimpse of what his life might have been like if his family had never left Louisiana. In 1956, when his grandfather died, he returned to the South for the first time since his family migrated north. The family traveled to Baton Rouge by train to attend the funeral. The trip was memorable for Gordon because he experienced legally mandated segregation and the ever-present threat of violence felt by Black southerners.

The family traveled via Chicago, where Gordon's aunt lived. They spent the night there and then boarded a train bound for New Orleans. "When we'd leave Chicago to go south, it was a segregated train," he said. "You had the engine, then you had the Black car, then you had the dining car, and the rest of the train. The White folks would go to the dining car and, when they were finished, the Blacks would go to the dining car. They would never come into contact with each other."

Their trip came just one year after fourteen-year-old Emmett Till was brutally murdered in Mississippi after he supposedly whistled at, touched, or flirted with a White woman at her family's grocery story (only in 2017 did the woman admit that some of her original claims were untrue). Gordon, like Till, was a teenager who lived in a northern city and traveled south to visit family. The similarities would have made any young Black male fearful. When the Gordon family arrived in Baton Rouge, they learned that a similar case was riling the Black community in Louisiana's capital. "All the ministers [were] fighting to keep a Black kid from getting electrocuted for whistling at a White woman or something," he recalled. "That was big news. That stuck on me. That made me militant."

Discrimination was strong in Boston, too, if more insidious than in the South. Most White-owned businesses would not hire Black workers. The few employers that would hire Black workers did not necessarily do that out of a belief that they should have equal opportunity. They hired Black people because they were cheaper. They would work for lower pay than White workers.

Most Black residents lived in Black-dominated neighborhoods like Roxbury and the South End. Few sought housing in other sections of the city, at least in part because they knew they would be denied for one reason or another. They shopped principally at stores in their neighborhoods. Gordon said he was subject to racism and discrimination growing up in the city, but, mostly, he kept his feelings to himself. Despite his self-described militancy, he never fought back against that racism because he didn't trust his own temperament.

"I wasn't going to stand for you calling me the N-word and all that kind of stuff," he said. "I'm not nonviolent. No way."

Gordon graduated from high school in 1957 and attended Bentley College for one semester. But then his father was laid off by the railroad and his mother got sick, so he had to go to work. Well-paying jobs for Black people without a college education were rare in the years before the Civil Rights Act of 1964 and subsequent efforts to end employment discrimination. Major Boston companies such as Gillette and Polaroid did not start hiring Black workers in significant numbers until the mid-1960s. Gordon got a job in Boston's garment district, working in the shipping and receiving department for a clothing manufacturer. "There were few places that would hire Blacks at the time," he said. "Most of us went to the garment district. Jews hired us."

He met his wife, Marinette, in the late 1950s and they married in 1961. He moved out of his parents' place, and he and his wife got an apartment on Crawford Street in Dorchester. The area where they lived was still primarily White and Jewish but was beginning to change. In 1960, Black residents made up only 5 percent of Dorchester's population. Ten years later, one-quarter of the neighborhood's residents were Black people, many of them likely southern migrants.[9]

Gordon's wife was also a migrant from the South. Her family had moved to Boston from Sumter, South Carolina. Her father had passed through Boston while serving in the military during World War II, and an uncle who lived there convinced him to relocate to the city after the war. Many Black men first experienced life outside the segregated South while in the military, and that prompted some of them to relocate to northern cities once their military service ended. Her parents, like Gordon's, told stories of life in the South and the factors that motivated them to leave the region. During the 1940s, her father and uncle worked as laborers for a White farmer. One hot summer day, the farmer told them to give his mules some water, and put them in the shade so they could cool off. Then he told the Black workers to get back to work.

"They treated the mules better than Blacks," Gordon said.

Gordon and his wife had five children over eleven years, three boys and two girls. As the family grew, they moved to a larger apartment in Roxbury, where they stayed until 1976. At the time, they lived their lives almost entirely within the Black community. They shopped at Dudley (now Nubian) Square in Roxbury, Fields Corner in Dorchester, and later on Blue Hill Avenue after it evolved from a Jewish district into Black commercial area. At the time, Boston's Black community had a greater variety of stores than it has today—grocery stores, clothing stores, shoe stores, anything they needed. "We never had to go downtown," he said.

Gordon bought the latest R & B records at Skippy White's record store on Washington Street in the South End (it was White-owned, but sold mostly Black music).[10] He got his hair cut at Charles Canada's Amity barbershop, where his father first took him on his seventh birthday. It was located initially on Tremont Street in the South End. Then, as the Black residents spread to Roxbury, it moved to Blue Hill Avenue. He and his wife ate southern barbecue at Slade's in the South End, once owned by Boston Celtics star Bill Russell. Gordon's mother worked there. He also liked Christmas Restaurant on Tremont Street in lower Roxbury, whose menu he described as "upper scale" soul food.

"No chitlins," he said. "None of that."

They could also stay in the Black community for entertainment. They went to nightclubs like Wally's Paradise on Massachusetts Avenue in the South End. One of Boston's most famous jazz clubs, it was founded in 1947 by a Black immigrant from Barbados. They saw touring R & B performers at Basin Street South on Washington Street in lower Roxbury. Gordon remembers seeing the O'Jays play there, as well as Diana Ross and the Supremes. "They weren't famous then," he recalled. They went for drinks to Big Jim's Shanty and the Patio Lounge. "All the clubs were in the neighborhood," Gordon said.

Gordon worked for six or seven years in the clothing industry—"too long," he said. "It was a dead end." He met a welder who said he could earn a higher income working in a skilled trade. He suggested Gordon inquire at Wentworth Institute of Technology, which offered welding courses. Gordon learned that the father of one of his friends worked as a welder at the Watertown Arsenal, a US Army weapons-manufacturing plant. He talked

General Dynamics Corp. shipyard in Quincy, where Charles Gordon began working as a welder about 1966. He worked for General Dynamics for twenty-two years. Historic American Engineering Record, Library of Congress, Prints & Photographs Division, HAER MASS,11-QUI,10-1.

to him. The friend's father earned three dollars an hour, a good wage at the time, equivalent to thirty dollars an hour today.[11] "To me, that was a gazillion dollars," he said.

In 1962, Gordon enrolled at Wentworth while still working in the garment industry. Two years later, he earned a welding certificate and got his first welding job at General Alloys, a metal manufacturing plant in South Boston. He was still wary of South Boston and remains so today. "I would not be caught in South Boston by myself at night," he said. "It was fine during the day. But after work, [you had to] get out of town."

After two years at General Alloys, he got a higher-paying welding job at General Dynamics, a defense contractor and shipbuilder in Quincy. He worked for General Dynamics for twenty-two years, gradually working his way up to jobs with greater responsibility. He became a supervisor, then a department head. Eventually, he transferred to a General Dynamics facility in North Kingston, Rhode Island, though he continued to live in Boston.

When he was not working, he began taking business classes at the University of Massachusetts, Boston. In 1983, he earned a bachelor's degree in management and economics. That enabled him to get a job in 1988 as a facilities manager for Harvard University. He retired from Harvard in 2002. Born in the segregated South, raised in poor Black neighborhoods in Boston by working-class parents, and laboring for many years as a welder, Gordon's advancement to a management position at the one of the world's elite universities would have seemed inconceivable to him when he was younger.

"I never imagined anything like that," he said.

Gordon believes his success was partly the result of his father's decision to leave Louisiana. Black people in the North still faced discrimination, but he is convinced that educational and employment opportunities were better in Boston than in the South. "There's a lot of discrimination," he said, "but it was a lot better than it was in Louisiana."

Gordon and his family were still living in Roxbury when Boston implemented court-ordered busing in 1974. His eldest son was bused to South Boston High School, which was the center of the White Irish resistance. His other children were also bused, but not to South Boston. He opposed busing initially because he thought that, rather than busing Black kids out of their neighborhoods, the city should improve schools in Roxbury and other Black areas—hire better teachers, improve the curriculum, raise the standards. But, in retrospect, Gordon believes that his children and other Black youth received a higher-quality education because of busing. He also believes busing had unintended consequences that made Boston a better place.

"It changed the nature of Boston," he said. "It made people who didn't vote, vote. It made people who weren't involved in the political system get involved. Good things came out of it."

As his kids grew older and his family needed more room, Gordon and his wife in 1976 bought a two-family house in Hyde Park. That move, like their earlier move to Dorchester, reflected changes underway in Boston's Black community. Black people began moving to Hyde Park in significant numbers in the 1970s, as White residents moved out, and today Black residents make up nearly half of the neighborhood's population.[12] In 2003, after all his children were grown, Gordon and his wife bought a house in suburban Randolph, a half hour south of downtown Boston, where they still live.

Randolph is one of the most racially diverse Boston suburbs. Black residents make up nearly half of the population there, higher than any other group. Randolph is also home to numerous immigrant Blacks, many of them from Haiti.[13]

Since coming to Boston, Gordon has always lived in areas where Black people predominated. As he advanced economically, he could have moved to more affluent areas that were largely White, but he chose not to do that. "We didn't try to blaze any new trails," he said. "We did not go to places where we knew Blacks wouldn't be welcome."

Like other individuals profiled for this project, Gordon said he socializes mostly with other southern migrants. There have long been divisions with Boston's Black community—between southern migrants, immigrants from the Caribbean and Africa, and, especially, Boston-born Blacks. Some Blacks can trace their roots in the city to the colonial era. Nicknamed the Black Brahmins, many are more educated and prosperous than comparatively recent transplants.[14] Native Blacks with a longer history in the city often looked down on southern migrants.

"There was a large Black population who were more well to do," Gordon said. "Most of us who came from the South were not that educated. They come from poor areas of the South. Those are ones who got discriminated on—badly, badly treated, by other Blacks. Many of the churches looked down on southerners."

Gordon, like all other people featured in this project, is a member of the Charles Street African Methodist Episcopal Church in Roxbury. He said Charles Street AME has long had a reputation as unwelcoming to southern migrants, even though it has many members who were born in the South. Gordon said tensions between Boston-born Black people and southern Blacks have diminished over time, but they still exist. His wife was reluctant to join Charles Street for that reason. He joined only because he had gone to school with the man who was the church's pastor in the 1970s. He said many southern migrants "wouldn't think of joining Charles Street."

He joined Charles Street after his mother died in 1979. When he was a boy, his family attended All Saints Lutheran Church in the South End, but as a "rebellious teenager," he stopped going to church. The death of his mother triggered a spiritual crisis within Gordon and prompted him to return to church. "I didn't belong to a church," he explained. "I thought, 'What am I going to do? How am I going to give her a Christian burial?' It was time. I saw her faith. I said I better get back to this faith."

Gordon said he never stopped believing. His family is deeply religious. Even when he stopped going to church, he still recognized the importance of God in his life. He taught that to his children, who went to church with his father. But after joining Charles Street, he resolved to take an active role in the church. He has sung in the church's choir for forty years and served as its assistant director for two decades. He's been a member of the church's board of trustees for fifteen years. He is the president of the brotherhood, a male organization within the church. He is currently associate director of Charles Street's food pantry.

"There's no life without faith," he said. "This is only a temporary world here. Everything I have and own, and ever will have, comes from God. I understand why we're here, and I understand that if we do right, then we will have what we are intended to have."

Given Gordon's antipathy toward the South, it is ironic that two of his children migrated there as adults. One son, Barry, moved to Houston because his wife got a job there. One of his other sons, Charles, married a woman from Atlanta and they moved to Georgia after a quarter century together in New England. She wanted to return home when they retired. They are not alone. There has been a return migration of Black people to the South since 1970. That has been a response to improvements in the treatment of Black people in the region, along with economic growth, particularly in booming cities like Atlanta.

But other Black people have returned to the South, especially in retirement, because housing and the cost of living are less expensive than in northern cities like Boston, and they miss aspects of the Black culture in the region. In fact, Gordon's son and daughter-in-law have tried to persuade him and his wife to return to the South.

"They're trying to get me to go down there," he said. "I'm not going down there! This is home."

Despite his self-described militant views about civil rights, Gordon has never been active in politics or the civil rights movement. He never marched and never participated in protests, not in the South, not in Boston. That is not a matter of apathy or ambivalence, but was intentional because he knows his own personality and feared how he would have behaved, particularly if he faced hostility because of race.

"I knew what I would do," he said. "I would not be nonviolent."

Gordon maintains strong views about civil rights and the treatment of Black people. But he disagrees with some of the methods Black activists have used to protest mistreatment. He also believes Black people are to blame for some of their continued difficulties. Black people who rioted in Los Angeles in 1991 after the beating by police of Rodney King, he said, should not have destroyed buildings in their own communities, but "should have burned down the White part of town." However, he opposes the use violence to achieve change, despite his own inclinations in that direction. "I'm a conservative person," he said. "I try to be a Christian. We believe in protesting, but we don't believe in rioting and all that stuff."

Supporters of the Black Lives Matter movement, he argued, would be better able to achieve change through voting than protesting. He said one reason Black people were mistreated in Ferguson, Missouri—where Michael Brown in 2014 was killed by a White police officer, stimulating widespread demonstrations—was because even though Ferguson was a majority Black community, many Black residents there did not vote, and most elected officials were White. Nearly all officers in the Ferguson police department were also White.

Gordon believes many problems still experienced by Black people are their own fault and cannot be blamed on Whites or discrimination. He said, for example, that too many Black people who have benefited from government social welfare programs have become dependent on such programs and content to live that way. "Too many of us just dropped out of society," he said. "I know people who grew up living in the projects, they're still living in the projects. They were on welfare fifty years ago. They're still on welfare. I think that's one of the problems within Black society, not only in Boston, but in a lot of places."

Because of his strong views, Gordon shudders to think what his life would have been like if his father had never chosen to leave Louisiana and he had grown up in the South. He watched from a distance, and largely the comfort of his Boston living room, all the high-profile events that marked the civil rights era—angry Whites accosting Black youngsters entering newly integrated schools, the beating of Black college students sitting-in at Whites-only lunch counters, police using firehoses and attack dogs to turn back Black protestors.

"I don't think I would have survived in the South," he said. "I hate to think about it. I'm not going to be beat upon with firehoses and dogs put on me. I'm not going to be spit on. If I grew up in a South like that, they would have had to lynch me."

3

Thomas Lindsay

Birmingham, Alabama, 1951

Growing up in Birmingham, Alabama, in the 1930s and 1940s, Thomas Lindsay was subjected to the usual indignities that all Black people suffered in the South when segregation was the law and racism was still common and accepted.

Lindsay has plenty of stories to tell about mistreatment by White people in a city considered by some at the time to be "the most segregated city in America."[1] He was accused of theft, harassed by police, bullied by White teens, his honesty tested surreptitiously by a White employer. He was not permitted to play golf, a sport he loves, at a legitimate course. He tolerated the situation as best he could and managed to escape. He was able to do that because he had an aunt, his mother's sister Leola, who lived in Boston.

The incident that prompted him to leave Alabama was comparatively minor, but it was the culmination of years of abuse and came at a time when he could finally make his own life decisions. Lindsay had graduated from high school and was working, but he was still living with his mother in the house where he grew up. A friend came over for dinner. Later, he walked his buddy to a bus stop so he could return home. They were stopped by police and questioned. Nothing came of it and the police officer eventually let them go on their way. But after a lifetime of being questioned, accused, threatened, accosted, mistrusted, and being treated like he was less than human because of the color of skin, Lindsay wanted out.

"I told my mama, 'I'm going to go up there where Leola is,'" he said. "'I can't take this no more.' If you were raised in the South, when it came to White people, you always had trouble."[2]

Lindsay was born in Birmingham in 1928, on the eve of the Great Depression. He was the second and last child born to Elizabeth and Henry Lindsay. His mother and father had been farmers in Georgia before migrating to Alabama. He had a brother, Richard, who was four years older than he was. He never knew his father, who left his mom before he was born. After she told his father she was pregnant with Thomas, he left their house one day and did not return.

North to Boston. Blake Gumprecht, Oxford University Press. © Blake Gumprecht 2023.
DOI: 10.1093/oso/9780197614440.003.0003

"She made his lunch, he left to go work, but he never showed up no more," Lindsay said. "He never came back to Birmingham. His own family couldn't find him. It was tough on my mother. It was tough in those days."

Elizabeth "Lizzie" Lindsay had only a sixth-grade education. She worked cleaning and cooking in the home of a wealthy executive of a Birmingham steel mill. Working as a servant for a White family was one of the few careers open to Black women without an education in the South at the time. In 1940, 60 percent of employed Black women in the United States were domestic workers.[3]

The Lindsays lived in a rented three-room house in Birmingham's Avondale neighborhood, east of downtown. His mother slept in the front room, while Thomas and his brother, Richard, slept in another room. They shared a bed. His mother woke the boys every day at 5:00 a.m. so they could make their beds and clean their rooms before they went to school, even though school did not start for hours. The boys didn't like it, but getting up early became a habit for Lindsay. "To be truthful, I still do the same thing," he said. "I still wake up at five o'clock. I don't even use a clock."

Every Sunday, they attended the St. James African Methodist Episcopal Church in Avondale. They put on their best clothes. The boys had to attend Sunday school before worship services. Like any young boy, Lindsay sometimes resented having to go to church and occasionally lied to keep from going. One day, he recalled, he told his mom he was sick, and stayed home while she and his brother went to church. As soon as they left, he dressed and went outside to play with his friends. Later, when he saw his mother and brother turn the corner at the end of his block on their way home, he hurried back inside the house. But his mother saw him. She did not say anything right away, but after she got home, she went into the backyard, where they had a peach tree. "She went and cut a little switch from the tree and gave me a whipping," he said. "I'll never forget that. I haven't missed church since."

In three interviews over three days, Lindsay's mother was never far from his mind, and he brought her up repeatedly. She clearly exerted a profound influence over his life. She remarried, but he said almost nothing about his stepfather. He said that even though the family was poor, his mother worked hard to make sure they always had enough food to eat and nice clothes for school and church.

"She was wonderful," he said. "I miss her to this day. She worked hard. I used to feel sorry for my mother. Sometimes tears come to my eyes."

Lindsay had plenty of fun growing up, too. Life for Black people in the South during the Jim Crow era was not all oppression and misery. Black people were

Thomas Lindsay at home in Hyde Park in 2021. Photograph by Gregory Groover; used with permission.

Highland Park Golf Course in Birmingham, Alabama, where Thomas Lindsay caddied as a youngster but was not permitted to play because of his race. Used with permission, Highland Park Golf Course.

prohibited from using public parks and swimming pools in Birmingham, but they made do. Lindsay instead learned to swim in a creek that ran through a wooded area near his family's home. Neighborhood kids turned an empty lot at a vacant ice factory into a playground where they played baseball, football, and other games. Lindsay and his friends learned to play golf, and earned a little spending money, by caddying for White golfers at the nearby Highland Park golf course. Black people were forbidden from playing golf there, though.

There were no Black golf courses in Birmingham, so Lindsay and his friends fashioned a small course with two or three holes on the grounds of the abandoned ice factory. Sometimes the men for whom they caddied gave them old golf clubs when they bought a new set. They gave them old golf balls, too. "I still play golf today," he said. "I taught myself to play golf. I love golf."

Segregation was a fact of life in Birmingham during the years when Lindsay grew up there. Alabama mandated segregation of schools in its

Interior of streetcar in Birmingham, Alabama, 1930s, showing a sign designating where Black passengers were required to sit. Birmingham in 1910 mandated segregation of passengers by race on buses and streetcars. Used with permission, Birmingham Public Library Archives.

1901 constitution. Birmingham in 1910 required segregation on buses and streetcars. The city library and zoo were closed to Black people. Blacks and Whites were even prohibited from playing checkers together.[4] But segregation in Birmingham was different than it was elsewhere. Most of the people profiled for this project grew up in small towns or in the country. Interactions between White and Black people in such places was often greater than in cities like Birmingham because they were not big enough to support separate facilities for Black people. White and Black residents of small towns shopped in the same stores, watched movies in the same segregated movie theaters, even though they typically lived apart and went to different schools.

Because Birmingham had a large Black population, it had a Black commercial district with many Black-owned businesses. Those businesses were concentrated along Fourth Avenue, north and west of the city's downtown, which became the focus of Black social and commercial activity. It had movie theaters, restaurants and stores, barber and beauty shops, dry cleaners, the city's oldest Black funeral home, a Black-owned bank, and a Black fraternal organization.[5] Lindsay went to movies with his friends at the Carver Theater and the Famous Theater on Fourth Avenue. He rarely went to movie theaters nearer to his home patronized by Whites, because Black moviegoers had to sit upstairs in the balcony, apart from White people, and enter using a separate entrance via a staircase that went up the side of the building.

"I never went there," he said. "I didn't like that."

He got his hair cut in Black-owned barbershops, including the New Deal barbershop in the Fourth Avenue district. As he got older, he went to dances at the Colored Masonic Temple. When he became an adult, he drank beer with his friends at the Little Savoy Café. Fourth Avenue was the location of the Alabama Penny Savings Bank, the first Black-owned bank in Alabama. One of its founders was W. R. Pettiford, pastor of the Sixteenth Street Baptist Church, located just outside the district, where in 1963 four young girls were killed when the church was dynamited by the Ku Klux Klan. Lindsay did not patronize the bank, though. "I wasn't making that kind of money," he said.

As Lindsay grew older, he began to have frequent problems with White people, and that caused him increasing frustration and ultimately prompted him to leave Birmingham and move to Boston. When he was a teenager, White boys often confronted him and his friends, "call me the N-word," he said, and threatened to beat them. He insisted he stood up to the bullies, but never got into any fights with them. "My mother told me to mind your own business and that's what I did," he said. "I've never been in a fight in my life." Lindsay said he and his friends were regularly stopped by police and harassed for no reason. "There was some tough police down there," he said.

One summer, though, he had a more serious run-in with law enforcement. He had gotten a summer job cleaning offices "to help my mother out," he said. One day, while he was working, police came to the office and arrested him, accusing him of stealing money from the office. He was taken to the Birmingham city jail, where he was interrogated. "They threatened me," he said. "They said, 'We're going to beat this out of you.' I said, 'You can kill me—I'm not going to own up to something I didn't do.' I didn't take no money."

Eventually, he was permitted to make a telephone call, and he phoned his mother. She told the White family for whom she worked what had happened, and one of them called the police to intercede on his behalf. Lindsay was released. Later, the owner of the business where he worked discovered that his son had taken the money.

Lassetter & Company, an art and school supply store in Birmingham where Thomas Lindsay worked in high school and after he graduated, before moving to Boston in 1951. Used with permission, Birmingham Public Library Archives.

Lindsay occasionally worked for the family where his mother was employed, mowing their lawn on weekends. One day, the woman of the house asked him if he would wash some windows inside the home. He agreed. While doing that, he entered a room in their house and saw two dollar bills on the floor. His mother told him to leave the money where it was.

"She's testing you to see what you do," his mom said. "She's checking you out, to see if you take anything."

"After that," he said, "I never had no more problems. She always trusted me."

Lindsay was never a good student, unlike his brother, who went to college after serving in the military during World War II (and whose son, Reginald C. Lindsay, graduated from the elite Morehouse College and Harvard University Law School, practiced law in Boston, and was appointed to a federal judgeship by President Bill Clinton). He regrets now that he did not try harder in school. He believes he could have made more of his life if he had. He never thought about going to college. He went to all-Black Thomas Elementary School in Birmingham and then Parker High School, which was said to be the largest Black high school in the world at the time. He dropped out in the eleventh grade, though he eventually returned.

"My brother was so smart," he said. "I don't know why he was so smart, and I wasn't. I could have put my head in the books more than I did. I thought about that as I got older. I could have gotten better grades."

But racism in Birmingham also limited Lindsay's dreams. Growing up poor and Black in the Deep South, his only ambition was to get a job, any job, to help his mother. There were few careers open to Black men without an education at the time. When he was in eleventh grade he dropped out of Parker High School and got a full-time job at Lassetter & Company, a school and art supply store in downtown Birmingham. He helped fill orders and deliver them to customers. By that time, his brother had left home. He was drafted during World War II, was stationed at Fort Devens in Massachusetts, and served overseas.

"All I wanted was to have some sort of little job to help out my mother," Lindsay said. "We were having a hard time. We came up the hard way, I'm telling you."

Lindsay eventually went back to high school and graduated about 1947. He continued to work at the art and school supply store after he earned his diploma, and continued to live at home.

His mother's sister, Leola, graduated from Miles College, a private Black liberal arts college located in a Birmingham suburb, and then moved to New England. She fled the South like so many other Black people, Lindsay said, because her career choices there were constrained because of her race. She married and lived initially in Rhode Island. Then her marriage broke up and she moved to Boston. Leola wrote letters to Lindsay and told him about her life there. Letters sent home by migrants have long been an important influence on family and friends considering migrating themselves. "My aunt used to write me," he said. "She would tell me about Boston."

Twice Lindsay took vacations to visit his aunt in New England, once to Newport, Rhode Island, and later to Boston. She showed him around the city and took him on a cruise to Cape Cod. They visited Harvard University. Those trips opened his eyes to the opportunities available outside Alabama. "I liked Boston," he said.

What Lindsay saw on his trips to New England, and the cumulative impact of being mistreated by White people in the South, inspired him to leave

Birmingham. Lindsay moved to Boston in 1951 at the age of twenty-three. He took the train from Birmingham to Boston and moved in with his aunt, who had an apartment in Roxbury. He got a job serving meals at Beth Israel Hospital, but disliked the job because he did not want to be around sick people all day.

He then got a job at the Durand Co., a candy manufacturer in Cambridge. He helped set up the machines that made candy, changing the equipment used to mold the different varieties of chocolate confections the company produced. He worked there for a decade or so. Eventually, his aunt moved into a nicer apartment and he took over the lease on hers. Hoping to advance as a machinist, Lindsay enrolled in a trade school at night to learn how to be a tool and die maker. He went to the school for two years, passed the exam for certification as a tool and die maker, but never worked in that field. "To be a tool and die maker you have to be real smart in math," he explained. "You can't make no errors. It's got to be precise. That was too high class for me."

Lindsay's girlfriend, Virginia Jackson, had remained in Birmingham when he moved north, but they kept in touch and hoped to reunite. After he had lived in Boston for a couple years, she moved to the city. She got her own apartment. She finished high school in Boston. They married about 1954 and rented an apartment in Dorchester. His wife got a job at the Honeywell Corp., working in an office and preparing orders. They eventually had five children, three girls and two boys.

After renting for a few years, Lindsay and his wife bought a "three-decker" house in Dorchester, following the same path as other Blacks and immigrants who buy three-family houses as an affordable way to become homeowners— they live on one floor and rent out the other two to pay the mortgage.[6] Lindsay's three daughters now own the house and live there.

Boston's Black population nearly doubled in the 1940s, as Black southerners poured into the city. Black residents began to take over neighborhoods in areas like Dorchester that had been all-White. Dorchester's Black population increased 1,360 percent in the 1950s. The neighborhood where Lindsay and his wife rented an apartment was mostly Jewish when they moved in.[7] "As soon as the Blacks moved in, they moved out," he said. "It was a quiet neighborhood."

By the mid-1960s, Lindsay had a growing family and needed to earn more money. A friend told him that Polaroid, the company that revolutionized photography with its instant cameras, was hiring. He had seen its cameras in stores. It was considered an exciting company. He applied and was hired. Founded in

Polaroid Corp. in Cambridge, where Thomas Lindsay began working about 1961. Polaroid increased its hiring of Black workers about that time, especially after it began participating in a voluntary Massachusetts program that sought to increase minority hiring. Lindsay worked for Polaroid for twenty-one years, retiring from the company in the 1980s. Photograph by Fay Foto; used with permission, Cambridge Historical Commission.

Cambridge in 1937, Polaroid has been called a "juggernaut of innovation," the Apple computer of its day. Founder Edward Land was even pictured on the cover of *Life* magazine with his "magic camera." Polaroid eventually employed twenty-one thousand people, most of them in the Boston area.[8]

Lindsay likely benefited from efforts by Massachusetts companies like Polaroid to hire more Black workers. The state of Massachusetts in 1963 created a voluntary program called the Massachusetts Plan for Equal Employment Opportunity to encourage businesses to increase the hiring of minorities. A Polaroid executive was a member of the committee that developed the plan. By 1966, ninety-six companies had agreed to participate.[9] "There were quite a few Blacks working there," Lindsay said.

He was hired to set up machines in Polaroid's film department. He worked in the company's Cambridge headquarters and later at its plant in suburban Waltham. Initially, he worked the 3:00 p.m. to 11:00 p.m. shift, but switched to overnights, working 11:00 p.m. to 7:00 a.m., which he liked, he said, "because I could come home and get my kids ready for school." He made more money at Polaroid than he did in his old job, and the company also provided better benefits—more vacation and sick time. He said Dr. Land "used to come around and give us a Christmas gift."

"I loved that job," he said. "Polaroid was a good company to work for."

Despite the racism Lindsay experienced growing up in Birmingham, he was never involved in politics or the civil rights movement in Alabama or New England. Black workers at Polaroid formed the Polaroid Revolutionary Workers Movement to protest the company's involvement with the apartheid government in South Africa, but Lindsay said recently he was not aware of the group.[10]

His nephew, Reginald Lindsay, the federal judge, who died in 2009, worked in the same law office as Deval Patrick, the state's first Black governor, and became only the second Black person to serve as a judge on the federal district court in Massachusetts. He majored in political science in college, worked for the Peace Corps and Lyndon Johnson's presidential campaign, and was appointed by Massachusetts governor Michael Dukakis to be the state's commissioner of public utilities when he was only twenty-nine years old.[11] He was outspoken, even as a judge. But his nephew's life did not inspire Thomas Lindsay to become politically active.

"I didn't have time for all that," he said. "I didn't care nothing about no politics. I had a family to take care of."

Lindsay's rising income enabled him to buy a two-story, single-family house with a yard in the Hyde Park section of Boston about 1970. Hyde Park was predominantly White at the time, but its Black population increased tenfold in the seventies. Black residents now make up nearly half its population.[12] The move to Hyde Park was a step up. He lives in an area of mostly single-family homes. He was tired of having tenants and wanted a house entirely his own. He lives on a dead-end street, a block away from a large area of hilly woods that have been proposed for development as a park. It is safer than his old neighborhood in Dorchester has become. "In Hyde Park we don't have no shootings," he said. "I've been here [a long time], and I never had no problems."

He and his wife went on traveling vacations every year. Once a year, they sat down and decided where they wanted to go. Sometimes they went to Cape Cod for a week. They took numerous cruises. They went overseas to France, Germany, and Belgium. They visited the Bahamas. Until Lindsay's mother died, they visited her in Alabama every few years. Three of his five children went to college, and all stayed in Boston. His eldest son, Ted, who was an engineer, died suddenly of unknown causes when he was in his thirties. "He was really smart," Lindsay said proudly.

Lindsay worked for Polaroid for twenty-one years, retiring from the company in the 1980s. He chose to leave when he did, he said, because Land had resigned in 1981, the company started losing money, and "the people that took Dr. Land's place didn't know what they were doing." About three years after he retired, he took a part-time job at Harvard University Press, processing orders, mainly to give himself something to do. He was "sitting around the house doing nothing," he said, and a friend who worked there told him about the opening. He worked there for about ten years.

Lindsay and his wife were married for sixty years. She died in 2013 from complications of diabetes after a long illness. He visits her grave daily. "I think about her every day because she was a nice person," he said. "You don't find too many girls as good as her."

Lindsay is healthy. He survived prostate cancer. Now in his nineties, he golfs often, when he is not bothered by back pain. He golfs most often at Franklin Park because it is near his home. But he and his golf buddies like to travel to Cape Cod and New Hampshire to play at different courses. He also regularly walks in a city park near his home. His son Nathaniel, a retired truck driver for the US Postal Service, lives with him.

When Lindsay first moved to Boston and lived with his aunt, they lived in an apartment less than a block from Charles Street African Methodist Episcopal Church. She brought him there the first Sunday he was in town, and he has been going there ever since, seventy years in 2021. He was raised in the AME church in Birmingham and has long been active at Charles Street. He served on its board of trustees. He sang in the choir. He was a Boy Scout leader. He has helped with its food pantry. Rev. Gregory Groover has been his minister since 1994.

"I've listened to Rev. Groover so much that I'm beginning to be like him," he joked.

Ever since that day in Birmingham when his mother caught him faking illness to avoid attending church, Lindsay has gone to church every Sunday.

Faith continues to play a strong role in the life of most Black Americans, and Black people are more likely to be Christians and attend church regularly than other groups, perhaps because they recognize how important religion was in helping their ancestors endure slavery. Lindsay's mother instilled in him a strong sense of spirituality, and that influence still shapes his worldview many decades later. His conversations include frequent references to God.[13]

"I'm at church every Sunday," he said. "When I go to church, I go to church to serve God. When I come home, I do the same thing. I don't run around, I don't drink, I don't get in anybody's business. I say my prayers before I lay down to sleep. I wake up and thank God for living another day."

Interviewed at the age of ninety-two, Lindsay appeared to recall less about his life in Boston than about his youth in Birmingham. At first that seemed surprising, but maybe it shouldn't. Trauma has the ability to permanently imprint the human psyche. Lindsay may recall less about his adult years simply because they were pleasant, if ordinary. Nobody called him names. Nobody threw him in jail or threatened him with violence. Lindsay lived his life—worked, got married, had a family, bought a house and then another, went to the movies and Red Sox games, traveled on vacation, experienced the usual heartbreaks but also joy. In those ways, he is like millions of others in Boston, regardless of color.

"God has been good to me since I've been up here," he said.

Lindsay credited his mother with teaching him the values that have made him the person that he is. "My mother taught me how to live," he said. "I always treat people nice. Even if you treat me bad, I treat you nice. Do what you do but do it in a nice way: my mother always taught me that. When you treat people nice, God is going to reward you."

Lindsay knows he benefited by leaving the South and moving to Boston. He says he was able to get better jobs than he could have gotten with only a high school diploma in Birmingham. He has made more money, which made it possible for him to buy nice homes. His kids went to college. He could do what he wanted, largely without limitations. He knows Boston is not perfect. He is aware of its racist reputation. He recognizes that the city still has shortcomings if you are a Black person.

A national survey commissioned by the *Boston Globe* in 2017 found that among eight major cities, Black people ranked Boston as the least welcoming to people of color—by far. The *Globe* then set out, in a seven-part series, to examine whether its reputation was deserved. The simple answer to that question was yes.[14]

Black people in Boston are underrepresented in positions of power (Boston elected forty-eight straight White, male mayors), in executive boardrooms, as students in its elite universities, and in the grandstands of its professional sports teams. The situation has improved somewhat since the *Globe* published its series. In 2020, for the first time ever, people of color became a majority on the Boston City Council. A year later, a Black woman, Kim Janey, a former community activist who grew up in Roxbury and was the city council president, became mayor when Mayor Martin J. Walsh was appointed to be President Joe Biden's labor secretary. Janey became the first person of color and woman to ever serve at Boston's mayor, but she failed to win election to the office later the same year, finishing fourth in a primary. Asian American Michelle Wu was eventually elected mayor.[15]

The *Globe* also published a series about Blacks in Boston many years before in 1983. In 2017, it found that conditions for Blacks had not improved much since then. Black people were still twice as likely as Whites to be unemployed. The share of Black workers who were officers and managers of businesses had barely changed. It found that landlords still discriminated against Black renters. Another Globe survey found that nearly two-thirds of Black Bostonians said they were treated unfairly because of their race in the previous thirty days.

"You're going to have trouble anywhere you go," Lindsay said. "Anywhere you go, if your skin is dark, you're going to have the same problem. In Boston, it's the same way. You have some White people up here that don't like you. It's like that everywhere."

But Lindsay has a more positive view of race relations in Boston than the *Globe* found in its surveys. "I've never had no trouble," he said. He's always lived in Black neighborhoods, but has worked elsewhere, and does not hesitate to go to predominantly White areas. "I just like Boston," he said. "You can go anywhere you want—ball games, museums, a Broadway show. You had the freedom to do what you wanted."

Some Blacks who migrated from the South to northern cities grow nostalgic for their former homes as they age. Some even move back to the South, especially in retirement. There has been a reverse migration of Blacks to the South since 1970. They miss the culture. They miss the food. They miss the weather. Lindsay is not one of them.

"I ain't missing nothing," he said. "I ain't never missed Birmingham. I missed my mother, that's all."

4

Lucy Parham

Morven, North Carolina, 1957

When Lucy Parham climbed aboard a passenger train bound for Boston in May 1956, the same month she graduated from high school in North Carolina, she had no intention of relocating to the city permanently. She came for the summer to help an aunt who was pregnant and already had two young children, but she planned to return home by September to enroll in college. Something changed in Parham, however, during the seven months she spent in Boston that altered the future course of her life, although she did not recognize that at the time.[1]

Parham grew up in the country, about three miles from the small town of Morven, North Carolina, which in 1950 had population of 601. It is in Anson County, sixty miles southeast of Charlotte and just north of the South Carolina state line in a region of piney woods and farmland. Cotton and tobacco were the dominant crops in the area.[2]

Born in 1937 to Bruce and Effie Love, she was the first of five children. Four of them ended up in Boston. Her father was a sharecropper, farming ten to fifteen acres of land that belonged to the Hardison family, which owned considerable property in and around Morven. Sharecroppers farmed land owned by others in return for a share of the income earned from what they raised. Parham's dad grew cotton and corn. He eventually bought that land as the Hardison patriarch grew older.

The Love family lived in a three-room house on the land they farmed. Lucy lived there with her parents, grandparents, a cousin, and her sister, Gracie, who was born two years after her. Another sister, Priscilla, was born when she was in high school. Parham left home before her other two siblings were born. The entire extended family slept in a single room that contained three beds. Lucy's parents slept in one bed, her grandparents in another, while Lucy shared a bed for most of the time she was growing up with her sister and cousin. The house had a kitchen with a wood stove and a living room, also heated by wood. They did not have indoor plumbing. Electricity was not extended to homes in her

North to Boston. Blake Gumprecht, Oxford University Press. © Blake Gumprecht 2023.
DOI: 10.1093/oso/9780197614440.003.0004

Lucy Parham in the nave at Charles Street African Methodist Episcopal Church in Roxbury, 2016. Photograph by Blake Gumprecht.

area until about 1947. Parham recalls watching TV for the first time that year at her uncle's house and seeing Jackie Robinson, the first Black person to play major league baseball, in the first World Series featuring an integrated team.

In addition to growing crops for sale, her father raised a few cows, pigs, and chickens, mostly for the family's use. They always had fresh eggs from their chickens and milk from their cows, and they made their own butter. They had a big garden, where they raised corn, cabbage, okra, tomatoes, string beans, and turnips. "I never had vegetables that came from a store until I came to Boston," Parham said.

All but two families that lived near them were Black, and many were extended family. Her uncle lived just up the road from her family's house. Her grandfather's nephew lived nearby. Her grandfather's sister and her family lived a little further away on the same road. The Hardison family lived in a "big white house," she said, and the man who oversaw their land, and supervised sharecroppers like Lucy's father, lived near them. Lucy's aunt lived "down from the big house." The daughter of her great-grandmother lived "across the creek," she said. Even nonrelatives who lived nearby, such as a woman she referred to as Miss Glennie, were "really like family," Lucy recalled.

Growing up, Parham helped in the cotton fields whenever necessary, "chopping" the plants with a hoe to remove weeds. Mostly she helped around the house, cooking, cleaning, and sewing. She helped her mother and grandmother can vegetables and fruits so they would have food over the winter. She washed clothes by hand. Her grandmother was particular about how that was done. They used three tubs, scrubbing the clothes in one, rinsing them in another, and then white clothes were boiled in a big black pot on an open fire. All of that was done outdoors.

Her life outside of home and school revolved around church. The Love family attended the Streater Grove African Methodist Episcopal Church in Morven. Lucy sang in the choir. She had plenty of free time growing up. She jumped rope and played baseball—the corner of their house was first base, and a tree served as second base. They fished in nearby streams. Her grandmother fished every day, but Lucy didn't much like fishing. They had a nice yard, full of chinaberry trees.

"We might have been poor, but I didn't know it," Parham said. "We had a nice house. We always had nice clothes to wear. We always had food. We had a car. We always had everything we needed."

The Love family did most of its shopping in Morven. The Hardison family had a commissary where their sharecroppers could buy food and supplies on credit, though prices in such stores were typically high. Sharecroppers often owed more than they earned from their crops when they "settled" with their overseers after the harvest, making it difficult to get ahead. Morven also had a hardware store, pharmacy, post office, clothing stores, and a couple of gas stations, she said. A larger town, Wadesboro, the county seat, is located eight miles north of Morven. The Love family traveled there to buy the girls clothes for Easter or the start of the school year.

Parham said race relations in Morven were congenial. White and Black people got along. She experienced no hostility from White residents that she recalls. She occasionally heard news stories on the family's old Philco battery-powered radio about racial violence elsewhere—cross burnings, lynchings, the murder of Emmett Till the year before she graduated high school. But she said nothing like that ever happened in the area where she grew up.

Black children in Anson County, North Carolina, in 1938, one year after Lucy Parham was born there. Photograph by Marion Post Wolcott, Farm Security Administration; Library of Congress, Prints & Photographs Division, FSA/OWI Collection, LC-DIG-fsa-8c29971.

"I have never known racism," she said. "We never had people running around shooting at people's houses or setting people's houses on fire. Where we was raised we didn't have any of that."

But even if Parham did not experience any hostility from White people growing up, she did experience racism, even if she did not recognize it as such. It was so much a part of life in the South that she took it for granted and accepted it. She attended all-Black schools. Restaurants in Morven and

Wadesboro would not serve Black customers in their dining rooms. They had to go to windows in the back for takeout orders. Morven was not big enough for a movie theater, but there was one in Wadesboro. Black and White moviegoers sat in separate sections at the theater.

Black people were expected to address White adults as "mister" or "missus." Parham remembers that once her father reprimanded her when she called their White postman by his first name. She acknowledged that poor White people in the area would call Black people "niggers." There was little interaction between races, other than in stores. "We knew we were Black, they knew they were White," she said. "You went your way and they went their way. We knew where we belonged, and they knew where they belonged." Black people in Anson County were subject to considerable racial violence when its schools were desegregated in 1966, but that was a decade after Parham left North Carolina. Homes of two Black families in Morven who chose to send their children to a formerly all-White school were bombed, as was a pool hall, presumably one patronized by Black people.[3]

Parham attended White Pine School, which was all Black, and then Morven Colored High School. She felt that she got a good education. Unlike other southern migrants, she never felt like her schools were inferior to the White schools in town. "We didn't think about that," she said. Southern states gradually increased their funding for Black schools, a strategy designed to prevent integration by showing that Black students received an equal education and that schools met the "separate but equal" standard established in the 1896 Supreme Court decision *Plessy v. Ferguson*. Black schools in North Carolina in 1950 received 93 percent as much funding per pupil as White schools, a dramatic improvement compared to earlier decades.[4] But even after the Supreme Court overturned the "separate by equal" principle in *Brown v. Board of Education* in 1954 and outlawed segregation, schools across the South remained separate.

Parham graduated from Morven Colored High School in May 1956 and planned to enroll that September at the Negro Agricultural and Technical College of North Carolina in Greensboro (now North Carolina A&T State University), two hours north of Morven. In the meantime, she traveled to Boston to help her aunt, her father's sister. Her aunt had settled in Boston with her husband after he was discharged from the military. He had been stationed in the Boston area while on active duty. Like other Black soldiers, he first encountered life outside the South while in the military, which may have influenced his decision to leave the region.[5] He and his wife had two children and were expecting a third.

Parham's parents asked her to spend the summer in Boston to help her aunt, taking care of her two kids during the day while she prepared to give birth and her husband was at work. Lucy agreed and took the train from Wadesboro to Boston's South Station. Darlene Clark Hine and Katherine Thompson have observed that many Black women left the South for similar reasons.[6]

She intended to stay in Boston for six weeks, then return home to prepare for college. She stayed with her aunt's family, who lived in Roxbury, which was then predominantly White (Roxbury's Black population share doubled between 1950 and 1960). They lived in a two-family house in a neighborhood with many double- and triple-deckers. Thousands of three-deckers (or triple-deckers) were built in Boston beginning in the 1880s as streetcar lines were extended outward from the city center. They became the predominant housing type in many parts of the city because they enabled more people to live within walking distance of streetcar lines.[7]

Having grown up in the country, what surprised Parham most on her arrival in Boston was not the high-rise buildings she saw when she exited South Station, or the throngs of people walking on the streets, but the preponderance of multifamily homes. She woke up the morning after her arrival, walked out onto her aunt's back porch, and looked in astonishment at all the triple-deckers that surrounded her. "It was amazing," she recalled. "I said to my aunt, 'Does one family live in that house?' She said, 'Noooo. There's three families.' So many people, so close together. No big yards. Back home everybody lived in their own house."

Parham's aunt gave birth that summer, but then she experienced health difficulties that forced Lucy to stay in Boston longer than planned. Her aunt had a gallbladder attack, which required surgery. When she finally came home from the hospital, she was weak and unable to lift her baby. Parham postponed her return to North Carolina and put off her plans to enter college so that she could help her aunt while she recuperated. She stayed through the fall.

When September came, her aunt's two older children went to school, so Parham had less to do during the day. By then, her aunt had regained her strength and could care for her newborn by herself. For that reason, Parham looked for work and got a full-time job as a seamstress making curtains for a Roxbury textile manufacturer. She remained in Boston so she could help her aunt at night and on weekends when all three of her kids were at home. She quit her job and returned to North Carolina at

Christmastime. Because it was the middle of the school year, she decided to delay enrolling in college until the following September. Instead, she looked for work in Greensboro. She had a cousin who lived there, and she stayed with him.

She went to a government employment agency there, but was disappointed when a staff member told her that the only job openings for Black women with just a high school education were for maids—cooking and cleaning in the homes of White families. Even in the mid-1950s, a greater number of Black women worked as domestics than in any other occupation. "The way she said it, 'The only thing we have for Black women . . . ,'" Parham recalled. "Even when I was in Morven, I was never exposed to stuff like that."

Parham returned to her cousin's house discouraged.

"Well, you know," her cousin told her, "that's just what happens down here."

Parham replied, "I don't want to do that."

By then, she had lived in Boston for more than a half year and had worked as a seamstress, which she preferred to domestic work. But she had also been sheltered from such concerns growing up in rural Anson County. During the seven months she lived in Boston with her aunt, she began to discover how much better race relations were in the city than in the South. There was a greater variety of jobs open to Black women. Black people could go wherever they wanted. She had also met her future husband, James Parham.

He was a chef who worked in Florida during the winter and New Jersey in the summer. In between jobs, he often traveled to Boston to visit his sister, who lived on the same block as Parham's aunt. Her aunt asked the woman, who was closer in age to Lucy, to show her around Boston. Her brother came along. They became friends. They did not become romantically involved right away, however. "I had begun to like it here," she said. "I could see the difference—that I had better opportunities."

After her difficulties finding suitable work in Greensboro, Parham decided in 1957 to return to Boston. She was twenty years old. She joined a steady flow of Black people leaving Anson County, many likely moving north. From 1940 to 1970, the county's Black population declined by nearly one-quarter.[8]

Upon returning to Massachusetts, Parham enrolled at Boston State College and got another job as a seamstress, this time working for B. F. Goodrich in Watertown making P. F. Flyers shoes, one of the leading athletic shoes of the era. Boston Celtics basketball star Bob Cousy had recently signed a deal to advertise P. F. Flyers nationally. She worked full time and went to school part time. She reconnected with her future husband. He, too, had decided to move to Boston, apparently because of her. Like Parham, he grew up in the South—in Georgia. They became involved. Parham and her husband married in 1958 and rented an apartment in Roxbury. Her aunt's brother-in-law lived in the same building and told them about it.

B. F. Goodrich, ironically, decided to move its assembly plant to North Carolina, reflecting changes underway in the clothing and footwear industries, as producers sought to take advantage of lower wages in the South. She was offered the opportunity to transfer there, but declined. Instead, she went to school full time until she and her husband had their first child.

Parham's daughter, Audrey, was born in 1959. She gave birth to a son, Steve, the following year. "I didn't waste no time," she said. The growing family needed more space, so they relocated to a larger apartment on Quincy Street in Roxbury. Later, they moved to an apartment in Dorchester. Parham's husband could not find work as a chef in Boston, so he got a job with Dy-Dee Diaper Service, then at Continental Can. With two children, they needed greater income, so Parham went back to work. She got a job at Gillette, the razor manufacturer in South Boston, as a machine operator. Gillette was expanding its workforce as it prepared to introduce its TechMatic razor and its first stainless steel blade.[9]

"At the time, you could count the Black folks at Gillette," she said.

There were not many. In fact, when she first sought work in Boston while living with her aunt, she was discouraged from applying at Gillette because, she was told, "They wasn't hiring Black folks." That changed when Gillette became one of the companies that signed on to the Massachusetts Plan for Equal Opportunity, a voluntary program designed to encourage companies to increase minority hiring. In 1964, Gillette participated in a job fair sponsored by Freedom House, a nonprofit based in the Grove Hall section of Roxbury, that sought to improve opportunities for Black people. John Oxley, a Gillette personnel manager who attended the job fair, was a Black man.[10]

Parham liked Gillette and ended up working there for nearly forty years, until she retired in 1999. Eventually, her husband got a job there as well, in the packaging department. "Gillette was a good job," she said. The company even paid for her tuition to continue her education. In 1965, she graduated from the University of Massachusetts, Boston, which later absorbed Boston State College, earning a degree in business management. While she was still

Gillette headquarters in South Boston in the 1960s. Lucy Parham was hired at Gillette about 1960, when the company had few Black workers. But it joined a voluntary state government program to increase minority hiring in 1963, and its Black workforce grew considerably after that. Parham worked for Gillette until her retirement in 1999. Photograph used with permission, Proctor & Gamble Co.

in school, she was promoted from a machine operator to supervisor. After she got her degree, she was hired by Gillette's marketing department, doing marketing to retail stores.

The sixties were a time of tumult in Boston's Black community, as in cities throughout the country—struggles to achieve school equality, rent strikes and protests against discrimination in hiring and housing, Martin Luther King Jr.'s march and rally on Boston Common in 1965, the Grove Hall welfare office sit-in and subsequent riot two years later. Parham watched, but she did not participate.

She is quiet and has a calm demeanor. She is careful when she speaks. She is not the rebel sort, not the sort of person to shout slogans or march, though she is strong willed and will speak her mind when provoked, as she did when she felt one of her daughter's teachers mistreated her because of her race. Her reasons for not participating in the civil rights movement were personal and driven by pragmatic concerns. "I had a very busy life," she said. "I got married and was raising a family. I was going to school full time and working. I didn't have time."

Parham was not apolitical, however. She occasionally campaigned for candidates she liked. Kevin White, who served as Boston's mayor from 1968 to 1984, including the difficult busing years, was "one of my favorite people," she said. She was also fond of Mel King, a community activist who was elected to the Massachusetts legislature and tried, unsuccessfully, to become Boston's first Black mayor when White chose not to seek reelection in 1983. But her most pointed and persistent political act has been to vote. Parham grew up in the South during Black struggles over voting rights there. Her parents and grandparents were never allowed to vote when she lived in North Carolina. She registered to vote in 1958, one year after she moved to Boston, when she turned twenty-one, which was then the minimum age for voting.

"I have never missed a time voting since I was old enough to vote," she said. "I vote because I grew up during a time when Black people couldn't vote. It should be important to everyone."

Parham's salary rose as she advanced at Gillette. The added income enabled her and her husband in 1972 to buy a three-decker in Mattapan, living in one apartment and renting out the other two units—a common path to home-ownership for immigrants and minorities in Boston still today. They took over the mortgage on the triple-decker from a friend of Lucy's who decided to return to North Carolina.

The movements of the Parham family within Boston over time reflected the changing geography of Black residents in the city. Black people moved from the South End to Roxbury and then Dorchester, as the population grew because of migration from the South and overseas. In the 1970s, they began buying homes in Mattapan, helped by the Boston Banks Urban Renewal Group program, a city agreement with local banks to increase lending to minority homebuyers in a designated area.[11]

Parham and her husband first moved to Roxbury as it was changing from a predominantly White neighborhood to a Black one. They rented an apartment in neighboring Dorchester as more and more Black people were moving there. Dorchester's Black population more than quadrupled in the sixties. They were also part of the wave of Black homeowners who transformed Mattapan. It went from being almost completely White, and mostly Jewish, to a Black neighborhood by 1980.[12] "I like where I live," she said. "It's a nice community. I know the people. Everybody takes care of their property."

Parham has never felt constrained by her race to stay within the Black community. She has always shopped nearby for everyday needs such as groceries. When she was younger, she was more likely to stay in the area, because Roxbury offered a wider range of businesses than it does today. Blue Hill Avenue was a thriving commercial district. She and her husband went to the movies at the Warren Theater on Warren Street.

Blue Hill Avenue declined after riots in 1967 and the departure of many Jewish merchants, as Jewish residents moved to the suburbs. But some of the changes in where she shops reflect transformations in retail nationwide, such as the building of shopping malls and the advent of big-box stores. You cannot shop exclusively in Boston's Black community anymore, though options have improved in recent years with new developments in Grove Hall and Nubian (formerly Dudley) Square.

After she moved to Mattapan, Parham shopped in Mattapan Square, where a friend owned a clothing store. But she always had a car and worked in South Boston, and never hesitated to travel elsewhere. She drove to the suburbs to buy clothes for her kids. "I went where I could get a good buy," she said. She lived in Black neighborhoods, but was also a citizen of the larger Boston region. She felt no reluctance to go to predominantly White parts of the metro area, whether to go to a baseball game at Fenway Park or shop in Braintree. Eventually, she and her husband bought a house in suburban Milton, where White residents make up three-quarters of the population.

"I've never had no problem," she observed. That was a phrase she said again and again.

Three of Parham's four siblings also moved to Boston. One summer, her sister Gracie, who was two years younger, traveled there with her son to visit. Not long after, she and her husband decided to move to the city. They lived with Lucy and her family until they could get established. "She liked it," Parham said. "She saw the difference in the pay. There's a big difference in the pay up here [compared to] the South. Still. Even now."

Parham's family regularly visited her in Boston. That influenced her siblings' decisions to relocate to the city. Her brother Sezzie and youngest sister, Theresa, moved to the city, too. Her parents, particularly her father, had greater difficulty adapting to some of the differences between the North and South.

Front porches are central to life in the South, a response to the warm climate of the region. In the days before most people had air conditioning, southern families sat together on the porch every evening because it was cooler than indoors. The Love house in Morven had a front porch, where the family sat often. Parham had a porch in her Boston house, but the family rarely sat on it. When her parents visited, her father noticed that and remarked about it one day. They passed through the porch whenever they arrived home. Puzzled that they did not sit on the porch, he asked Lucy about it. But Boston is not the South, and Parham, like other Black migrants, adapted to the different culture and mores when she moved north.

Her father gave up farming as he got older. He and his wife moved to Greensboro, where he got a job with a company that made telephone and power-line poles. Every morning, his wife, who never worked outside the home, would cook him a hot breakfast and make him a big lunch to take to work—not a sandwich, but large meals, like fried chicken, or steak with potatoes and gravy. Once while visiting Boston, Parham's father noticed that Lucy did not get up in the morning to cook for her husband. At the time, Parham was working the night shift and her husband was working during the day. He got up in the morning, ate a light breakfast, and made himself a sandwich to take for lunch.

"Must have been about the third day, my father says, 'You don't get up and cook him breakfast?'" Parham recalled. "I said, 'No, I don't get up and cook him breakfast because I work, too.'"

Parham continued to visit North Carolina once or twice a year, but as time progressed she knew fewer and fewer people there because so many of her family members and friends had moved away, some elsewhere in the South, but many of them, like her, to the northern cities. In fact, so many graduates of her high school left the region that reunions are often held away from Morven, even outside of the South. Morven Colored High School closed after Anson County schools were integrated. Because the school was small, reunions include all graduates, not just a single graduating class. Recent reunions have been held in Charlotte and Atlanta, but also in New York and Connecticut.

"We're all over the place," Parham said.

Both her parents are now dead, so she visits North Carolina less often. She does not miss the South. Although she recognizes that the region has progressed in its treatment of Black people, she's never contemplated returning, like many Black southern natives have done, not even in retirement. "I couldn't live down there," she said.

While Parham acknowledged that Boston remains a largely segregated city, with most Black people concentrated in one part of town, apart from White residents, the only time she has experienced problems because of her race was when Boston schools implemented court-ordered busing in 1974. Opposition to busing was strongest in predominantly Irish neighborhoods like Charlestown, Hyde Park, and South Boston, and two Italian neighborhoods, the North End and East Boston. White residents made up at least 95 percent of the population in all those neighborhoods in 1970.

During busing, Parham said, Gillette escorted its employees, including many Black workers, from the nearest subway station to the company's plant in South Boston to ensure their safety. She recalls that when hostilities were at their peak, someone threw a beer can at her. The Parham family was living in Mattapan at the time. Parham's daughter was bused to Hyde Park High School. Hyde Park is adjacent to Mattapan, but while Mattapan had a mixed population, nearly all residents of Hyde Park at the time were White people.[13] It has become more racially diverse since then, and today Black residents make up nearly half the population.

Shortly after the school year began, Parham said she contacted her daughter's teachers to introduce herself and ask them to telephone her, or send her a note, if Audrey was experiencing any difficulties. She worked the night shift at the time, she told them, so could easily be reached during school hours. But first-quarter report cards came out and Audrey received an F in conduct in one of her classes. The teacher had never contacted Parham, despite her request. That made her angry and she went to the school to speak to the teacher. She arrived to find White parents lined up in front of the school. She said White antibusing protestors staged demonstrations outside the school all year long, as they did throughout the city.[14] "I had to walk between them to the school," she said. "They were screaming, they were hollering, they were acting ugly. I didn't say anything."

Parham went to the office and met with the principal, who then summoned the teacher. Parham asked her why her daughter had received a failing grade for her conduct. She said to the teacher, "My daughter may not be an A student in all her classes, but one thing she's an A student in is conduct. We make sure of that."

Parham asked the teacher why she did not contact her if Audrey's conduct was disruptive.

"I didn't have time," the teacher told her.

Parham took a deep breath before speaking, but then, she said, delivered a scathing rebuke.

"You are a teacher?" Parham said. "And you're getting paid out of my tax money? And you don't have time to call parents?" She paused, then added, "I will do whatever I have to do and go to wherever I have to go . . ."

The teacher left and the principal apologized to Parham, she said.

"That's all right, don't be sorry," she told the principal. "Just make sure she do her job. If she don't want to teach these Black kids, she don't need to be in this system."

She then demanded that the principal update her regularly about her daughter's progress.

"I need a report every week," she said, "because I won't come to you next time. I will go over your head. Yes, I will."

Parham remains convinced that the teacher disliked her daughter, and gave her a failing grade, because she was Black.

"She was racist," she said.

Yet Parham insisted that the tensions that boiled over during busing were an exception and that she has experienced no other difficulties in Boston because of her race. Unlike some Black Bostonians, she was never afraid to go to South Boston. After all, she worked at the Gillette plant there for nearly four decades.

Parham's most lasting association since moving to Boston has been with her church. When she first came to Boston and lived with her aunt, her aunt's family did not attend church. A friend of her aunt's, who grew up in North Carolina with Parham's mother, was a Jehovah's Witness and she invited Lucy to one of their services. She didn't like it. It was quite different from her experience attending the Streater Grover AME church in Morven. She then set out to find an AME church in Boston and chose Charles Street AME, which is in the neighborhood where she first lived. She has been a member of Charles Street ever since.

"We are a friendly church," she said. "We are very open."

Parham has belonged to the church for more than sixty years. She became an officer in the church within a year or two of joining and has been an officer ever since. She is currently a steward in the church. Stewards, she said, oversee spiritual activities. She also oversees the church kitchen, which she jokingly refers to as "Lucy's Kitchen." She is known for exerting tight control over what goes on there and makes sure it is kept in good shape and thoroughly cleaned after events.

Parham grew up in a religious family and her devotion has never wavered. Her sister was an AME minister who was on the staff at Charles Street. She believes her faith has provided more than comfort, more than security. She has twice survived cancer and she credits her belief in God for that.

"I'm still here," she said. "I think the Lord healed it. I have an A1 doctor, but he can only do what he was taught."

In 1980, after their kids were grown, Parham and her husband bought a large house in suburban Milton. She wanted a single-family home, but was still working so she did not want to live too far from Gillette's plant in South Boston. Milton is more racially diverse than most affluent suburbs near Boston and has become a common destination for better-off Black families. Parham's husband died in 2006. In 2019, she sold her Milton house and moved back into her Mattapan triple-decker "for safety reasons" and to be nearer to family, since she is now in her eighties, though in good health. She lives on the first floor. Her daughter and grandson live on the second floor. Her granddaughter lives on the third floor.

"My grandkids are here, so I have a ball," she said. "My grandson—some of the questions he asks! It's a lot of fun."

She believes strongly that her life and the lives of her children have been better because she moved to Boston. Her daughter works as a paraprofessional in the Boston school system. Her son attended an elite prep school in Connecticut, Avon Old Farms, on a basketball scholarship. He also went to Springfield College on an athletic scholarship. He is a Boston police officer.

"Boston is a good place to live," she said. "All my family is doing well. I was always a person that if I wanted something, I went after it. My grandfather on my mother's side, that's the type of person he was. He always told us: you can be who you want to be. That's what I tell my kids—you can be anything you want to be."

That may be possible today for Black people in North Carolina, too. But it was not when Parham chose to leave.

5

Ollie Sumrall Jr.

Quitman, Mississippi, 1959

In October 1942, while three-year-old Ollie Sumrall Jr. slept in his bed at his family's home in Quitman, Mississippi, a group of White men abducted two Black teenage boys from the Clarke County Jail across town. The teenagers had been accused of threatening a White girl. The men drove them to an abandoned bridge over the nearby Chickasawhay River, put nooses around their necks, and hanged them.

It was not the first time Black people had been hanged from the bridge.

In December 1918, four Black men and women, two brothers and two sisters, both sisters pregnant, one just sixteen years old, were hanged from the bridge after their White boss was shot to death. Between 1888 and 1942, at least ten Black people were lynched in Clarke County, not counting the unborn children of the sisters.

The bridge became known locally as "the hanging bridge." The historian Jason Morgan Ward later wrote that it "boasted a history as gory as any lynching site in America." Langston Hughes penned a poem dedicated to the memory of the 1942 lynching victims called "The Bitter River."[1]

Growing up in Clarke County, Sumrall heard stories about the lynchings from his father and others. He heard stories about the bridge. His father used those stories as object lessons to teach his children how to behave around White people. Those stories instilled fear in the mind of the young Sumrall, as they likely did for many Black residents of Clarke County. That fear and the racial hatred that was all around him shaped his personality and every aspect of his behavior—where he went, the ways he spent his time, how he acted, what he said, and to whom he spoke.

Born in the land of the free, Sumrall never felt free in Mississippi. "That's why I left," he said.[2]

Sumrall was born in 1939 in Quitman, the seventh of ten children, and the youngest boy, born to Ollie and Girlia Sumrall. His parents moved to Mississippi from a small town in Alabama, about a half hour east of

North to Boston. Blake Gumprecht, Oxford University Press. © Blake Gumprecht 2023.
DOI: 10.1093/oso/9780197614440.003.0005

Ollie Sumrall Jr. in front of Charles Street African Methodist Episcopal Church in Roxbury, 2021. Photograph by Gregory Groover; used with permission.

Abandoned bridge over the Chickasawhay River in rural Clarke County, Mississippi, where at least six Black people were hanged in the early 1900s. It became known locally as "the hanging bridge." Ollie Sumrall was three years old and sleeping in his bed in nearby Quitman when two of those people were hanged in 1942, and he grew up hearing stories about the lynchings. Photograph by Andrew Lichtenstein; used with permission.

Quitman. He does not know how they ended up there, though they had many relatives in Clarke County. When Ollie Jr. was a baby, his father worked for the Gulf, Mobile, and Ohio Railroad, laying track. Eventually, he saved enough money to buy a two-acre lot in Quitman, where he built a house for his family. He bought an additional hundred acres bordering that lot and began to farm. He raised corn, cotton, peas, and peanuts to sell. He was unusual among Black farmers in Mississippi at the time because he owned his land. Many were tenant farmers or sharecroppers, struggling year in and year out, while their White landlords prospered from their work.

Machines had transformed American agriculture, but Black farmers like Ollie Sr. practiced a primitive form of farming because they could not afford the expensive equipment. He owned horses and mules, but not a tractor. He put his mule in a harness to plow his fields. He hitched his mule to a wagon to haul his crops downtown to sell. The entire family helped in the fields. Ollie Jr. spent most of his free time there, plowing, picking peas, pulling peanuts from the soil, and placing them in burlap bags. Beside the family house, Sumrall's father grew a wide range of vegetables and fruits for family meals in a kitchen garden. He also raised pigs, turkeys, and chickens.

"He grew everything we ate," Sumrall said.

Although his mother occasionally cooked, cleaned, and washed clothes in the houses of White families, mostly she stayed home to raise her large family. "She had plenty to do at home," he recalled.

Ollie adored his mother's cooking, a characteristic that seems ubiquitous among Black men of his generation. She cooked chicken with gravy, rice with gravy, butter beans, collard greens, and sweet potato pie, typical Black southern food. "I don't think anybody could beat my mother's cooking," he said. "I liked it all, except the cabbage."

The Sumrall family lived in a white frame house on the north side of Quitman in the Black section of the city. There were so many Sumralls living in the area—one of his grandfathers had twenty kids—that it became known as "Sumrall town." Ollie Jr. had aunts and uncles, nieces and nephews, and cousins who lived nearby. The house had six rooms, including four bedrooms, and a big front porch. Ollie shared a bedroom with three brothers, though he always had his own bed. There was a piano in the living room.

"My family wasn't poor," he said. "My dad farmed all the time. He did pretty good. We didn't worry about nothing. He sent two kids to college."

Sumrall's mother and father were deeply religious. Every Sunday morning, the entire family attended the Pearlie Grove Baptist Church, a few blocks from their home. Ollie Sr. parented with a light hand, according to his son, and required little of his children. He did not force them to help in the fields. He did not push them to go to college. But he did require them to go to church every Sunday. Ollie's father was an officer in the church. Ollie's brother, Arthur, played piano during services. His sister, Oudia Faye, was a member of the choir. Ollie went to church every Sunday, but his parents' strong religious beliefs didn't rub off on him until much later, long after he moved to Boston.

The elder Sumrall awoke every morning before dawn to work in the fields so that he could take advantage of the coolest temperatures of the day. When it got too hot to work, he came home, sat on the front porch, and read his Bible. "Daddy was a very religious man," Sumrall said. "He was in church all the time. My mother and father, all they talked about was religion."

Quitman was a typical small county seat and market center in the Jim Crow South. The town's population was just under two thousand in 1950. Black people made up about a third of residents and lived on the north side. White residents lived nearer to downtown.[3] Black people worked in a sawmill in town or on farms. Some were employed at a large textile mill in Stonewall, northwest of Quitman. Agriculture was important in Clarke County, but the northern half of the county around Quitman was hilly and less dependent on cotton than other parts of Mississippi.

Quitman was rigidly segregated. Black and White youth attended separate schools. The public swimming pool was off limits to Black people, as was a beach in a nearby state park. Black people were allowed to fish at the park only if they accompanied a White person. Sumrall sometimes went there with a White man who employed his mother. The town was too small to have many Black-owned businesses, other than juke joints. Black and White shoppers patronized the same stores, but Black customers knew to allow Whites to be served before them, even if they arrived later. Black people were expected to be off the streets downtown by nightfall.

The bus station in Quitman had separate waiting rooms, ticket windows, and restrooms for Black and White people.[4] There were designated White and "Colored" water fountains in public buildings. "I wondered why," Sumrall said. "All of us are made the same."

Black moviegoers were required to sit upstairs at the Majestic Theater downtown, while Whites sat downstairs. Black people had to enter the theater via a fire escape that went up the side of the building. Sumrall went to movies there about once a month until he was in high school and became more socially aware. But he and a friend decided to stop going to the theater because of the restrictions. "We said it isn't right," he said. "We never went back."

As in the rest of the South, White-owned restaurants forbade Black customers from entering through the front door or being served in their dining rooms. They were required to go to the back door for service. Sumrall said White restaurants in Quitman typically had a single, small table in the back for Black diners, but only four people could be seated there at a time. Sumrall got tired of that, too. He said he ate at a White-owned restaurant only once for that reason. "That didn't suit me," he said. In the late 1940s, a Black brick mason, Rufus McRee, a distant cousin of Sumrall's, built a brick hotel in town. The McRee Hotel also housed a restaurant, grocery, beauty salon, and

The McRee Hotel in Quitman, Mississippi, built by a Black brick mason, Rufus McRee, a distant cousin of Ollie Sumrall, in the late 1940s. It housed a restaurant, grocery, beauty salon, and barbershop and became a center of Black life in the city. Used with permission, Historic Resources Inventory, Historic Preservation Division, Mississippi Department of Archives and History.

barbershop. It became the center of Black community life in Quitman for two decades.[5]

The public infrastructure in Quitman was different in the White and Black sections of town. There were streetlights and sidewalks in White sections, but not in Black areas. White homes had electricity and running water, but Black homes did not for much of the time Sumrall was growing up. Many streets in Black sections were unpaved. The Sumrall family obtained water from a pump beside their back porch. There was an outhouse nearby. Their only lights were kerosene lamps. To heat water for baths, they built a fire beneath a big black pot in the backyard and carried water into the house one bucket at a time.

The McRee Hotel was the first Black-owned building in town to have running water. The Sumrall family finally obtained electricity and indoor plumbing in the early 1950s, when Ollie was about thirteen or fourteen years old.

"Whites had it all," Sumrall said. "Blacks didn't have anything."

Black adults were prevented from voting in Clarke County for decades. Civil rights legislation enacted by Congress in 1957 and 1960 authorized the Department of Justice to file lawsuits to help Black people obtain the right to vote. One of the first such voting discrimination suits targeted Clarke County. The Justice Department sent a young, Harvard-educated lawyer, Gerald M. Stern, there to investigate and he later wrote about that experience. Stern reported that "the White political structure of Clarke County did not admit any Negroes to register to vote for at least thirty years" and that "none of the Negroes in Clarke County had ever heard of a Negro's being permitted to register."

White government officials in Clarke County, and throughout Mississippi, used a variety of tactics to prevent Black people from registering. Applicants were required to fill out a lengthy application (investigators found that White voters often were not). They were required to interpret one of 265 sections of the Mississippi constitution, typically an especially difficult section (Whites seldom had to pass any such test).

County officials often made excuses to discourage Black people who sought to register. They would claim they were out of registration forms. Or they told them they would have to register when the registrar was in the office, but said he was out. Whites were permitted to register with the deputy clerk. Black people told Stern that sometimes they were simply refused without any reason given. One Black man, Samuel Owens, a Black school principal for fifty years, so respected in the community that his school was named for him, told investigators he had been prevented from registering seven times in four years.

When the federal lawsuit was heard in court in 1962, Clarke County's registrar of voters, A. L. Ramsey, a frail, eighty-two-year-old White man who had been registrar since 1953, testified that when Black people tried to register, he asked them to go home and reconsider. "Well, during that time, that was when we were having a lot of trouble over the country," he told the court. "Mississippi wasn't having any trouble. I would always just tell them that I wasn't going to refuse them the opportunity to register, but then I would just like for us to consider this matter, that due to the fact that they were having trouble in other parts of the country and that we folks here in Mississippi, White and colored, were getting along together and they were our friends and we were their friends and we weren't going to have any trouble either way, and then I just suggested to them that they go back home and consider this matter and think it over and come back later."[6]

Such was the racial climate in which Sumrall was raised, and it had an oppressive impact on him. It continued to shape his life even after he moved to Boston.

Growing up in Quitman, Sumrall rarely left his home, except to go to school or church. He had few friends. He mostly kept to himself. That was intentional. Staying at home and being alone were defense mechanisms to ensure his safety. During the week, he would go to school, come home, work in the fields until dinner, eat, take a bath, and then go to bed. On Saturdays, he might play basketball or baseball. On Sundays, he went to church. He rarely went downtown or to stores. "It was safe there at the house," he said. "I didn't go nowhere."

Sumrall's father had taught him about Clarke County's troubled racial history. He heard rumors about other horrific acts. Some of the stories he tells do not appear to be true, at least based on the well-developed historical record about Clarke County's racial past. The threat of violence was used to intimidate Black people in Clarke County, and that may have encouraged unsubstantiated rumors to spread. He said, for example, that he heard when he was ten or eleven that White men killed multiple Black boys and dragged their bodies through the streets behind a vehicle. He said that a Clarke County sheriff, who had been implicated in earlier lynchings, "died a hard death." None of that appears to have happened, but it had a chilling effect on Sumrall nevertheless.

"It scared us," he said. "That's why I didn't do anything. That's why I didn't go anywhere."

Sumrall's father instructed his son to avoid interacting with White people. If a White spoke to him, his father said, he should always show proper respect. If he went to a store, he should allow White customers to be served before him. Like Black parents of males throughout the South, his father reserved his strongest warnings for young Ollie about White women. Stay away from them, he said. Don't look at them. Don't talk to them. Don't respond to them in any way. Black males throughout the South knew that if they even looked at a White woman in the wrong way that they could end up dead.

Sumrall developed a fear of White women as a result that would influence his behavior even after he moved to Boston. "As a kid growing up, my dad told us to leave White people alone," he said. "They were very prejudiced. He told us to mind our own business, don't say nothing to them, that way you won't get in any trouble. That's the way we were raised up."

Still, in a small town in the Deep South where White residents made up most of the population and there were few Black-owned businesses, it was impossible to avoid Whites altogether. The young Sumrall kept silent wherever he went. "They call you 'nigger' in a minute—'Nigger, where you going?'" he recalled. "I didn't open my mouth. I kept walking." If he ran an errand for his parents, say to pick up a bag of sugar at a grocery, and somebody called him "nigger," he would not respond. He simply turned around and walked back home without getting whatever he came to the store to buy. "That's how I got along," he said. "Don't say nothing and keep my mouth closed."

Sumrall said that not all White people in Quitman were racist. His father occasionally worked for a White man who lived near them and owned a large farm. His father helped him in the garden and mowed the family's lawn. Ollie became friends with his son, who was a couple years older than he was. The family erected a basketball net in their backyard. Ollie would play basketball with the son, or they shot marbles. "They didn't care about no color," he said. "They didn't feel like they were no better than nobody else. They didn't figure they were better than the Blacks. They said, 'We all have to live together.' We didn't have no problem."

As those experiences suggest, Sumrall's memories of his childhood are not entirely negative, despite the racism all around him. He had fun. He played baseball and basketball. He fished. He shot marbles. He had a girlfriend when he was in high school. He had a loving family, with many brothers and sisters, which helped insulate him from all that was bad about Quitman. "I had a nice boyhood," he said. "We just lived the way the Lord wants us to live. God likes peace. God doesn't like arguments. He wants us to be happy. I was on the happy side."

There do not appear to have been any lynchings in Clarke County after the two teenage boys were hanged in 1942, perhaps because past killings had drawn national attention. The FBI investigated those lynchings, but nothing came of it. The National Association for the Advancement of Colored People sent undercover investigators to Clarke County. The *Chicago Defender*, a Black newspaper with a national audience, twice sent reporters to the county and wrote three articles about hangings there.[7]

But White people in Clarke County continued to use violence, and violent threats, to control Black residents, particularly after a local civil rights movement emerged in the early 1960s. Black people who spoke to federal attorneys investigating voting rights discrimination were threatened. After Black people boycotted White-owned businesses in the town of Shubuta and then staged a march through the city, police officers attacked marchers with clubs. A cross was burned on the lawn of the house where a local civil rights leader lived.[8]

In the summer of 1966, a mimeographed flier circulated in Clarke County that warned Blacks in stark terms [mistakes retained from the original]: "NIGGERS BEWARE! All niggers will be shot and killed if any demonstrations accure in Mississippi. All kinky head darkies better stay on your guard, and cut out all this smart allic demonstrations. If you find your car windows dash in and it burn up, or your wife hanging on a light pole, or kids strung up in the outdoor toilet, it will be alright."[9]

One of Sumrall's cousins in Quitman, John Otis Sumrall, who grew up next door to the McRee Hotel, was one of the leaders of civil rights efforts in Clarke County. He was once jailed for punching a sheriff's deputy. Ollie was four years ahead of John Otis in school, so he may not have seen the potential for social change that became apparent just a few years later. Ollie never had any desire to challenge the White power structure in Quitman or become involved in the civil rights movement. He never became politically active in Boston either.[10] "I didn't think it was worth it," he said.

Progress was slow for Black people in small towns in the Deep South, but they did benefit from incremental improvements. There were no Black high schools in Clarke County until after World War II, but southern states gradually increased their funding for Black schools as a way to avoid integration. In 1896, the US Supreme Court, in *Plessy v. Ferguson*, ruled that segregation by race was legal so long as facilities were equal. White and Black schools in the South during the Jim Crow era were rarely equal, but southern states thought they could better convince judges that they were by making funding more equitable.[11]

Between 1910 and 1950, states such as Alabama and Louisiana more than doubled their per pupil funding for Black schools as a ratio of funding for White schools. Still, Mississippi was considered the most racist state in the South and lagged other states in boosting Black school funding.[12] In Clarke County, though, school officials closed most of the county's most decrepit Black schools, many of them one-room cabins in the country, and built new schools. With state funds, the county also built its first two Black high schools. In 1955, one year after the Supreme Court overturned the "separate but equal" doctrine in *Brown v. Board of Education* and outlawed segregated schools, Clarke County spent $91 per Black student and $168 each for White students.

When Sumrall entered high school, Quitman's Black high school was relatively new. The state Sovereignty Commission, formed to investigate civil rights efforts in the state, observed that the county's Black high schools were "newer and nicer than White school buildings."[13] Sumrall agreed with that assessment. Unlike Black students elsewhere, he said he never had to use dirty, outdated textbooks passed down from White schools. Though he acknowledged that Black schools were inferior to White schools, he insisted they provided a good-quality education.

To prove his point, he noted that his brother, Arthur, got a sufficient education in Quitman to go to college and medical school, become a physician, and have a long and successful career as a dermatologist in Indianapolis. Sumrall himself was held back after the tenth grade, which suggests that his school was challenging and sought to make sure Black pupils received an adequate education.

Because Sumrall struggled in school, he never considered going to college. In high school, he worked at an auto body shop in Quitman. He thought if he stayed in town after he graduated he could continue to work at the body shop. His father quit farming the year before Sumrall finished high school, once he turned seventy. He was physically worn out from decades of working on the railroad and in his fields, his son said. But Ollie Jr. never had any desire to take over his father's farm. None of his siblings chose to farm either. "I wouldn't want to do no farming," he said. "I just didn't like it. The sun is hot. You had to get up early and go out in the fields. I didn't want that type of life."

Sumrall graduated from Quitman's Black high school, Shirley-Owens High School, in 1959. For Black males in Mississippi at the time, there were few career options other than farming. Quitman had its sawmill and a cotton gin. Stonewall had its textile factory, where they made blue jeans. He was not interested in any of those options. Once upon a time, he had dreamed of becoming a musician, but then "got girl crazy," he said, and never learned how to play the piano as intended. He decided instead to leave Quitman and leave the South.

"I was just tired of Mississippi," he said.

The destinations of Black migrants who left the South was strongly influenced by geography. Historically, Black people in the Southeast migrated to cities like Washington, Philadelphia, and New York because they were closest. Migrants from Louisiana and Texas, in contrast, often headed to California. Most Black migrants from Mississippi ended up in Chicago because it was a straight line north, and they could travel there easily. Migrants traveled initially aboard the Illinois Central Railroad, which ran from New Orleans to Chicago. Later they went on buses that traveled north on Interstate 55.[14] Boston had few Mississippi-born Black people, because it was a long way away. Quitman is 1,341 miles from Boston, but Chicago is only 756 miles.

Sumrall had a friend, Flossie Moore, who had migrated to Chicago and encouraged him to move there. They had grown up on the same street. She was two years ahead of him in school. She eventually married Sumrall's cousin. "She wrote me a letter and told me to come to Chicago," he said. "Flossie told me she would find me a place to stay if I come there." Sumrall's father offered to pay his bus fare. "If I can send my two kids to college I can send you to Chicago," he told his son.

Black people had been leaving Clarke County for decades, owing at least partly to its history of violence against them, and everyday mistreatment. The county's Black population declined by nearly half from 1910 to 1970. In thirty years following World War II, the county lost nearly three thousand Blacks.[15] Some Black migrants followed the same path as family and neighbors, helping to create distinct ethnic enclaves in faraway cities. In 1927, a traveling preacher from Shubuta in southern Clarke County relocated to Albany, New York, bought land, and encouraged Black people from back home to join him. Black migrants from Shubuta helped create Albany's Rapp Road community.[16]

Gerald Stern, the Department of Justice attorney who traveled to Clarke County in 1961 to investigate voting rights discrimination and interviewed many local residents, wrote, "High school graduation day—for those who finish high school—is often their last day in Clarke County. It's the kind of place people leave."

By the time Sumrall graduated from high school in May 1959, two of his siblings had relocated to Boston and a third was planning to join them. But Ollie still intended to go to Chicago, at least until his brother and family came to Quitman for a visit. Sumrall's oldest brother, Job, left Quitman to join the military, serving in the army. Toward the end of his service, he was transferred to Fort Devens in the Boston suburbs. He was stationed there when he was discharged. Like many Black men, he first experienced life outside the segregated South in the military.

Job liked Boston, his brother said, so he decided to stay there after his military service ended. He got a job at American Biltrite, a rubber-manufacturing plant in Chelsea, where he made heels for shoes. He lived in Roxbury with his family. Sumrall's sister, Betty, had also moved to Boston with a friend after graduating high school. She worked in a nursing home. She later married and had a family in Boston, staying there until she got sick a few years ago.

In June 1959, Job drove to Quitman with his wife and two young children for a two-week visit. Sister Fay, who still lived in Quitman, planned to go with them when they returned to Boston. But Fay got pregnant and decided at the last minute not to go. One night, shortly after Job arrived in Quitman, he and Ollie were sitting on the porch talking. Since Fay was no longer planning to move to Boston, Job now had an empty seat in his car for the return trip. Ollie asked him if he could go to Boston with him. He was nineteen years old. "C'mon, let's go," Job told him.

Ollie thought about it and the night before his brother was scheduled to leave, he decided to move to Boston. He packed a suitcase and they left the next day. So much for the idea that migrants plot and scheme for years before moving. The decision to migrate is sometimes more spontaneous. "I didn't know anything about Boston," Sumrall said. "I didn't know nothing about it."

Ollie and Job drove to Boston without stopping, except for gas and meals. Blacks traveling in the Jim Crow South had difficulty finding motels that would allow them to stay the night. They took turns driving. When one drove, the other slept. Sumrall moved in with his brother and his family. They had an apartment in a three-family house on Warren Street in Roxbury, the same street on which Charles Street African Methodist Episcopal Church is located.

Boston was a fundamental change for a young man who had spent his entire life in a small town in the Deep South. Before coming to Boston, the farthest Sumrall had ever traveled from home was to Tuskegee, Alabama, a three-and-a-half-hour drive, where two of his siblings went for college. He noticed differences in Boston right away. When he went to a corner store to buy a soda, he learned that carbonated beverages were called "tonics" in Boston and that you had to pay a return deposit on bottles. You never had to do that in Mississippi. Shortly after he arrived in Boston, he experienced his first hailstorm.

But the biggest change for Sumrall was being apart from his mother and father for the first time. One day he was sitting alone on the back porch of his brother's apartment and he broke down, crying. "I didn't like it at first," he recalled sixty years later. "Tears come out of my eyes. I said, 'What am I doing here?' I got lonesome for home."

Sumrall got a job at the Regal Restaurant in Roxbury, on the same street where he lived, through his brother's wife, who had an uncle who worked there. He washed dishes at first, but over time did a little of everything. He became a short-order cook. He liked it.

One day, a White woman who was eating at the restaurant became friendly with him. They got to talking and she eventually asked him if he would like to go to a movie sometime. What a change that represented from his life in Mississippi, where he was forbidden from even eating in the same restaurants as White people. In Boston, he quickly discovered, he could go to any restaurant he desired, eat beside Whites sitting at the next table, and talk to whomever he chose.

But the exchange frightened him, because he had been taught in Mississippi that he should never, ever speak to a White woman, except to say, "Yes, ma'am" or "No, ma'am." Attempting to bridge that divide was perhaps the greatest violation of social codes that existed in the Jim Crow South. Even though he had left the South, the racial code that Sumrall learned in Mississippi was still imprinted on his psyche. He never went out on a date with the woman. "It didn't feel right," he said. "I thought about the things happening down south. All that was in my mind. I thought it might be the same way. I said, 'No, this ain't right,' so I never did go."

The racism that shaped Sumrall's lifestyle growing up in Mississippi also had permanent impacts. In Quitman, he chose to stay home and keep to himself for safety reasons. In Boston, he behaved the same way. It had become part of his personality. "I still like to be by myself," he said.

Sumrall worked at the restaurant for three years, until it closed following the death of one of its owners. He then got a job at a tire store in Cambridge, changing tires and doing mechanical work. He worked there for more than a decade. The job paid better than the restaurant. He continued to live with his brother and his family, even after they moved to another apartment and eventually bought their own two-family house in Dorchester. He always had his own bedroom. He was part of the family, got along well with his sister-in-law and the kids. They encouraged him to stay. He did not get his own place until he married.

Sumrall grew to like Boston. He liked that he could walk out his front door and take a bus most anywhere. He went to the beach. Basketball had always been his favorite sport and he became a Boston Celtics fan at a time when the team won ten titles in twelve years, led by outspoken Black center Bill Russell, whose family had migrated from Louisiana to California. He went to many Celtics games at the Boston Garden. He appreciated the ways in which Boston was different from the South. "I had more freedom," he said. "I could do things here I couldn't do in Mississippi."

Sumrall met his first wife, Dolores Drew, in the mid-1960s through her brother, one of his coworkers at Cambridge Tire. The siblings lived together and Ollie met her one day when he visited his friend. She had moved to Boston from North Carolina several years before. They married about 1968 and got an apartment on Warren Street in Roxbury. They quickly had two children, Joseph and Sharon. Because they both worked full time, they sent the kids to North Carolina to be raised by their maternal grandmother. But the marriage failed, and they broke up in 1972. "She was one of those kind that like to go out," he said, "and I didn't."

About a year after his marriage ended, he met his second wife, Martha Jones. Like Dolores, she had moved to Boston from the South. She grew up in Selma, Alabama, a two-hour drive from Quitman. They met at a cookout, then went, ironically it would turn out, to a nightclub. She was a nurse at a Veterans Administration hospital. They moved in together. She had four kids from previous relationships, and they raised them jointly. They eventually had two kids of their own, Dwayne and Michael. They did not marry until after their kids were born.

"She was a nice girl," he said. "We hit it off. She didn't like to hang out in clubs and bars. All the rest of them, they like to hang out and get high. It wasn't for me."

About 1973, Sumrall left his job at the tire shop and went to work at a liquor store in Roxbury, even though, he said, "I couldn't stand liquor." In 1986, he got a job as a security guard at Roxbury Community College. He liked that job and worked there for twenty-six years, retiring in 2012. Ollie and Martha lived at first in a Dorchester apartment. Then, in 1978, Sumrall bought a two-family house on Ford Street in Dorchester, where he still lives. He now lives there with his two sons. A stepdaughter lives in the other half of the house.

Sumrall was not religious growing up, despite the efforts of his mother and father, but eventually their influence had an impact. Although he did not go to church during his first two decades in Boston, about 1980 he reconsidered. His family had always attended a Baptist church in Mississippi, but he said there were no Baptist churches near his home in Boston. A friend

Mounted Boston police separate Black and White beachgoers on Carson Beach in South Boston in 1975. Ollie Sumrall stopped going to Carson Beach during this time because racial conflicts became common. Photograph by George Rizer, *Boston Globe*; used with permission, Getty Images.

told him about a church just down the street from where Sumrall was living. That church was Charles Street AME on Warren Street in Roxbury. Sumrall started attending Charles Street and has done so ever since. He did not see the differences between Baptist and AME churches as important, though his wife continued to attend a Baptist church.

"My mother and father always wanted me to go to church," he said. "I started going and never stopped. I don't know what changed. God can change anybody."

He and his wife were married for more than thirty years. They visited the South every year—spending two weeks with her family in Selma and two weeks with his in Quitman. Martha died in 2012 after a long illness. She suffered from diabetes, was on dialysis, and succumbed to heart failure. "We had a good time," he said.

Although Sumrall appreciated Boston's advantages over Mississippi from the moment he arrived, he also quickly discovered, like most Black people, that Boston's benefits were relative and that racism was prevalent in the city. That surprised him at first. He expected it to be better. But he saw racism in the way that some Whites looked at him. He could see it in their eyes and in the way they treated him. He lived through the busing years, when racism in Boston was most overt and ugly. There was a time when he would not go to Carson Beach in South Boston, the closest beach to his home, because Blacks were expected to remain on one side of the beach, and fights between White and Black beachgoers were common. Sometimes police had to separate them.[17]

Sumrall believes racism in Boston has diminished over time but still exists, even if it is expressed differently than in the South. "Down there they let you know that they're racist," he said. "Here they hide it. They don't want you to know that they're racist. They do it in a sneaky way. It wasn't as great here as I thought it would be, but I learned to live with it."

In Sumrall's more than six decades in Boston, he has always lived in Roxbury or Dorchester in the heart of Boston's Black community. He has never considered living anywhere else. All but one of his jobs was also located in that part of Boston. Like most of the people profiled for this project, he chose to remain in Black neighborhoods because he prefers them, not because he was prevented from living elsewhere by housing discrimination. He likes where he lives because it reminds him of the South, minus the White people. Most of his friends over the years have been southerners. Many of those he met through his church. It is telling that both of Sumrall's wives were southern born and bred. Because of that, his adjustment to Boston was relatively easy and quick. "Most of the people I've been associated with here were from the South," he said. "Even my neighbors, they're from somewhere down south. I enjoy them. It feels like home. I never knew too many people from Boston."

Asked if he gave up anything significant in leaving Mississippi and moving north, Sumrall responds bluntly. "Yeah, I gave up being around White folks," he said. "I can avoid them here."

Sumrall's life may appear unremarkable. It may not seem to be a resounding confirmation of the benefits of the Great Migration. What he has gained has been more subtle and personal. He achieved his goals. He made enough money to buy his own home. He has a loving family, with many grandkids and great-grandchildren. Most of his children live nearby. He got what he wanted—except the Cadillac he coveted when he was younger. "Too expensive," he said.

Moving to Boston has allowed Sumrall to do what he wants, go where he chooses, speak his mind, and, above all, to be the person he wished to be. It has allowed him the freedom to live without fear. His desires were simple, but he could not fulfill them in Mississippi.

"If I had to do it all over again, I'd come right to Boston," he said. "I have a good life up here. It turned out very nice."

6

Elizabeth Hall Davis

Columbia, South Carolina, 1963

To Elizabeth Hall Davis, the Boston she first experienced in 1963 did not seem much different from the segregated southern city she left behind.

Davis grew up in Columbia, South Carolina. She worked as a teacher there before following her mother north. In Columbia, she lived in an all-Black neighborhood, taught at Black schools, and rarely interacted with White people. The same was true in Boston, for the most part. "In Columbia, I was around all Blacks," she recalled. "And when I came to Boston I was around all Blacks."

That did not bother her, though. She had never known anything different. But she did earn more money in Boston and she liked that. She discovered over time that Boston provided greater freedom and opportunity of all sorts for her and her children.

"It was worth it," she said. "It worked out for me."[1]

Davis was born in 1929 in the Columbia home of her maternal grandparents. A Black midwife helped with the delivery. Born Elizabeth Hall, she was the only child of Robert Hall and Martha Ann Spigner. It's uncertain whether they were married. Her father died when she was three or four years old. She does not remember him. She and her mother then moved in with her mother's parents.[2] They lived in a small house in the Ridgewood neighborhood of Columbia. Her mother worked as a servant for "wealthy" White families—cooking, cleaning, and taking care of their children. Elizabeth's grandmother did laundry in her home for White families. There were few other career options at the time for uneducated Black women in the South. According to Davis's daughter, when Elizabeth got older she would help her grandmother, picking up dirty laundry from White homes and later delivering the washed and folded clothing.

Davis said her family was "not poor, just average," but she described a childhood that was lacking in certain regards, but probably typical for working-class Black people in South Carolina at the time. "I didn't have toys or many good things to play with," she said. "I would make toys, take cans or pull up grass or whatever—pull up some grass and say this is going to be

North to Boston. Blake Gumprecht, Oxford University Press. © Blake Gumprecht 2023.
DOI: 10.1093/oso/9780197614440.003.0006

Elizabeth Hall Davis in 2015. Photograph by Blake Gumprecht.

my doll. The roots would be the hair." Davis's father had been a minister, according to her son, and she was raised in the Baptist church. She played the piano in church and taught Sunday school when she got older.

Ridgewood was a Black neighborhood. Davis attended all-Black schools. Black residents lived apart from White residents and rarely encountered them. Black people shopped mostly at Black-owned stores. She recalled that the only time she was around White people growing up was at the annual South Carolina State Fair in Columbia.

Black schools in the Jim Crow South were generally inferior to White schools, but she did not recognize that as a child. She did notice that all her schoolbooks were "hand-me downs," likely dated and passed down from White schools when they got new textbooks. Her mother and grandparents taught her how she should act around White people, how to speak to them, and about unwritten social codes that Black people were expected to follow. They taught her about Jim Crow laws that mandated separation of the races. She took a city bus to high

Elizabeth Hall Davis
when she graduated
from Benedict College
in Columbia, South
Carolina, in 1949. Used
with permission, Elizabeth
Hall Davis.

school, but she knew that when she boarded the bus that she had to go to the back, like other Black riders. "My parents taught me, 'This is the law, we go by the law,'" she said. "I didn't question it. That's just the way things were."

Davis's mother had only a sixth- or seventh-grade education, but she could read and write. She insisted that her daughter concentrate on her education and go to college, so that she could have better opportunities than her mother had. Elizabeth's daughter, Danné Davis, is an associate professor of education at Montclair State University in New Jersey. She wrote about her parents in the academic journal *Genealogy*. She said about Elizabeth, "Her mother scrubbed floors to keep [her] from scrubbing floors."

"I can attest to never seeing my mother clean floors," Danné wrote.[3]

Elizabeth graduated from Booker T. Washington High School in Columbia, then studied at two Black colleges, Benedict College and Allen University. They are adjacent to each other in Columbia and students could take classes at both. Her mom and grandparents scraped together the sixty dollars a month needed to pay for tuition. Sometimes she missed class because she did not have the ten cents required for bus fare. Once, when she told one of her professors why she missed class, the teacher gave her bus fare for the rest of the week and offered to help in the future when necessary.[4]

Davis earned a degree in elementary education from Benedict College in 1949, intending to become a teacher. Earning a college degree elevated her into the elite of southern Black society at the time. In 1950, only 2 percent of adult Black women in South Carolina had graduated from a four-year college. There was no more respected career for a Black woman than teacher, particularly in the South, where most still worked as domestics.[5]

While she was in college, Elizabeth met her future husband, Lafayette Davis. They were introduced by one of her classmates, who later taught at the same school in Columbia. Five years older than Elizabeth, Lafayette had only a sixth-grade education and worked as a bellhop at the Columbia Hotel.[6] He was the youngest of five children. His parents owned a neighborhood market in Columbia that also sold hot food. Elizabeth called it a soul food restaurant, but her son said that is "an embellishment." He acknowledged his grandfather was "a pretty good cook" and said his dad learned to cook from him while growing up. Lafayette also worked in the mess hall while he was in the military. Those experiences would shape his work life in Boston.

Davis got her first teaching job at a Black elementary school in Fountain Inn, South Carolina, a small town near Greenville in the northern part of the state, about ninety minutes northwest of Columbia. A friend of her family was the principal there. She said she taught fifth grade, but a class photo from the period shows her with a second-grade class. She rented a room in a family house near the school and returned to Columbia to live every summer. She taught in Fountain Inn for about five years. Her future husband drove there on weekends to visit her. They became engaged one Christmas, she said, but made no immediate plans about when they would marry. At the end of the school year, her fiancé drove to Fountain Inn to bring her back to Columbia for the summer and told her they were getting married.

When Lafayette arrived at the home where Elizabeth rented a room, he said to her, "You might as well take everything because you're not coming back."

Surprised, Elizabeth said, "What you mean I'm not coming back?"

"We're going to get married," he said.

"What you mean 'married'?" she replied. "I haven't said anything to my momma."

"Well, I said something to her," he said.

Elizabeth Hall Davis (back row, left) with her second-grade class at a Black elementary school in Fountain Inn, South Carolina, in 1951. Used with permission, Elizabeth Hall Davis.

Interviewed initially when she was eighty-six years old, Davis has an imperfect recall about some important dates and events in her life. Her children remember some details differently. Elizabeth and Lafayette married in July 1953. She said they were married at a courthouse in Fountain Inn, though it is not a county seat, so that seems unlikely. Later she said they were married in York, South Carolina, which is not near Fountain Inn or Columbia. She said she returned to teach the following year in Fountain Inn even after they got married, but that, too, seems doubtful.

Real estate records indicate that Davis and her husband bought a small house in Columbia in 1953. Her husband served in the US Army from 1938 to 1946 and was able to obtain a home loan from the Veterans Administration, one of many benefits Congress provided to World War II veterans in the Servicemen's Readjustment Act of 1944, known as the GI Bill. Research by Davis's daughter found that Lafayette Davis was born in 1924, which, if true, meant he was only fourteen years old when he joined the army. Birth records for Black people in the South at the time were often nonexistent, so he may have lied about his age to join the military. Or he may have been older than records indicate.

The house they purchased was a celery-green, 546-square-foot single-family home in the Greenview neighborhood, an all-Black area then on the northern edge of Columbia. The house had been built the year before and they were the first people to live in it.[7] After quitting her teaching position in Fountain Inn, Elizabeth got a job teaching fifth grade at Lower Richland School, an all-Black elementary school southeast of Columbia. She and her husband owned a car, which she drove to the school. The Columbia Hotel was downtown, so her husband likely took public transportation to his bellhop job.

She gave birth to her first child, a son, Marquis, on July 4, 1954. She resumed teaching that fall. Her mother-in-law took care of her son while she was at work and eventually moved in with the young parents. Marquis lived in Columbia for his first nine years, and he recalled it as a typical 1950s boyhood. He had little understanding of race relations at the time. He lived in an all-Black neighborhood and went to an all-Black elementary school, just as his mom had. All his friends were Black. He said that his parents used to spell out "White"—"W–h–i–t–e"—when they talked about White people around him. Although Columbia was segregated, he had little memory of that because he was rarely around White people. However, he does recall once as a child going to Sears with his mother and almost taking a drink from a Whites-only water fountain, not realizing that he was forbidden to use it.

"You can't use that," his mom snapped at him.

Marquis replied, "Why? What did I do wrong?"[8]

Davis was inspired to move to Boston by her mother, who she said moved to the city about 1950 to work as a live-in servant for a Jewish family in Brookline. She seemed uncertain about the date, however, and it may have been later than that. She said her mother's employers traveled to Columbia to recruit servants, though she's uncertain how they connected with her mom. Marquis says his grandmother had a friend from South Carolina who had moved to Boston to work as a domestic, which may have influenced her decision.[9] At some point, Davis visited her mom in Boston, and her mother encouraged her to move to the city. But Davis was reluctant at first because she had a teaching job in South Carolina and Boston schools had few Black teachers at the time. As late as 1963, only forty of thirty-six hundred teachers in the Boston school system were Black. It had no Black principals.[10]

"I want you near me," her mother told her.

Elizabeth dismissed the idea. "I got a job," she said. "I'm teaching, and I'm not going to find a job up there because they're not hiring Blacks.'"

Nevertheless, she discussed the possibility of moving to Boston with her husband and he was receptive to the idea, particularly since Elizabeth no longer had any immediate family in South Carolina. Her husband visited Boston and he liked it, she said. Elizabeth's mother continued to try to persuade her to come north. She told her daughter that she and her husband could stay with her until they got established.

"She said Boston is a better place," Davis recalled. "She said, 'You'll find a job.' Believing what she said, I came."

Davis family members disagree about what happened next. Elizabeth says she and Marquis moved to Boston about 1963, but said her husband stayed behind in South Carolina. But both her kids say their dad moved first, which, given gender roles at the time, seems more likely. Plus, Elizabeth was teaching, so it seems doubtful she would have left in the middle of a school year.

According to Danné Davis, her father moved to Boston in 1962 after his mother died. She said he lived initially with Elizabeth's mother and stepfather, Lonnie Brabham. Davis never mentioned having a stepfather when I interviewed her. It is unknown when they met and married. Both of her children called Brabham "Popsie." Danné said she did not know until after her grandmother died that Brabham was not her grandfather. Because of his experience as a cook growing up and in the army, Davis's father was able to get a job cooking at the Hayes-Bickford restaurant chain. He was employed as a cook for the rest of his working life in Boston.

According to Danné's research, her father traveled back to Columbia to visit Elizabeth in January or February 1963, when Danné was conceived. At the end of the school year in June, her mom resigned her teaching position. She and her son then moved to Boston.[11] Danné was an unusual variety of migrant: conceived in the South, she made the trip north in her mother's womb.

Elizabeth was different in key ways from other migrants profiled for this project. She was thirty-three years old when she moved, considerably older than the others. She was already married and had a child, with another on the way.

Although Elizabeth said her mother originally moved to Boston to work as a live-in domestic, her son says that when he arrived in Boston, his grandmother and Brabham worked as caretakers for a landlord who owned several apartment buildings in Brookline. They lived in the basement of one of those buildings, Marquis said. His grandmother cleaned apartments after tenants moved out and her husband performed minor building maintenance and disposed of trash from the buildings.

When Elizabeth and her son arrived in Boston, they moved in with her mother, Brabham, and Lafayette in that basement apartment in Brookline. Brookline was quite a change for the young Marquis after growing up in the segregated South. That's when he first realized he was different. Most of his friends in Brookline were White and Jewish. "One of them said, 'We're just the same, except you're colored and I'm White,'" Marquis remembered. "I had no idea what that was. I had no concept."

Other than that passing remark, though, Marquis never felt he was treated differently in Brookline because of his race. Once that summer, in fact, his friends had to go home because they had to attend Hebrew classes. He asked if he could go with them, not knowing what Hebrew was. "We did everything else together," he said, "so why not?"[12]

When Elizabeth registered her son for school in September 1963, she also asked about what she would have to do to apply for a teaching job. The principal of her son's school provided her information. The first step was to take a written exam. Davis did not take the test right away because she was eight months pregnant. She gave birth to Danné in October 1963. Her parents' employer then helped the family find an apartment on Huntington Avenue in nearby Jamaica Plain.

She and her family adjusted quickly to life in Boston, in part because her mother and stepdad preceded her. They made friends easily because her parents knew people in the city. They joined her mother's church, Charles Street African Methodist Episcopal Church in Roxbury. "I liked it," she said, "first of all, because my mother was here. It gave me an opportunity to be close with her. And she had a relationship with my children."

The teaching exam required by Boston public schools was notoriously difficult. It was a writing test rather than a multiple-choice test, unlike exams employed by many school systems at the time. Steven Taylor, author of a book about the desegregation of Boston schools, has argued that "Black teachers were weeded out" by the exam, which was later replaced by a national exam.[13] Davis took the exam in December 1963 and was notified the following spring that she passed. She interviewed for a teaching position at the Christopher Gibson School in Dorchester. Most students at the school were Black, she said, but the school had only one other Black teacher, a southern migrant like herself. The principal, who was White, offered her a job teaching first grade. She took it.

"She said, 'We give beginning teachers first grade and we put them in the basement,'" Davis said. "All that was trying to discourage me. I said to myself, 'I want a job. I don't care where she puts me.'"

When she reported for work in September 1964, the principal told her that she would be teaching third grade rather than first grade. "Instead of giving me the first grade and putting me in the basement, she gave me the third grade, which was opposite her office," Davis recalled. "Everyone was saying, 'Yeah, she wanted to keep an eye on you,' because she didn't have any other Black teachers."

Despite her concerns, Davis did well and quickly discovered the advantages of moving north. Her first teaching job paid twice what she made in South Carolina, she said. She earned tenure and ended up teaching at Gibson for a decade.

The Gibson School was the same school where writer and educator Jonathan Kozol taught from 1964 to 1965, when he was fired, in part, for reading a Langston Hughes poem, "Ballad of a Landlord," to fourth graders. Kozol was strongly critical of the school and its treatment of Black students in a book he wrote about his experiences, *Death at an Early Age*, which became a best-seller and won the National Book Award.[14] Kozol drew a discouraging portrait of the school, saying the building was overcrowded and so rundown that it was hazardous. One day, the glass from a window was blown out and nearly landed on his pupils. He said teachers regularly beat students, and he accused several of being racist.[15]

Davis taught with Kozol and said of his book, "It's a good book. It's a sad book." She contends that it was not entirely accurate, though. "Some of it was true," she said, but "some of it was exaggerated." She acknowledged that many of his overall criticisms were valid, and agreed with Kozol that Black students in Boston received an inferior education compared to White children. "Oh yeah," she said. "I figured that was true."

Perhaps because she was accustomed to segregated southern schools, where Black students got even less than they did in Boston, she didn't complain or try to advocate for change. She may have also been disinclined to speak out because she recognized her new job and life were significant improvements over what she had in South Carolina. "I was glad to be here because it was an advancement for me," she said. "I'm making more money. I'm living in a better neighborhood than I did in South Carolina. I felt very proud to be here. I didn't have any problems. All I ever knew is to go to church, go to work, and go back home. That's all I did. All I wanted to do was make a better living for my children."

Davis's husband left his job at the Hayes-Bickford restaurant chain to work as a cook at Filene's, the Boston department store, which was beginning to expand into the suburbs. He worked at stores in Chestnut Hill and Braintree. Danné Davis wrote that "for years" her dad was the only Black employee in the kitchens where he worked, and that all the servers were White women.

His mother was classified as "mulatto" in census records, biracial in today's nomenclature, and he had relatively light skin. Danné wondered in her article if his light skin helped him get a job in a place that employed no other Black workers. He worked at Filene's for twenty years, but was injured when he fell on the job. He was never able to go back to work and instead received disability payments.[16]

After about a decade teaching at the Christopher Gibson School, Davis transferred to the Lucy Stone School in Dorchester. She continued to teach third grade there. Black students made up about 90 percent of the student body, she said, but the school had a White principal. Davis worked at the Lucy Stone School for thirty years, retiring in 2002.

Davis and her husband in 1967 bought a three-story, twenty-five-hundred-square-foot house in Dorchester. They were part of a wave of Black migration to the neighborhood. Dorchester's Black population more than quadrupled during the sixties. The house is only three blocks from the Lucy Stone School, so her daughter walked to the school (Elizabeth always drove). Charles Street AME is a short distance away.[17] "It was convenient," she said. "I was working in the area. I was attending church in the area. I like the neighborhood. I like the people. There wasn't any fighting or shooting."

She still feels that way. Davis chose to remain in the large house even after her kids grew up and left home, and her husband died in 1999. She has now lived there for more than fifty years. "We haven't had any serious problems in this neighborhood," she said. "Everybody seems to get along with one another. I feel safe when I go out."

Davis mostly stays in the area. She shops for groceries at a Stop & Shop on Blue Hill Avenue. She goes to a Walgreens in Codman Square for prescriptions. She also shops in Codman Square for other everyday purchases. When she was younger, she would take the train or bus to downtown Boston to shop for clothes at department stores like Filene's and Jordan Marsh. Later, after those stores opened suburban outlets and she bought a car, she drove to shopping malls in Chestnut Hill or Braintree. She was comfortable shopping in suburban stores where most other shoppers were White, but it seems doubtful she would have felt that way in South Carolina when she left there.

Davis never had any favorite restaurants or nightclubs near her home, she said, because she and her husband seldom went out at night and the family rarely ate in restaurants. "I was a homebody," she said. "I didn't go out to socialize. I was brought up like that. I was more of a church person."

Davis was working at the Lucy Stone School in 1974 when Boston was ordered by a US district court judge to implement busing to integrate its schools. Because Lucy Stone had mostly Black students, White children were bused there, and some Black students from Lucy Stone were bused to predominantly White schools. "It didn't really affect me as a teacher because all I had to do was be in the classroom," she said. "I didn't have any problems. I had no problems with the parents at all."

Neither of Davis's children was bused as part of court-ordered desegregation. When busing was first implemented, Danné attended the Lucy Stone School, but, because she walked to school, she was not bused. Marquis had already graduated from Boston English High School, then one of Boston's elite public high schools. Students were required to score well on an examination to be placed there. Davis does not have strong views about busing, and she was ambivalent about whether Black students benefited from it, but that may reflect her political outlook more than anything else.

"I don't consider myself a political person," she said, "just a person that wants to make sure the rules are obeyed, that people are respected, and that children are treated equally."

She has always voted, she said, but unlike most people featured in this book, she also voted when she lived in the South. She was never active in the civil rights movement in South Carolina or Boston. When Martin Luther King Jr. led a march from Roxbury to a rally on Boston Common in 1965 to protest school segregation, she attended the rally where he spoke, but did not march. She supported civil rights efforts in her own way. For example, she said she helped lead educational programs for children at her church to celebrate the birthdays of civil rights leaders such as Harriet Tubman, Booker T. Washington, and Rosa Parks.

"If it wasn't affiliated with the church," she said, "I didn't participate."

Although Davis's daughter, Danné, was not bused as part of court-ordered busing, she was later bused to suburban Wayland as part of a voluntary and innovative busing program created in 1965, nine years before the city of Boston was required to bus students to desegregate its schools.

The program, the Metropolitan Council for Educational Opportunity (METCO), buses Black students from Boston's inner city to mostly White schools outside the city. It grew out of a grassroots effort by two Roxbury parents to place Black students in schools in mostly White neighborhoods within the city of Boston. Later, school leaders in two

A mother waves goodbye to her son as he rides a school bus from Roxbury to suburban Braintree in 1966 as part of an innovative voluntary busing program, the Metropolitan Council for Educational Opportunity, which has enabled thousands of Boston inner-city youth to attend suburban schools. Elizabeth Hall Davis's daughter attended suburban schools as part of the METCO program. Photograph by Dan Sheehan, *Boston Globe*; used with permission, Getty Images.

suburban municipalities, Brookline and Newton, asked if they could participate. Those officials, along with Boston civil rights leader Ruth Batson, chairman of the Massachusetts Commission Against Discrimination, developed METCO.

In 1966, the first year METCO operated, 220 Black students from the city of Boston rode buses to schools in seven suburbs. The program was funded by the US Department of Education and the Carnegie Corp. The following year, the state of Massachusetts took over funding the program. Ten years after its founding, thirty-seven suburban school districts were receiving Black students from the city.[18]

When she entered sixth grade in 1976, Danné attended the Oliver Wendell Holmes School in Dorchester. Now an educator herself, she recalled the school as overcrowded and not very challenging. In fact, she said, she and some of her friends, unhappy with their art class, attempted to take over the class and teach it themselves. One day her mom visited the school and her daughter's classroom. She noticed Danné was wearing her winter coat during class. She asked the teacher about it, and was told Danné and her friends always wore their coats in class. That bothered her and made her think something was wrong.

"At that moment, my mother said she needed do something different because that wasn't a good situation," Danné remembered.

Her mother knew Jean McGuire, executive director of METCO, so was able to secure Danné a place in the program even though it often had long waiting lists. She began attending school in Wayland the following year as a seventh grader. She rode the bus every day from Dorchester to the Wayland, an hour-long trip. For the young Danné, who grew up in mostly Black, lower-income neighborhoods in the city, going to school in the suburbs was an eye-opening experience, though not entirely positive. Raised in a small family, her brother a decade older than her, Danné was accustomed to being by herself. She said she was shy compared to other Black kids who rode the bus with her, many of whom came from large families. They perceived her as "aloof," Danné recalled, and ridiculed her. "It wasn't a happy time," she said. "It was traumatic."

Going to school in a wealthy suburb, where houses were large and mothers seldom worked outside the home, was a culture shock for her. All METCO students were assigned host families in the place they attended school in case they got sick or needed assistance during the school day, because their families were so far away. She was surprised when she learned that the daughter of her host family owned a horse. "That was amazing," she said.

Ironically, White students in Wayland were nicer to her, she said, than the Black students on her bus. She played lacrosse and soccer, and became friends with one of her White lacrosse teammates. She went to her friend's house some days after school and occasionally stayed overnight, particularly when the lacrosse team played games away from Wayland and returned too late for her to ride the bus home. She quickly noticed how different her friend's home life was from her own. Her friend's mom often had fresh-baked cookies waiting for them when they arrived after school. Rather than plopping in front of the TV, they would then go up to her friend's bedroom and work on homework until dinner. Her friend's dad was an engineer and often brought home prototypes of his projects.

"The expectations of children and the way in which the families engaged was different," Danné said.

Though METCO was intended to provide Black urban youth better educational opportunities, Davis said that the way the program was administered in Wayland was less progressive and, in her view, racist. She said that "all of the Black and brown kids" were channeled into vocationally oriented courses. While her lacrosse friend was taking Latin and other college-prep classes, she was taking typing, stenography, home economics, and wood shop. "It bothered me," she said. "What are you supposed to do with that stuff?"

As she neared graduation, her White classmates were applying to elite private colleges such as Williams and Bryn Mawr. But her Wayland guidance counselor suggested that she apply to Tougaloo College, a historically Black institution in Jackson, Mississippi. She was flabbergasted. Danné ignored the guidance counselor's advice. But because she had not taken a college-prep curriculum in high school, she struggled to gain admittance to Northeastern University. She eventually was admitted and earned a BS in criminal justice, then taught in Boston public schools, and went on to earn a PhD in education from BWoston College.

While in high school, Danné complained to her mother about the unequal education that she and other minority students received in Wayland, but said her mom was unmoved. "I say to my mother, 'If I bring home a wooden car [made in wood shop], why would you think that was okay?'" she said. "'Why would you think it okay for me to learn typing skills? Why?' She was happy I was in Wayland and that I would finish high school—the fact that I wasn't in

Boston and whatever turmoil was happening there. I was still safe. That was okay as a goal for her."[19]

Her mother may view issues of race differently because she grew up in a different time and place, and so her expectations may have been lower. Boston was such an improvement over what she knew as a child and young adult in South Carolina that she appreciated what she had achieved and did not push for anything greater. But Danné grew up in Boston, looked around her, and knew that more was possible.

Elizabeth Hall Davis has lived in the same Dorchester house for more than a half century. She has gone to the same Roxbury church even longer. Even though she has lived and worked almost entirely in Black sections of Boston, she said she has enjoyed greater freedom than she would have in South Carolina—to go to the theater, for example, or shop at suburban malls. Despite Boston's reputation for racism, Davis said she has never experienced any hostility due to her skin color, although she acknowledged she will not go to certain parts of the city, such as South Boston, because they are perceived as racist. "I haven't had any problems," she said, "but I do know people who've had problems."

She does not believe Boston is a racist city even though it is sometimes considered one. In making that point, she noted that her son, Marquis, married a White woman. They met at Simmons College in Boston, where she was a student and he was working as a janitor. They live today in Grafton, near Worcester, and have two grown children. He is semiretired after a career in corporate sales working mostly for technology companies.

Davis said that her son's in-laws were shocked at first when their daughter told them she was dating a Black man. She grew up in Sturbridge, Massachusetts, a small town in central Massachusetts that is overwhelmingly White, and is famous as the home of Sturbridge Village, a living history museum that seeks to replicate a rural New England village from the 1800s. "I remember her saying that she told her mother, 'I have a friend I want you to meet,'" Davis said. "And her mother said, 'I would love to meet him.' And she said, 'I just want youW to know that he's Black.' She said her mother almost passed out when she told her."

They have now been married for three decades and Elizabeth said both families get along well. "I feel very comfortable when I'm in her parents' environment," she said. "They feel comfortable when they come and visit me."

Davis still has relatives in South Carolina, but she visits there less frequently than she did when she was younger because many of her family and friends have relocated, and others have died. Like many Black people who came north as part of the Great Migration, she said her relatives who remained in the South have encouraged her to return, particularly now that she is retired. She talks several times a week to a cousin in Columbia who has tried again and again to persuade her to move back there.

But Davis says she has never seriously considered leaving Boston. She likes her home. Her son still lives in Massachusetts. Her daughter lives in New Jersey, but visits often. She has many friends in the city. She likes Boston and sees no compelling reason to return to South Carolina.

"Just let me stay here and die," she said.

7

Willie Pittman

Shady Grove, Alabama, 1963

When Willie Pittman traveled north from Pike County, Alabama, as part of a migrant harvesting crew in 1963, he was following the example of multiple generations in his family. His relatives had been migrating north for years—to Chicago, Detroit, Washington, DC, as well as Boston. Already he had a brother and sister in Boston. Eventually, six of seven kids in his family migrated to the city. Even his dad relocated there.

Pittman did not intend to relocate to Boston when he left Alabama. Work on the harvesting crew was only a summer job. He figured he would pick crops for a few months to earn a little money, then return home. He still had vague plans to go to college in Alabama. But when the crew reached upstate New York, he thought of his siblings in Boston, and decided to visit them.

He liked it and stayed.[1]

Many migrants travel well-worn paths, following family and friends who migrated before them, a process known as chain migration. They may think, "Johnny did it, my aunt did it, why not me?" The presence of family or friends in a place increases the likelihood that a migrant will go to the same place because that makes the adjustment process easier. New migrants may be able to live with people they know until they get settled. Those people may help them find a job or permanent housing. True migration pioneers, people who are the first in their family or social circle to move to a place, are rare. Move somewhere where you do not know a soul and you will quickly learn how difficult that can be.

Pittman was born in 1945 in Pike County in a part of the South known as the Black Belt, so named because its soils are black, richly fertile, and ideal for the cultivation of cotton, but also because Black people make up a majority of the population. Most are the descendants of slaves who worked on cotton plantations there before the Civil War. He was the third of seven children born to Charles and Juanita Pittman. He grew up on a small farm in Shady Grove, Alabama, an unincorporated community fifteen miles northwest of Troy, the county seat and home to a small teachers college. The Pittman

North to Boston. Blake Gumprecht, Oxford University Press. © Blake Gumprecht 2023.
DOI: 10.1093/oso/9780197614440.003.0007

Willie Pittman at his home in Brockton in 2015. Photograph by Blake Gumprecht.

family owned the land they farmed, unlike many Black farmers in the South who were sharecroppers or tenant farmers and struggled to make a living.

Many of Pittman's ancestors were enslaved persons, but one was not, which explains how his family came to own that land. His great-grandfather, Jeff Trotter, was the son of a White farm owner and a Black woman, perhaps one of his father's former slaves. Trotter was born in 1867, two years after the end of the Civil War.

"These three White guys, cousins, they were all Trotters," said Laniel Pittman, Willie's youngest brother, who has studied the family's history and now lives on the family land. "They went around to these Blacks and impregnated a bunch of them. There's a lot of Trotters around here."

As Jeff Trotter reached adulthood, Laniel explained, his father began giving him some of his land, a few acres at a time. The son built a house on the land. His property gradually grew. He raised his family in that house and it eventually became the Pittman homestead. Trotter's daughter, Willie Pittman's

Black farmer cultivates a field in Pike County, Alabama, in 1939. Willie Pittman grew up on a farm in Pike County about this time. Photograph by Marion Post Wolcott, Farm Security Administration; Library of Congress, Prints & Photographs Division, FSA/OWI Collection, LC-USF34-051718-D.

grandmother, was an only child and eventually inherited that land. She married, and she and her husband had seven kids. Pittman's mother, Juanita Moore, was the second born. His mother gained control of the family property because all her siblings migrated north—to Chicago, Detroit, and Washington, DC. "They spread all over," Willie said. "They didn't want to farm. So she became . . . the sole guardian of the land." Pittman said that his family farmed about thirty acres, but his brother Laniel said the property was much larger than that, perhaps 120 acres. They grew cotton, peanuts, corn, and cucumbers.

Charles Pittman, Willie's father, was handicapped, so he was a "housefather," according to Willie. He was injured while harvesting timber from the family land when a branch from a falling tree struck his hip. The accident left him with a permanent limp and kept him from doing all but the easiest farm work. Instead, he did all the cooking and housework for the family. His wife and their seven children worked in the fields. They also worked for a neighboring White farmer who had a larger farm and higher-quality land, helping him when they were finished with their work to earn extra cash.

They did not own any farm machinery. They did all the work by hand, though they did own three mules, which made them better off than most nearby Black farmers, Pittman said. They used the mules to plow fields, transport their crops via wagon to market, and haul firewood. "[We] had to walk behind the mules, like people walked behind oxen in the olden days," Pittman recalled. "It was hard work. I have no love lost for farming. I don't know how we stood it. How did we stand being in that hot sun?" The farm produced a modest income. Laniel Pittman said the family was "poor," but, because they owned land, "we had it a little better than most other Black people."

The Pittman family lived in the house Jeff Trotter built. Pittman's mother was born in the house and lived there until her children built her a new home on the same land in 1968. The Trotter house was larger than most Black homes in rural Alabama at the time. In typical southern style, it had a porch that spanned the entire front of the house. Inside, a hallway extended from the front door to the back, and there were two large rooms on both sides. Each room served multiple purposes. There were two beds in every room. The dining room had a long wooden table that could seat eight to ten people. "It wasn't like the queen of England," Laniel said, "but it was long."

The house was built of wood but was unpainted, and, by the 1960s, the unprotected wood had begun to buckle and deteriorate, prompting the Pittman children to tear it down and build a new house for their mother. The Pittman family stopped farming after the children grew up and left home. One by one they migrated to Boston, all except Pittman's youngest sister. His father was too handicapped to work outside the home. His parents eventually divorced and his father moved to Boston, where he lived alternately with his eldest daughter, Portia, and oldest son, Johnny, until he died in 1983.

Pittman's mom stayed on her family's land. She worked as a maid for a White family in Montgomery for twenty-two dollars a week. "Ain't that pathetic?" Laniel asked. She then got a job as a cook in a high school in nearby Goshen after Pike County schools were integrated. The Pittman family still owns the land, which has been divided among family members. The land is now covered with pine trees, and family members harvest those trees occasionally for cash. Laniel, who served in the navy for twenty years, lives in the house the children built for their mother.

Growing up in the country, the Pittman family traveled to Troy to sell their crops and shop. Troy had a population in 1960 of about ten thousand.[2] It was home to Troy State College, which did not admit Black students until 1967. Troy was segregated when Willie grew up. Like many southern towns, it had a Confederate monument on its town square. The bus station had "white" and "colored" washrooms. A dime store downtown had a modern, chrome water fountain for White customers, but a "rusty spigot" for Black people. Black moviegoers had to sit upstairs at the Pike Theater, as in theaters throughout the region. The balcony was derisively called "the buzzard's roost."[3]

The city had a separate Black business district, centered on Love Street, which had been named for an eccentric, illiterate widow who used to roam the town with a whip and butcher knife telling drunks to go to church. Love Street was home to Black-owned restaurants, nightclubs, beauty salons, and barbershops. On Saturdays, Black farmers would transport their cotton to the White-owned cotton gin in Troy, then walk over to Love Street, purchase provisions, get their hair cut, and hang out on Love Street for the rest of the day, often late into the night. Growing up, Pittman was intrigued by the lively social life on Love Street, but most of the businesses were geared to adults. He used to peek inside Juanita's, a bar, as he passed with his parents. "I'd look in there to see what was going on," he said.

Pittman never went to Troy on his own even when he was old enough to drive because neither he nor his friends had access to a car. He did not get his haircut there. "My father cut my hair," he said. "We didn't have money to be going to no barbershop."

Schools in Pike County were segregated until the late 1960s. Pittman attended Ansley School, which educated area Black youth from the first through twelfth grades. It was a short distance from a school for White students, Shellhorn School. Shellhorn was prominently located on a county highway. Ansley sat down a hill from Shellhorn, and back in the woods, invisible from the road. Asked if that was intentional, Earnest Green, a local minister and member of the Pike County Board of Education, who attended Ansley, said, "I imagine so."[4]

Ansley School was situated in the country, midway between Shady Grove and Troy. Built of cinder blocks and painted green, it had six classrooms, with two grades sharing each room. It had no indoor plumbing during Pittman's time there. Teachers and students alike used outhouses. The school did not even have a gym. The high school basketball team played its games outdoors. The court was set in a depression and the crowd sat on the dirt slopes around it. The court was not paved. It was dirt. "They had little children with rakes," Green recalled. "Whenever they had a time out, they'd level it up. It was fun."

Even as a kid, Pittman knew his education was inferior to that received by White students, who went to the nicer, and more substantial, brick Shellhorn School up the hill. "The Whites had the better schools," he said. "They had a book in the fourth grade that us Blacks (would use) in the fifth or sixth grade. We were always two books behind them."

Although Jim Crow was still strong in Alabama when Pittman grew up, he said that interactions between White and Black people were common and that he had White friends. As a teenager, he played on a town baseball team in Shady Grove. The team was composed mostly of Black players, but there were two Whites on the team. Pittman became friends with one of them, who lived near him. "We were at each other's houses all the time," he said. "We played baseball and stuff together. I never paid any attention to the segregation. It hardly ever crossed my mind."

But he did notice other ways that Black people were disadvantaged in rural Alabama. He and his brothers all played sports. They liked baseball and basketball best. Willie said he was a good baseball player—"I could hit and I could run"—but his brother, Charles, was better. He believes his brother could have played professionally if he had grown up somewhere else and was White. Charles played for an all-Black high school in the countryside that played exclusively against other Black schools, and for a mostly Black town team that played its games "in a pasture," Willie said. Professional scouts never showed up in such places.

"He could have went far, if he could have been seen," Pittman said. "Nobody came down there to look at no country boys play baseball. He could throw a ball at least a hundred miles an hour. He could throw that ball! He had an arm on him."

Pittman did not finish high school, though he never mentioned that in two interviews. His brother, Laniel, said he stopped going to school after the tenth grade. Willie said he intended to go to college, but his plans abruptly changed, and he never returned to school. By that time, two of his siblings had already moved to Boston. His oldest sister, Portia, moved there in the early 1950s. Growing up, she dated a man who had family in Boston. After high school, they moved to the city and married there. By the time Willie relocated to Boston, they had three children. Portia was a secretary. Her husband worked for American Biltrite, a rubber manufacturer in Chelsea. Pittman's older brother, John, moved to Boston about 1958. He, too, got a job at American Biltrite. "We can get you a job there," John told Willie.

Pittman's brother and sister told him there was plenty of opportunity in Boston for Black people. In the rural South where he grew up, there were few jobs for Black men other than farming or working for White farmers. But Willie had helped on his family's farm from the time he was a young boy, old enough to hoe a row of cotton, and he knew he did not want to work in agriculture. "I didn't want to be a farmer," he said. "That's a lot of work! A farmer's work is never done. When you're through with your crop in the field, there's still barns and fences, and everything to be mended. I didn't want no part of that."

Civil rights leader and longtime congressman John Lewis also grew in rural Pike County. Born five years before Pittman, he was the son of sharecroppers. Like Willie, he had to work in the fields with his family, and that shaped his young mind, influencing his developing interest in civil rights. "I hated picking cotton," Lewis wrote in his memoir, "and not just for what it was— literally backbreaking labor: planting, picking, chopping, fertilizing, row after row, often on your hands and knees, from one end of a field to the other, sunup to sundown, year in and year out, the blazing Alabama sun beating down so hard you'd give everything you owned for a little piece of shade and something cool to drink. I hated the work itself, but even more than that, from a very early age, I realized and resented what it represented: exploitation, hopelessness, a dead-end way of life."[5]

Like Pittman, Lewis experienced the segregation of Troy while growing up. He was later denied admission to Troy State College. His discussions of segregation in Troy in his memoir are strongly critical. He was especially angry that Black people were not allowed in the public library. "That killed me," he wrote. "The idea that this was a *public* library, paid for with government money, and I was supposedly a U.S. citizen, but I wasn't allowed in. Even an eight-year-old could see that there was something terribly wrong about that."[6]

Lewis also had relatives who moved north—to Buffalo, Detroit, and Newark, New Jersey. He visited Buffalo with an uncle at age eleven and, he wrote, "started obsessing about it, about what it would be like to live up north." After college in Nashville, he worked in New York and Washington, DC, but the desire to fight for civil rights drew him back to the South. He was one of the original Freedom Riders, who rode buses throughout the region in 1961 to test segregation. He was beaten by a state trooper in 1965 while on a voting-rights march out of Selma, Alabama, in what became known as Bloody Sunday. After working in President Jimmy Carter's administration, he returned to the South to stay in 1980 and that year won election to the

Atlanta City Council. In 1986, he was elected to Congress from Georgia's Fifth District, a seat he held until his death in 2020.

Pittman took a decidedly different path than Lewis, influenced by his siblings in Boston. His brother and sister told him how much better life was in Boston than in Alabama. They told him there were well-paying jobs for Black men, even without an education. They told him that Black people enjoyed much greater freedom there than in the South.

"They said up here, you can go where you want to go," he recalled. "You want to go to the movies, you go right into the movies. You want to go to a restaurant, you can go to the restaurant. If you want to go to a hotel, you go to the hotel. You couldn't do that down there. That sounded attractive."

When the school year ended in 1963, Pittman was feeling antsy, though he did not know for sure what he wanted to do. He had long planned to attend Tuskegee Institute, one of three colleges in Alabama open to Black students at the time. But Tuskegee was known as an agricultural school and he knew he did not want to do that, though it also offered technical degrees. That summer, he and a friend got a job on a migrant farmworker crew that traveled from place to place harvesting crops. They traveled first to Trenton, South Carolina, where they picked peaches. They stayed there for a month and a half. They headed next to Penn Yan, New York, to pick tomatoes and Concord grapes. But Pittman did not stick around long enough to pick any grapes.

He looked at a map one day and discovered he was only about six hours from Boston. He had some cash in his pocket. He got a ride to a Greyhound bus station and bought a ticket. "Boston ain't that far away," he said. "Here I come."

When he arrived in Boston, he got off the bus downtown. He was amazed at the tall buildings. He'd never seen a building taller than two stories back home in Alabama. He also noticed "all the pretty girls." Pittman went to Boston only intending to visit his brother and sister. He called his parents when he arrived and told them where he was. His dad told him to be sure to be back home by September for school. "I wasn't sure," he said. "I didn't plan on coming up here."

But he never left Boston. He moved in with his sister and her family in Roxbury and ended up living with them for a year. He decided after about a week to stay permanently. He got a job with the brother of his sister's husband, painting houses. He was nineteen years old when he relocated. "I liked it," he said, "and I seen that there was opportunity."

He bounced from job to job for three years. After painting houses for four or five months, he got a job at a Goodyear tire store in Roxbury, unloading trucks and helping around the shop. He stayed there four or five months. Then he got a job at a bakery supplier in suburban Randolph, carpooling there with coworkers from Boston. He drove a forklift, and filled bags with flour and cans with jelly. "As soon as I find something better, I moved up," he said.

After living with his sister's family for about a year, Pittman got his own studio apartment in the South End. Later, he moved to an apartment in Roxbury. He said he adjusted "real fast" to life in the city.

But he discovered that race relations were not as advanced in Boston as his brother and sister had led him to believe. He said that in Alabama there was greater interaction between White and Black people than there was in Boston, where they lived largely separate lives. "I thought there was more segregation in Boston when I got here than down there," he said. "In Boston, you got Roxbury, you got South Boston—Black, White. I thought it would be more integrated. Down there [in Alabama] we were all mixed up."

In 1966, unhappy with his job at the bakery supply company, Pittman again began looking for work. He took a day off, telling his boss he was going to register for the draft. He applied at a shoe manufacturer. He applied at a caterer. Then he went to South Boston to apply at the razor blade manufacturer Gillette. He had no phone, but the next day there was a knock at his door. He received a telegram from Gillette asking him to come for an interview the following Monday. Gillette hired him and he stayed there for thirty-five years. He retired from Gillette in 2004.

After Congress created the Equal Employment Opportunity Commission in 1965, companies like Gillette began to actively recruit Black workers. Gillette was also one of twenty-two Boston companies that in 1963 signed on to participate in the Massachusetts Plan for Equal Employment Opportunity, promising to increase hiring of Black workers.[7] "A whole lot of Blacks came in 1965," Pittman said. "When I came in 1966, there were tons of Blacks that came in and from then on."

Pittman worked at first as a "general laborer," cleaning grease off razor parts after they were manufactured. He was promoted to the quality control department after two years. He inspected razor blades after they were sharpened. Later, he made sure the blades were treated properly. After twenty years in quality control, he was promoted to a supervisory position as a group leader in the production department, where he worked until his retirement. "They treated me good," Pittman said. "They had good benefits."

Pittman met his wife, Virginia, shortly after he moved to Roxbury. She had migrated from Oglethorpe, Georgia. She worked as a teacher's aide. She was living with her sister in an apartment on the same street as Willie. He passed by her home every day on the way to and from work. Sometimes she was outside and they would talk. Eventually, he worked up the nerve to ask her out. Before long, she became pregnant, so they married in 1966. They moved into a two-story townhouse on Warren Street in Roxbury. Their daughter, Regina, was born soon after. They had a son, William Jr., in 1967.

Pittman's brother, Charles, moved to Boston that year. He also worked initially for American Biltrite, the rubber manufacturer in Chelsea. Another brother, James, also relocated to Boston, but did not like it and returned to Alabama. Willie's youngest brother, Laniel, moved to Boston after graduating high school but left after three months because, he said, "it was too closed in for me. There were too many people." The only one of Pittman's siblings who never moved to Boston was Caroline, the youngest, who married in Alabama and lived in Troy until her death.

Pittman family members who left Alabama were part of an exodus of Black residents from Pike County. The county lost a greater percentage of its Black residents between 1940 and 1970 than any other county that was home to migrants profiled for this project, and four-fifths of counties in Alabama. The Black population in Pike County declined 43 percent in thirty years.[8]

So many Pittman family members left the South that when one side of his family had a reunion recently, they held it in Washington, DC. Willie said that the reunion drew family members from Chicago, Detroit, Washington, and other northern cities. "We didn't have nobody from Alabama," he said.

Pittman and his wife raised their two kids in Roxbury, but they went to school in the suburbs. They were bused there, like Danné Davis, the daughter of another person profiled for this project, as part of the same innovative voluntary busing program, the Metropolitan Council for Educational Opportunity. By 1976, METCO was transporting minority Boston students to thirty-seven suburban school districts.[9] Pittman's wife worked as a monitor on METCO buses, so they were able to place both their children in the program at a young age. Pittman's daughter, Regina, went to school in Concord, twenty miles northwest of Boston. His son, Willie Jr., attended school in Lexington, also northwest of the city. Both went to school in those wealthy suburbs from first grade until they graduated from high school.

Willie Jr. attended Southern Connecticut State University on a football scholarship, but he was injured, lost his scholarship, and dropped out of school. He then went to a trade school and is an electrician for the Massachusetts Bay Transportation Authority, Boston's public transit system. Regina went to business school and has worked as a clerk. Pittman has no doubt that his children received a better education because of the METCO program than they would have in Boston city schools. "Much better," he said.

Although his children were not affected by court-ordered busing in Boston, Pittman was, indirectly. Pittman said he never experienced any direct hostility in Boston because of his race, except during the busing years. Protests, fighting, and violence occurred all year long after busing was implemented in 1974. White protestors in South Boston threw rocks and bottles at buses carrying Black students. Shots were fired at Boston police cars and the Boston Globe building (the *Globe* was perceived as a pro-busing newspaper). Two White students were stabbed in schools. Fearing for their children's safety, many parents kept their kids home.[10]

Pittman worked at Gillette in South Boston, where White resistance to busing was strongest. Tensions often spread beyond the schools and bus routes. Pittman recalled a close call he experienced on his way home from work during the busing era. He worked the overnight shift at Gillette and decided to walk home one Sunday morning after he got off work. He was crossing the Broadway Street bridge over the Fort Point Channel at the entrance to South Boston, when a carload of White teens passed him. They looked back at him and then car slowed.

"There goes a nigger," he heard one of them say. "Let's get him."

The car stopped and Pittman feared that the teens were going to attack him. He had no way to protect himself, but remembered he had a metal Afro comb in his jacket pocket. He quickly grabbed it and pointed it outward through his jacket to suggest that he was holding a gun. He kept walking toward them. "They thought I had a gun," Pittman said. "They jumped in their car and took off. They saw that I wasn't scared. I said, 'Oh boy!' because about forty feet down was the water. I thought they were going to grab my ass and throw me in the water."

Black-White relations in Boston have improved since then, though the city is still highly segregated, and most White people live, work, and shop apart from Black people. A study by two sociologists found that Boston was still highly segregated in 2010.[11] Social scientists measure segregation using a measure called the Index of Dissimilarity. The index measures the proportion of residents who would have to move for a city to be fully integrated. In 1980, Boston had a White-Black dissimilarity index of 0.798, meaning that nearly four in five residents would have to relocate for Boston to be completely integrated. That number dropped to 0.678 in 2010, a 15 percent improvement in thirty years.

Even so, Boston was the eleventh most segregated metropolitan area in the United States in 2010 among the fifty metropolitan areas with the largest Black populations—more segregated than southern cities such as Atlanta, New Orleans, Birmingham, and Memphis. The five most segregated metro areas were all in the North. In 2015, four out of five Black residents of the city of Boston lived in just four neighborhoods, Roxbury, Dorchester, Mattapan, and Hyde Park. Black people made up less than 6 percent of residents in twelve of twenty-two city neighborhoods. Despite Boston's ever-increasing Black population, Black people are seldom seen in many parts of the city.[12]

Although Pittman was surprised by how segregated Boston was when he arrived in 1963, and said little had changed in that regard, he was never active in the civil rights movement. He joined the National Association for the Advancement of Colored People, but mostly went his own way. Like other Blacks profiled for this project, Pittman seemed to accept segregation and the way Black people were treated in the South when they grew up, and did so in Boston as well, perhaps satisfied that their lives have been somewhat better in the North. They have not challenged the system. They stay in Black neighborhoods. They rarely go to White areas, and most have never tried to obtain housing in predominantly White sections. They avoid parts of Boston where they feel they would be unwanted. They are not active in politics. They do not do anything that might make their lives more difficult.

"All I wanted to do was try to better myself," Pittman said.

Pittman still had relatives in Alabama, including his brother, and visited about once a year, though not as often as he did while his mother was alive. He said in 2015 that race relations in his home county had improved "100 percent" since he grew up, more so than they have in Boston. "It's more friendly, more sociable," he said of Alabama. "It's nothing to see people walk and say, 'Hey man, how you doing?'—White, Black, whatever. They're more sociable. [Blacks and Whites] socialize more there than they do here."

In 1996, Pittman and his wife moved out of the city of Boston, even though he continued to work at Gillette. He took over the payments on a small house in Brockton from a coworker. Brockton, thirty minutes south of Boston, is racially mixed. Black residents make up nearly a third of the city's population, and there are many Black immigrants from Cape Verde, Haiti, and Brazil.[13] Pittman retired in 2004. His health, and the health of his wife, deteriorated. A longtime smoker, he contracted tuberculosis in the 1970s. In 2016, he spent six weeks in the hospital for pulmonary fibrosis. When he returned home, he had to use an oxygen tank to help him breathe.

"I have trouble breathing," he said. "My breathing went down to nothing. It ain't fun."

Pittman died in 2018. His wife had died six months earlier. But, before he died, reflecting on his life, Pittman was clearly satisfied with the move that began when he boarded that Greyhound bus on a lark in 1963, headed for Boston.

"I think I had a better life here," he said. "I had a pretty decent job—with no education. I did pretty good."

8

Geraldine Walker

Clay County, Alabama, 1963

Geraldine Walker still has nightmares about that day when she was thirteen years old. She still experiences trauma because of what happened. She still bears the scars. She still goes to therapy for it.

Unlike some Black people, Walker never adjusted to life in the racist South. She never accepted being treated like a second-class citizen. She still feels the horror of her life there. She has nothing nice to say about her childhood in Alabama.

"It was a horrible life," she said. "It really, really was."[1]

Walker was born in 1945 in rural Clay County, Alabama, ninety minutes southeast of Birmingham. She was the fifth of seven children born to Leroy and Nazree Wilson. Her father was a sharecropper. They lived in what once had been a slave cabin, working for the same White family that operated a plantation on the land using slave labor before the Civil War.

After emancipation, many plantation owners still owned large parcels of land, but they no longer had a resident labor force—enslaved people—to work for them. Black southerners, meanwhile, gained their freedom but little else. Sharecropping was a labor system that developed because White landowners still needed workers to farm their land, while Black people (and poor Whites) needed work. But for many Black farmers, sharecropping was not much better than slavery. The system was stacked against them and most never progressed economically. The landowner provided sharecroppers land to farm, supplied them tools, and sold them seed and other provisions on credit, usually at inflated prices. Once the crop was harvested, the landowner and sharecropper split the profits.

After the crop was sold, landowners (or their overseer) met with sharecroppers in what became known as "the settle." That is when they would show the sharecropper a ledger for their account. But when the owner or over-seer calculated what the sharecropper earned and then subtracted what was

North to Boston. Blake Gumprecht, Oxford University Press. © Blake Gumprecht 2023.
DOI: 10.1093/oso/9780197614440.003.0008

Geraldine Walker at her home in Dorchester in 2016. Photograph by Blake
Gumprecht.

owed, the sharecropper often received little or no money. Many sharecroppers
were perpetually in debt and could never escape the cycle of poverty.[2]

Walker's father farmed about forty acres owned by a White landowner
named Levy Blair. He raised cotton, but also corn, peanuts, peas, string beans,
potatoes, and sorghum. He did not own a tractor or any other machinery. He
had to borrow the landowner's mules to plow his fields. He purchased seed
and other supplies on credit from Blair. "Every year, by the time you paid
that off, you didn't have anything left," Walker explained. Blair, she said, "was
getting just about everything."

The Wilson family lived in a crumbling, four-room shack. Geraldine's
parents slept in the living room. She and her four sisters slept in another
room. She shared a bed with two of her sisters. Her two brothers occupied
a third room. The only other room was the kitchen. The structure had but
two windows. The house did not have running water or a bathroom. They

used an outhouse. They relied on a well her father had dug, but it eventually ran dry, and, starting when she was eight years old, Walker had to haul water from a nearby stream. The house lacked electricity until Walker turned fourteen in 1959. There were cracks between the planks that formed the outside walls of the house that were large enough to see through.

"You could feel the wind in the wintertime," she said.

Like other poor Black farming families, the Wilsons had enough food to eat because they had a kitchen garden and grew their own vegetables. Her father also raised pigs and chickens. The children picked "all kinds of berries" in the nearby woods. Sometimes her mom made pies from those berries. The Wilson family fished in nearby streams and caught catfish, pickerel, brim, and bluegill that they ate. Her father also went "turtle-gigging." He would kill any turtle he caught and remove its shell, and her mother cleaned it by soaking it in salt and vinegar. She boiled it, then sautéed the meat with onions and green peppers, making gravy from the fat. She served the turtle with gravy on top.

"I can't say we starved," Walker said. "We ate a lot of fried cornbread with peas."

Walker said her family was "very, very poor," so poor that she had two pairs of shoes, one for school and one for church, but otherwise had to go barefoot. Her mother made dresses for her out of large burlap sacks in which flour was sold. All the children were expected to work around the house and in the fields. Walker awoke before dawn to help her mother make breakfast and prepare lunch for her father to take with him to the fields or when he cut pulpwood for extra cash. She would "get the eggs, feed the pigs, wash the clothes."

The children still had time for fun. Her father built the girls a miniature house where they pretended to cook, clean, and care for imaginary children. She and her siblings played in a creek and had contests to see who could swallow the largest number of live minnows. Walker claimed she could swallow twenty fish in a row and was tougher than any of her brothers or sisters. "I could climb trees, shoot, and fight better than all my siblings," she said. "I could shoot a slingshot. I could shoot my father's shotgun. I was the strongest. I could throw a rock and kill a chicken."

Most of their neighbors were poor White families, likely sharecroppers, too. The closest Black people "were miles away," she said. Black farmers helped each other at harvest time, even though they lived far apart. The owner of the land her father farmed lived about a quarter mile from their home. Walker became secret friends with the daughter of Levy Blair, the White man who owned the land where her father sharecropped. They would

sneak into the woods to play. But friendships between White and Black children were forbidden at the time, she said. One day the girl's father caught
them playing together and told Walker's father.

"I got a beating for that," she said.

The nearest town to her family's home was Millerville, unincorporated
and with a population of a few hundred. It was about a three-mile trip. They
had to walk there or take a mule and a wagon. They did not acquire a car,
a beat-up old Packard, until Walker was sixteen. Millerville had a post office, two stores, and a mill that ground the corn her father grew. But even in
that small town they suffered discrimination. If they went into a store to buy
supplies and a White customer came in after them, they had to step aside so
that the White shopper could be served first.

Larger but further away was the county seat, Ashland, which had a population of 1,610 in 1960.[3] Ashland was segregated like all towns in Alabama
during the Jim Crow era. Contrary to the usual pattern at southern movie
theaters, though, Black people sat downstairs in Ashland's theater, according
to Walker, while Whites sat in the balcony. "They'd start throwing stuff on us,"
she said. "They was very evil."

Walker attended an all-Black elementary school in Ashland through the
sixth grade. She went to middle school in Lineville, six miles further from
their home. The children rode a bus to school, and when Walker got off the
bus with her siblings on returning home, White kids sometimes threw rocks
at them. She left school after the eighth grade and never went back. She said
she did not drop out, but was "pushed out." "We wasn't learning anything,"
she said. "It was a nasty school."

Walker said that her family suffered from racism and discrimination in
everything they did. She said that her paternal grandmother was lynched
"because she was going with a White man." Her father was then raised by
family friends and did not learn that he had siblings until he was an adult.
Walker sometimes helped her mother when she cooked and cleaned for
White families in the area. Even though they prepared the White family's
food and she set their table, when it came time for her and her mom to eat,
they had to eat outside on the porch. As a girl, Walker could not understand
that. Her parents taught her how to behave around White people—to step
aside when they approached on a sidewalk, let them go first in stores, and always show deference when addressed. "You couldn't cross that line," she said.
"It was a way back life. We were still in the slavery times, essentially. Where
I was raised up, it was a very prejudiced place."

Once when her mother was washing clothes for a White family, Walker said, her robe caught fire and she was burned over 90 percent of her body. She had to be rushed to the hospital, but her children were not allowed to visit her there because of their race. Eventually, her mother was sent home. She recovered after being nursed back to health by family members and Black friends in the area, who used folk remedies to treat her wounds. Walker said they mixed cow manure and butter, then spread it on her body every day. Ironically, her mom later worked as a cleaner in the hospital her children were not allowed to enter.

Her father struggled to get ahead as a sharecropper in hopes that one day he could buy his own land. He made sorghum syrup to sell, grinding it by hand, riding a horse round and round to power the mill that squeezed the syrup from the sorghum cane. He cut pulpwood for extra cash and transported it twenty miles to a paper mill in the town of Sylacauga. He was also a bootlegger, using the corn he grew to make whiskey in a still. Walker's father was eventually able to buy a small parcel of land and build a house. White people tried to prevent her father from getting ahead, Walker said, and once, when she was ten, the Ku Klux Klan burned a cross in the family's yard. Her parents believed that the man who owned their land ordered the cross burning to punish her father for selling bootleg liquor and intimidate him so that he would not buy his own land.

"It really, really scared me," Walker said. "I see these people come up. I peeked through one of them little cracks [in the house walls]. They had on these sheets. I asked my father, 'Why did they burn that wood in the yard?' My mom said, 'That's a cross, like Jesus died on a cross. That was the Ku Klux Klan.' That took me for a ride for years."

But Walker's worst experience came after she dropped out of school. She went to work as a servant for a White family that lived about five miles from her home. Seven people lived in the house—a mother and father, their two adult male children, their wives, and their two kids. She had been working there about six months, when one day after breakfast, most of the family went for a walk. But one of the adult sons remained in the house. She was cleaning the kitchen, she said, when he came up behind her, held a gun to her head, pulled her into another room, and raped her.

She fled the house immediately, hurrying home through the woods. She never told her parents what happened because she feared how her father would react. She thought he might go to the White family's house with a shotgun and get lynched in response. Instead, she told her parents that the family's dogs frightened her so she could not work there anymore. They did not press her about it, she said. She never went back. "I'm still going through it sometimes now at the age of seventy," she said. "I still get counseling. Sometimes I go to bed at night and I can hear the gun going off in my head."

The fear of being raped by White men was common among Black women in the South, particularly for those who worked in White homes. The rape of Black women by Whites began during slavery, when rape was not considered a crime because enslaved women were property, and continued throughout the Jim Crow era, when Black women remained powerless and such crimes were rarely punished. Elizabeth Clark-Lewis interviewed eighty-one domestic workers who moved from the Deep South to Washington, DC, in the first half of the twentieth century, and she wrote that the fear of rape was a "universal concern" for young Black women in the South and their families. "You'd know how to run," one woman told her, "or always not be in the house with the White man or big sons."[4]

Darlene Clark Hine and Kathleen Thompson have written that "the threat of rape was held over Black women as the threat of beatings and lynchings were held over Black men" and contend that "the climate of terror" was a "primary motivation" for Black women to migrate north. Danielle L. McGuire went even further, arguing that "African-American women's long struggle against sexual violence" was a key force behind the civil rights movement.[5]

Walker moved to Boston in 1963, when she was eighteen years old. Her sister, Murine, migrated to Boston several months earlier. Murine had been working in nearby Sylacauga when she saw an advertisement in a newspaper from a labor recruiter seeking Black women to work as live-in servants for White families in the North. Murine telephoned the personnel agency and later met a local recruiter. She took a job with a family in Newton Centre, a wealthy suburb west of Boston. Murine wrote letters home telling the family how different life was in Boston than in Alabama. Black people could go anywhere that Whites could go, she told them. Public facilities were not segregated by race. She said that she never heard the word "nigger."

"They treat you with respect," Murine wrote.

Once, Murine came home to visit and Walker marveled at her sister's clothes and shoes. She had begun to talk differently, too, speaking better English. Several months later, Murine told her family that two sisters of the people for whom she worked needed servants. They offered jobs to Geraldine and one of her sisters. For decades, the most common employment for Black women in the South was domestic work, but Black domestics could earn more money for the same work in the North and were generally treated better. Fewer and fewer Black women in northern cities worked as servants as employment discrimination diminished, but still in 1960, about 14 percent of Black women in Boston were private domestic workers.[6]

In November 1963, Walker and her eldest sister, Mollie, took a Greyhound bus to Boston to work as servants. Walker had given birth to a son two years before, but she left him in the care of her parents. She and Mollie went to work for families in Newton Centre. She remembers vividly the day she arrived in Boston.

"I felt like I came out of a cave," she recalled. "I'd never been out of the state. I'd never been nowhere but right there in the woods."

Walker was so accustomed to life in the South that she did not know how to act at first in such a different social environment. She recalled that when she arrived in Boston, she looked around the bus station for a "colored" restroom, but could not find one. "It was so different," she said. "I said to my sister, 'Am I in the wrong bathroom?' It was shocking."

Walker lived with her employers in Newton Centre and earned thirty-five dollars a week. She cleaned. She washed. She cooked all their meals. She said the family "treated me very, very good," but her tenure proved short because of problems that developed with her employers' teenage sons.

Walker regularly sent money home to her parents to help them. She and her sisters each sent them fifteen dollars a week. Since they lived with their employers, they had few expenses. But Walker discovered that her parents were not receiving the money she sent home. She suspected that one of her employers' sons was stealing it. One day, she put an envelope addressed to her parents in the mailbox, and then watched the mailbox. She saw one of the boys go to the mailbox, remove the envelope, and open it. She confronted him. He confessed to stealing the money, she said, and agreed to pay her back all the money he had taken if she would not tell his parents. He did that and she did not tell.

But not long after that incident, she experienced more problems with the teenagers. One night, her employers went out for the evening, leaving their two sons home alone, while Walker stayed in her room. They invited some of their friends to the house and raided their parents' liquor cabinet. They began drinking and carrying on, turning up the stereo loud. Traumatized after her rape in Alabama, Walker feared for her safety. They started banging on her door. She did not know what to do. She had no way to contact the boys' parents, so she called her sisters. One of them called the police. Officers came and broke up the party, sent the boys' friends home, and asked them where their parents were. They called the boys' parents, who came home. The parents immediately came to see Walker in her room to see if she was okay. They were concerned.

Walker was angry and told the parents that they were wrong to leave their teenage boys home alone with so much liquor in the house and available to them. She told them she could not work there any longer. She stayed the night, but in the morning a cousin from Alabama, who lived in Dorchester, picked her up. She never went back to Newton Centre. She lived with her cousin until she could get back on her feet. She got a job pressing clothes in a laundry in Boston's South End. Later, her father visited from Alabama and brought her son, Victor, with him. Her son ended up staying.

Walker met her future husband, David Walker, through her cousin, who was friends with him. He was a native Bostonian. They met at a party at her cousin's apartment. Like her, he was raising a child on his own, a daughter. They married in 1966 and she moved into his apartment on Blue Hill Avenue in Roxbury. She said she married him so that she would have someone to help raise her son, not because she was in love with him. He was sixteen years older than she was. They remained married until his death. "I married my husband at that time to help me take care of my child," she said. "It turned into love."

Walker bounced around from job to job. She left her first laundry job to do the same work at another laundry. She then got a job as a cashier at Filene's department store in downtown Boston. She worked there for about seven years. In the 1970s, she studied to earn a GED certificate at the Women's Service Club in the South End. Founded in 1919 to help Black soldiers in Boston, the organization expanded its purpose over time to provide a variety of social services and educational programs to Black women. When Walker earned her GED, the organization was run by Boston civil rights pioneer Melnea Cass, whose family migrated from Virginia when she was a young girl.[7]

Walker has never been politically active because her life did not allow it. But she is not apathetic, either, and has lent her support to civil rights efforts in small ways over the years. She could not do more because she worked full time and her husband was a longshoreman who worked the night shift. She had to stay home with their two children. "I never had the chance," she said. "There was a lot of things I couldn't do. I had to be home with the little ones."

However, she did participate in a march in Boston after Martin Luther King Jr. was assassinated in April 1968. Like most American cities, Boston experienced unrest in the days following King's assassination, though it was more successful than other cities in preventing large-scale violence. The day after King's assassination, demonstrators gathered on Boston Common, and then a crowd of five thousand people, mostly of them White, marched a half-mile to Post Office Square. About three hundred Black people broke off from the main group and marched instead to Roxbury. Walker joined that march, though her work schedule prevented her from participating in other events in subsequent days, including a large rally at White Stadium in Franklin Park that was militant in tone.[8]

"I had never done anything like that before," she said. "I wanted to let them know I'm here, I'm against what happened, and what was going on. It really felt like I had accomplished something within myself."

Walker occasionally attended meetings of the National Association for the Advancement of Colored People on issues such as school desegregation and housing discrimination. The education she received from the Women's Service Club inspired her to volunteer at that organization for several years. She also volunteered for an organization she said was called Women on the Move that fought housing discrimination in Boston.

All of Walker's brothers and sisters eventually moved to Boston like she did, though her parents remained in Alabama. Her oldest brother, Willie, lived in Boston until he died; he worked at the Necco candy factory in Revere. Mollie, who accompanied Geraldine to Boston, worked at a dry cleaner and likewise remained in the city until her death. Another sister, Evelena, worked as a school crossing guard after she moved to Boston and remained in the city for the rest of her life. Three of her siblings who relocated to Boston eventually returned to Alabama. Murine, the first Wilson child to migrate, remained in the city for two decades before returning home and marrying there. Her brother, Billy, lived in Boston for thirty years before returning to Clay County. Geraldine's youngest sister, Sarah, lived in Boston for a decade, but also returned to Alabama.

Once one of the Wilson children relocated to Boston, their parents pushed all the others to do the same, Geraldine said, because they knew their opportunities in Alabama were limited, but also because they wanted all their children to live in the same place. "That was mother and dad's rule—that all the children stay together," she said. "Mom said you all have to take care of each other."

Geraldine Walker in 1983. Used with permission, Geraldine Walker.

After earning her GED certificate, Walker trained at the Women's Service Club to be certified as a home health aide. She worked as a home health aide for twenty years. She was inspired to do that because she saw many older people who struggled to take care of themselves as they aged, often forgotten by their family and children. "They need a bath, they need clothes, they need food, they need a hot meal," she said. "I've seen some horrible things in the way they treat old people. That made me start doing that."

Walker and her husband never had any children together, but shared in responsibilities for raising the kids each had before they married. She considers her husband's daughter as much her child as her son. Both children still live in Boston and have families of their own. She has nine grandchildren.

She eventually stopped working as a home health aide because, she said, the state of Massachusetts cut the number of hours aides could work, making it difficult to get the work done. About 2000, she got a job as a lunch monitor at the Sarah Greenwood School, an elementary school in Dorchester. She worked there for ten years. Her experiences at the school inspired her and a friend to train to become foster parents. Her reasons for doing that were similar to what prompted her to become a home health aide—she saw a need. Many children in the school lived in foster homes, she said, but were treated poorly.

"We had a lot of kids coming in there, their clothes were dirty, they were hungry, they didn't have a quarter or fifty cents to pay for lunch," she said. "I thought we could make a difference. We have made a difference."

Even though she is now in her seventies, Walker continues to work as a foster parent and has done that for more than two decades. She has typically had two kids at a time, and they stay with her for six months to two years, until they return to live with their parents or are adopted. She estimates that she has had sixty foster children pass through her home over the years, though some only stayed a few days on their way to somewhere else. She has remained close to many of her former foster children. They call her often, visit, and sometimes bring her gifts. One paid for an airline ticket so that she could travel to Alabama to visit relatives.

When Walker was growing up in Alabama, her parents often required her to take care of a half-dozen kids—her two younger sisters but also the children of other Black parents who were working in the fields. She said her work as a home health aide and a foster parent have provided her great personal satisfaction. "I did this all my life," Walker said. "My mom told me when I was growing up, 'God sent you to take care of older people and children. That's your calling.' Not everything I done turned out like I wanted. This is the only thing that came out like I wanted. When you see that somebody loves and cares for you, that's the best feeling in the world."

The two constants in Walker's life since she moved to Boston have been children and church. She was raised as a Baptist in Alabama and joined the Morning Star Baptist Church in Mattapan after moving to Boston. She belonged to that church for two decades, but one day she asked a new pastor there if he would give her a ride home or to the subway station. He would not because he said it would not look right. That bothered her. One of her girlfriends was a member of Charles Street African Methodist Episcopal Church in Roxbury, and told her that the church had many members who were born in the South like she was. She attended services there one Sunday and liked it. She joined Charles Street AME and has now been a member there for twenty years.

African Methodist Episcopal churches are known to be more sedate than Black Baptist churches or Pentecostal churches. Walker knew that before she went, and was apprehensive about Charles Street as a result, but she found it different from that reputation, perhaps because so many of its members are from the South.[9]

"Some AME churches, they sit there like statues," she said. "I would say this is a swinging church. We have all kinds of music. They sing like we does down in the South."

Walker has long been active in the church. She's been an usher since she first started going to Charles Street. She is also a missionary—visiting elderly in nursing homes, helping the sick and shut-ins, provided care baskets for homeless people. "I love Charles Street," she said. "I feel so much at home there."

Walker has lived for more than a half century in Boston's Black community. She has always been a renter and has moved around, living at ten different addresses in Roxbury, the South End, and Dorchester. Although she has lived nearly all her time in Boston in Black neighborhoods, she said that she did that by choice, not because discrimination prevented her from moving elsewhere. In Alabama, when she was growing up, Black people had little freedom in where they lived.

"When I came into Roxbury, I thought it was the best thing in the world," she said. "It was my folks, my people. I don't find nothing wrong with that because that's your choice. Down there [in Alabama], you didn't have but one choice: you stayed on that farm back in the woods."

Walker has seen Boston's Black community change over time, for better and worse. She does not drive, which has given her the opportunity to observe those changes more closely, at the sidewalk level or from the seat of a Massachusetts Bay Transportation Authority bus, than would be possible for someone who typically speeds by in a car. It is a different perspective. Because she's lived all over, Walker has personal knowledge about a greater number of areas within the Black community than most people. After moving out of her employer's home in Newton Centre, she lived for more than a decade in Roxbury, first with her cousin, and then with her husband and their two children. She shopped mostly along Blue Hill Avenue, which had become the commercial spine of the Black community.

Blue Hill Avenue had been a Jewish shopping district until Black people began moving into the area and Jewish residents fled to the suburbs. Blue Hill Avenue was home to grocery stores catering to Black tastes, Black-owned beauty salons and barber shops, barbecue restaurants, record stores selling R & B and jazz, as well as car dealers, furniture stores, and dress shops. You could get most anything there.[10] Walker ate with her family at Ma Dixon's restaurant in Grove Hall, started in 1943 by a Black woman who migrated from Georgia. It specialized in fried chicken, collard greens, and other Black southern foods. Walker bought meat at Carl's and Eddie's market. She went to Kasanof's Bakery for sweets. On hot summer nights, she took her kids to the Family Hut for ice cream.[11]

"Blue Hill Avenue was beautiful when I first came to Boston," she said.

In 1967, Walker was living with her family in a fourth-floor apartment on Blue Hill Avenue when police forcibly removed mothers who were staging a sit-in at a welfare office in Grove Hall. That incident stimulated three days of rioting up and down Blue Hill Avenue, which destroyed some businesses and damaged many more. Protestors burned Cohen's Furniture Mart. They smashed windows and looted more than two dozen stores—hardware stores, shoe stores, liquor stores. Teenagers overturned police cars, and threw bricks and rocks at officers. Snipers shot at police from the roofs of buildings. A Boston fireman responding to a fire was shot in the hand. Nearly one hundred people were arrested and sixty were injured.[12]

The riots stimulated a decline in Blue Hill Avenue from which the district never recovered. Many businesses did not reopen. Empty storefronts and vacant lots proliferated. Blight spread. Crime in the area increased. "We lost so many stores," Walker said. "We lost buildings. They just tore it up."

Several years later, Walker was mugged after leaving a liquor store on Humboldt Avenue, a few blocks west of Blue Hill. The muggers threw her to the ground and took her purse. She was employed at Filene's in downtown Boston, and had agreed to work two hours extra that night. That meant she arrived home after dark. After being mugged, she refused to work late and stayed home when it was dark. Walker had once felt comfortable walking to stores in the neighborhood by herself at night, or going for a stroll.

"After that, I didn't feel safe anymore," she said.

In the mid-1970s, Walker and her family moved to a seven-story apartment building on Washington Street in the South End. The neighborhood was home to Boston's oldest Black community. Black people began moving to the South End in the 1870s, pushed off the north slope of Beacon Hill by high rents and deteriorating housing conditions. By 1914, about 40 percent of Boston's Black population lived in the area.[13]

The South End was never exclusively a Black neighborhood. It was always home to diverse groups of people, including waves of immigrants—Germans, French Canadians, Lebanese, Italians, Chinese, and others. Most came for a few years, and moved to better-off areas as they advanced economically. But Black residents stayed and became the "most stable" group in the neighborhood. By the 1950s, third-generation Black families were common.[14]

When Walker moved to the South End, it was a neighborhood in transition. It had declined in previous decades, as once-luxurious redbrick rowhouses were converted to apartments and rooming houses, then allowed to deteriorate. The city targeted it for renewal, clearing one section entirely of buildings. The South End became the site of the largest urban renewal project in the nation, but the city was forced to change its plans in response to protests.

In the end, urban renewal stimulated the large-scale gentrification of the South End, as middle-class Whites moved in and rehabilitated the historic rowhouses. Between 1960 and 1980, some twenty-five thousand residents were displaced from the neighborhood, forced out by escalating real estate prices and rising rents. Most of the people who were displaced were poor and working class, and they included many Black residents. Walker ultimately left the South End for the same reasons. The South End's Black population declined from more than eleven thousand in 1950 to fewer than four thousand in 2015.[15]

The South End was still a center of Black culture when Walker and her family lived there, home to nightclubs like Louie's Lounge and Wally's Paradise, reportedly the first Black-owned nightclub in New England, and restaurants such as Slade's barbecue, once owned by Boston Celtics star Bill Russell, and Bob the Chef's, where Walker and her family went for down-home southern cooking. "That was the hip place to move," she said. "You was moving on up."

The South End was a neighborhood of small, mostly independently owned businesses—corner markets, luncheonettes, bars and liquor stores, pawnshops and discount stores, and countless beauty salons. Walker stopped at Morse Fish Co. on Fridays for whitefish, catfish, and porgy. She went "all the time" to Skippy White's record store for the latest soul and R & B records by singers such as Otis Redding, Bobby Bland, and B.B. King. She liked to eat at Dotty's Lunch. All were located on Washington Street, where she lived.

Few businesses near where she lived were Black-owned. Those that were tended to be small, service businesses, such as beauty salons. There was a Black-owned drug store, Douglass Square Pharmacy; a Black-owned boxing gym, Baby Tiger School of Boxing; and two Black-owned funeral homes. Walker's husband took his shoes to Dave's Shoe Repair, which was Black owned and a block away from their apartment on Washington Street. She was a quick train ride away from downtown Boston. The elevated Orange Line, since relocated underground, went right down the middle of Washington Street. She would go to Filene's or Jordan Marsh downtown, she said, "when you'd want to find something special to wear."

It was when she was living in the South End that Walker first heard about Melnea Cass's Women's Service Club. It was on Massachusetts Avenue, three blocks from her apartment. That's where she earned her GED certificate, trained to be a home health aide, and later volunteered.

She moved out of the South End in the mid-1980s "because they started going up on the rent too much," she recalled. "It was too much money." By then, her kids had grown and left home. Her husband's health had begun to deteriorate. He eventually moved into an old-folks home and died in the late 1980s. She moved in with a friend in Dorchester for a few years, then got her own apartment.

Walker has now lived in Dorchester for more than thirty years. Since 1997, she has lived in a two-bedroom apartment owned by the Boston Housing Authority on Columbia Road. She likes where she lives. She likes her neighbors. The neighborhood has changed around her while she has lived there.

Although she says shopping options have improved in Boston's Black community, she's more likely these days to travel to suburban shopping centers than to shop in her neighborhood, except for everyday needs. That merely reflects changes in American retail. She takes the bus to the South Bay Center, along Interstate 93 on the east side of Dorchester, where there are big-box stores like Best Buy and Marshall's, and a twelve-screen movie theater. She also takes the bus to the Dedham Mall, southwest of Boston. Occasionally, her son will drive her to B.J.'s Wholesale Club and Walmart south of the city. "A lot of things would be much cheaper out there," she said. "You save a lot of money."

Walker lives a half mile from Franklin Park, Boston's largest park, where there are athletic fields, playgrounds, a zoo, picnic areas, walking trails, and extensive natural areas. Growing up in the country in Alabama, where she spent much of her youth outdoors, she has long been drawn to the park. She played baseball there when she was younger. She often took her grandchildren fishing at a pond there or to the zoo. For many years, she walked the perimeter of the 485-acre park for exercise. Charles Street AME regularly held cookouts there.

"I like to live in that park," she said.

The most conspicuous change that has occurred in Boston's Black community in recent years is that it has become increasingly multicultural. When migration from the South slowed, immigration of Black people from the Caribbean and Africa increased, spurred by changes in US immigration laws. One-third of Black residents in Boston today are immigrants. Forty percent of people in three predominantly Black neighborhoods speak a language other than English.[16]

Boston is home to twenty thousand immigrants from the Dominican Republic, most of whom live in Roxbury and Dorchester. There are seventeen thousand Haitians, who are concentrated in Dorchester and Mattapan. There are thousands of Black immigrants from Jamaica, Cape Verde, Trinidad and Tobago, Nigeria, Ghana, and Barbados. There are also thirteen thousand Puerto Ricans, who are US citizens but share characteristics with the other immigrant groups. They have a complex racial identity, but many have African ancestry.[17]

There are African clothing stores in Grove Hall, West Indian and African markets, Haitian and Dominican churches, and restaurants serving the food of every place from which the immigrants have come. To get a taste of how Black Boston has changed, one can walk up and down the aisles of Tropical Foods on Melnea Cass Boulevard in Roxbury, which seeks to serve them all.[18] Walker has watched those changes from her front door, and they have impacted her personally. In the more than two decades she has lived in her apartment, the composition of residents in her complex has changed. Most are now immigrants—chiefly Dominicans, but also Haitians, Jamaicans, Nigerians and other Africans, plus Latinos from Central America.

"I am the only American in this building," she said.

But she is fine with that. The changes have also impacted her own family. She has a daughter-in-law from Ghana and nieces who are Puerto Rican and Cape Verdean. She interacts all the time with the immigrants in her apartment complex. "If they need somebody to babysit their kids, it's always me, 'Nana,'" she said. "We get along very well. We help each other."

But all is not well in Boston's Black community from Walker's perspective.

She goes to Franklin Park less frequently today than she once did, and the reasons are indicative of what she sees as a declining quality of life in Boston's Black community. The park, she believes, has become too crowded. You must now purchase tickets to the zoo in advance if you want to make sure to get in. You must also reserve picnic sites. The pond in the park, she says, has become a dumping ground, and she would no longer eat fish caught there. "You'd probably get ptomaine poisoning," she said. She doesn't go for walks in the park anymore, she said, "because there are so many perverts."

Crime has become an increasing concern for her, but she says attitudes have also changed. Roxbury, Dorchester, and Mattapan are the three most dangerous neighborhoods in the city, but that is not new. They are also Boston's poorest areas, and poverty breeds crime. Drug trafficking is widespread. Gangs and drug dealers seek to control turf, and sometimes law-abiding citizens get in the way. Walker says you now must be careful about everything you say and do. Unintentional missteps, such as bumping into someone by accident, may receive angry responses.

Walker's concerns may seem like the typical fears of an elderly person—crime rates in Boston have declined significantly since the 1970s—but her perceptions are common among people living in Boston's Black community. A survey conducted in 2008 by the Boston Police Department found that fewer than one-quarter of residents in Roxbury, Mattapan, and north Dorchester felt safe in their neighborhoods. Residents of many White neighborhoods were more than twice as likely to say they felt safe.[19]

Walker used to walk on Sunday to services at Charles Street AME, which is six-tenths of a mile from her apartment. But now she takes a cab. "It's very scary," she said. "I don't feel safe anymore. You have to watch at all times. Life is so different."

She also gets discouraged talking about race relations. She knows Black people are still not treated equally in the United States—not in the South, not in Boston, not anywhere. She knows the perils that all Black people face just living their lives. She has taught her children, her grandchildren, and her foster children what she thinks they need to know to survive. She has instructed them in how to act if they are pulled over by police while driving. Do not get out of the car. Open your window just far enough to hand the officer your license and registration. Place your hands on the steering wheel. Do not do anything that might arouse suspicion, but do not allow your car to be searched either. She tells them if they see police activity anywhere to turn around and go the other way.

"There are so many things, even today, that we have to teach our children about racism," she said.

Walker has occasionally experienced racism in Boston, most of it subtle. When she was employed at Filene's as a young adult, she worked alongside a White woman who, she said, "always had something negative to say to me." Like most Black people, she sometimes goes into stores and knows she is being watched or followed because of her race. Walker said that many Bostonians will say that they are not prejudiced, but their behavior—the way they act around Black people, their implicit fear of Black males, their reluctance to venture into Black neighborhoods—demonstrates otherwise.

"When is it going to end?" she asked.

Like other people featured in this book, she has noticed on trips to the South that race relations there have advanced more than in Boston. For all the South's faults, she appreciates that racial attitudes there are more transparent and sometimes prefers that. "You knew where you stood with them," she said. "Up here, up north, you don't know. They look at you, they smile in your face, they say they care about you, they like you. But . . ."

Walker recognizes that Boston is still a largely segregated city and that Black people often feel unwelcome in predominantly White parts of the metro area. She said her son and his wife once tried to buy a house in the suburbs, but that White real estate agents always came up with reasons not to show them certain homes, or they would fail to return their telephone calls. They ended up buying a house in the Hyde Park section of Boston, where Black people make up more than half the population. She is well aware of Boston's reputation for racism. When told that maps depicting the distribution of Boston's Irish and Black populations showed little overlap—where there are Irish, there are few Blacks, and vice versa—she replied, "You noticed that, too?"

Like many Black Bostonians, she avoids certain White neighborhoods, especially South Boston. White residents of that traditionally Irish neighborhood, led by lifelong resident and longtime Boston School Committee and city council member Louise Day Hicks, violently opposed court-ordered busing in the 1970s, and their protests were often openly racist.

"I never had anything to do with South Boston," Walker said. "Miss Louise Day Hicks, years ago, she got me not to go to South Boston."

Despite all that, Walker has no regrets about moving north. She has struggled economically more than the other migrants portrayed in this project. She has never made much money. She has never owned her own home. She lives in public housing. She readily acknowledges that her life has sometimes been difficult. But she believes strongly that she has had a better life in Boston than would have been possible if she had remained in Alabama.

"I've had a great life," she said. "I have good friends. I have a good church. I felt that I could accomplish anything I wanted. I can go anywhere I want. I couldn't ask for no better life than I have right now. I came here and my whole life turned around."

Asked what she gained by moving north, her answer was simple, but knowing the details of her life, her statement carries much greater meaning.

"I felt free," she said.

9

Barbra Hicks

Bradford, Alabama, 1964

Barbra Hicks's oldest brother and two of her sisters moved to Detroit. Another brother moved to Ohio. Her younger sister moved to St. Louis. Two of her siblings moved to California. Her girlfriends growing up in Alabama moved to New York City to work as domestics. The same employment agency that recruited them also offered Hicks a job in New York.

If Hicks were like most migrants, she would have gone to one of those places. The advantages of going where you know someone are many. The alternative promises loneliness, anxiety, and struggle. Where will you stay until you get settled? How will you find a job? Where will you go to church? How will you move that furniture up three flights of stairs all by yourself? But Hicks didn't go to New York or California or Detroit. She chose Boston, even though she had never been there, did not know anyone in the city, and knew almost nothing about the place, except that it is in New England, which she learned in school was "all stony, beautiful."

She is the only person featured in this project who was a true migration pioneer—she moved to a place where she had never been, had no family or friends, and did not know anybody.

"I'm different," she said. "I'm a leader. I don't follow."[1]

Hicks was born in 1944 as Barbra Davis. She grew up in Bradford, Alabama, a coal-mining camp in the Appalachian foothills, twenty miles north of Birmingham. The town no longer exists; it disappeared after the mine closed in 1957. She was the seventh of nine children born to Henry and Ethel Davis. They had their first child when they were fourteen years old. All their children eventually left Alabama.

Henry Davis was a coal miner and remained a miner his entire working life. Ethel did "day work" in the homes of White families, cleaning and taking care of their children. She also worked at a dry cleaner and later cleaned offices. Hicks's father woke at dawn to work in the mines but got home in mid-afternoon. He ate dinner, then left the house again to do construction work to

North to Boston. Blake Gumprecht, Oxford University Press. © Blake Gumprecht 2023.
DOI: 10.1093/oso/9780197614440.003.0009

Barbra Hicks in 2015. Photograph by Blake Gumprecht.

earn extra money. He even built an in-ground cement swimming pool for the family at their home. "Dad and mother worked very hard," Hicks said. "They tried to give us everything we needed. We never wanted for nothing."

The Davis family lived in a four-room wood-frame house owned by the mining company. Mom and dad slept in the front room, which served as the living room during the day. Five boys slept in three beds in a second room. Four girls shared two double beds in another. They lived in the Black section of town, known as "The Bottom," because it sat at the bottom of a valley. It was on the west side of the Louisville and Nashville Railroad tracks, which divided the community. White residents lived in better homes on a hill to the east of the tracks.

All roads in Bradford at the time were dirt, Hicks said. Black workers who labored in the mines were poor. Black families regularly sifted through the discarded rock in slag heaps of mine waste for chunks of coal that they could use as fuel for cooking and heating. Houses in "The Bottom" were built close together, and the Black families that lived there were friendly with one another and helped each other often, Hicks recalled. "It was a community and a family," she said. "Everyone watched out for each other, no matter what."

Worker housing in the coal-mining town of Bradford, Alabama. Barbra Hicks grew up in Bradford, where her dad was a miner. They lived in a four-room wood house owned by the coal-mining company. Photograph by Carl Mydans, Farm Security Administration; Library of Congress, Prints & Photographs Division, FSA/OWI Collection, LC-DIG-fsa-8b28931.

Hicks said that although the town was segregated, the mines were not. Black and White miners worked alongside one another underground. It was not uncommon for Black and White miners to work together, though they were often segregated by job category. Whites miners typically held jobs that required more skill and paid higher wages, such as machine operator, while a Black miner might work alongside them as a helper.[2] Evidence that mine operators viewed their Black and White employees differently is a 1939 photograph taken of Bradford mine employees. It shows 159 workers, but not a single Black person.[3]

Hicks said her father occasionally complained about how Black workers were treated in the mines, but he and other Black miners felt powerless to do anything about it, particularly since he had such a large family to support. "He dealt with it," she said. "He had nine crumb snatchers."

Bradford was too small to have separate businesses for White and Black people. Both shopped at the company-owned store. There was a community hall that showed movies. Seating was not segregated as at movie theaters elsewhere, but some showings were reserved for White moviegoers and others for Black customers. Black people were forbidden, Hicks said, from entering the White residential area in Bradford unless they had a specific destination. There were unwritten rules about where they could walk. As elsewhere, they were expected to show deference to White adults.

Hicks's parents taught her and her siblings how to behave around White people. "My parents would tell us, 'This is what you do,'" she recalled. "'Just keep your head straight ahead, don't look back, coming or going.' Our instructions were to say, 'Yes, ma'am,' 'No, ma'am,' 'Yes, sir,' 'No, sir.' Keep the peace. Don't cause trouble. And this is what we did."

Even if they followed the rules, Hicks said, Black people were mistreated. White kids picked on the Black kids because they could. They called them "nigger" and scolded them if they were walking on the wrong side of the road. They would throw rocks at them. If they passed them on the street, the White kids would push them. Sometimes they would spit on them. "It was terrible," she said. Her brothers, Hicks said, would not put up with such treatment and often got in fights with White kids, despite frequent warnings from their parents. They were lucky: they escaped with nothing more than bruises and never suffered more serious retribution later, which was common throughout the South.

Hicks said that the Ku Klux Klan was active in the area and occasionally her parents would lock all the doors, close all the windows, turn out all the lights, and instruct their children to be quiet because they heard rumors that the KKK were "nightriding." "They didn't want to see Black people out at night," she said.

When Hicks was young, she liked to play marbles with her siblings, dig holes under their house (which was built on piers), or go fishing in a nearby pond. She went to an all-Black elementary school in Bradford that went through the eighth grade. Her siblings then attended Hooper City High School, an all-Black school in Birmingham. Hicks said she did not have many friends growing up because her parents were strict, and they expected all their kids to help around the house. She awoke early to make her father's lunch. When she got home from school, she was expected to do her homework and Sunday school lessons, clean the house, help cook dinner, and wash dishes afterward. On Sundays, they often spent the entire day at the Shady Grove Baptist Church. Her father was active in the church and Hicks was secretary for her Sunday school.

As Hicks grew older, she worked to earn money so she could help her parents. She babysat for White children. She cleaned the houses of White families. She did yardwork. "Whatever was needed, I did it," she said. "I was always working."

The Bradford mine, owned by Alabama By-Products Corp., closed in September 1957. Hicks's father then got a job at a coal mine near Jasper, about an hour west of Bradford. The family moved to Jasper, which was much larger than Bradford. It had a population in 1960 of nearly eleven thousand.[4] They lived in a "bigger" and "better" house, Hicks said. By that time, only five of the Davis children remained at home. Hicks's grandmother had moved to Detroit after she divorced. When Hicks' oldest sibling, Henry Jr., graduated from high school, he moved there to attend Wayne State University. Two of Hicks's sisters later moved to Detroit. Two other brothers worked on tobacco farms throughout the South.

Hicks attended Walker County Training School, an all-Black high school in Jasper. Once she reached high school age, her parents became more protective, imploring her not to get pregnant and establishing rules about when and where she could see boys. She was only allowed to see them at home, only on Sunday nights, and they had to leave by 9:00 p.m. If another boy visited her sister at the same time, they all had to sit on the same sofa in the living room. Dad sat in the den, next to the living room, where he could hear everything that went on. When a boy left, he had to say goodbye inside the house. They could not even go out on the front step. Promptly at 9:00 p.m., her mother would let them know it was time for the boys to go. "My mom was the clock watcher," she said. "She would bang on the wall."

Hicks graduated from Walker County Training School about 1961 and entered Tuskegee Institute, one of three Black colleges in Alabama, to study nursing. Her sister Cathleen also attended Tuskegee, intending to become a child psychologist. But colleges at the time still exerted tight control over undergraduates, particularly women, and the rigid discipline reminded Hicks too much of the household in which she was raised. She didn't like it. She also grew bored with her classes. Hicks went to college, she said, because "I wanted to see the world," but she soon realized that Tuskegee was just another small town in Alabama, smaller even than Jasper. She thought college would mean greater freedom, but it did not. When she came home at Christmastime during her sophomore year, she told her parents how she felt. She returned to college after the holidays. That spring, however, she told her sister that she wanted to quit school and leave Alabama.

The following summer, she informed her parents that she was going to drop out and relocate. They tried to talk her out of it, but she could not be dissuaded. "I prayed about it," she told her parents. "I'm old enough now. I know all about it. I can do it. I don't want to go back to Tuskegee. I want to explore. I want to do something for me."

Hicks had several girlfriends who had left Alabama and moved north to work as domestics for White families. They had gotten their jobs through an employment agency in Birmingham. They all went to New York City. By then, three of her siblings had relocated to Detroit, following her grandmother. She had aunts, uncles, and cousins in Detroit, too. Every summer, she traveled with her parents to Detroit to visit family. But she had no interest in moving there. "I didn't like it," she said.

She visited the same Birmingham employment agency that had placed her girlfriends in jobs in New York City. They found her a job in New York. But she told them no, she didn't want to go there. She wanted to go to Boston. She knew little about Boston at the time. "Nothing!" she said. "Nothing!" In grade school, she had seen photos of New England in picture books. "Beautiful," she recalled. In college, she had read about the Kennedys. There was little more to her interest in Boston than that. But she also had a strong desire to blaze her own trail and chose very deliberately not to follow the paths of her family members or girlfriends.

"I was the one, the seventh child, the different one," she said.

Hicks left Alabama at the height of the civil rights movement. Many pivotal episodes in the civil rights era took place in Alabama—the Montgomery bus boycott, Bull Connor turning firehoses on protestors, the bombing of Birmingham's Sixteenth Street Baptist Church, Martin Luther King's letter from the Birmingham jail, the marches from Selma. That only intensified her desire to migrate. Some Black people chose to stay and fight. Others, including Hicks, decided instead to leave. "I couldn't live like that," she said. "The way people were treated, the way my parents were treated. They'd grit their teeth and just accept it. This is the way we were brought up. I said, 'I can do better.'"

The same employment agency that found her girlfriends jobs in New York secured for Hicks a job working as a live-in "governess" for a wealthy family in Brookline, an affluent Boston suburb. The agency paid for her bus ticket from Birmingham. A representative of her employer's family picked her up at the bus station and drove her to the house where she would be working. Hicks arrived in Boston about 1964, when she was twenty years old. She worked for the family of Peter Fuller, who ran a Cadillac dealership on Commonwealth Avenue in Brookline and several other auto dealerships for his family. He was the son of Alvan T. Fuller, who was governor of Massachusetts from 1925 to 1929.

She came to admire Peter Fuller, who was described in his *Boston Globe* obituary as "a character out of a Hemingway." A boxer in his youth, he later owned racehorses, one of which won the Kentucky Derby. Fuller was also a strong champion of civil rights in Boston. He served as chairman of a program developed by the Boston chapter of the National Association for the Advancement of Colored People to improve education, voter registration, and job opportunities for Black people in Boston's inner city.

His civil rights activities sparked controversy on the eve of his horse's Kentucky Derby win in 1968. He gave Coretta Scott King, Martin Luther King Jr.'s widow, the $65,000 purse from an earlier victory after the civil rights leader was assassinated. The move was believed to have angered members of Kentucky's conservative horseracing establishment. Fuller received death threats and one of his stables was set on fire. His horse was later stripped of its Kentucky Derby crown because it tested positive for a banned painkiller. Fuller suggested that someone may have sneaked into the horse's stall and given it the drug, or that test results may have been altered.[5]

Fuller owned a six-thousand-square-foot mansion in a wooded section of Brookline. Built in 1914, the house has nine bedrooms and six and a half bathrooms. Hicks said Fuller had seven children when she arrived and a sizable domestic staff to care for the family and its property. She still remembers the morning she arrived at the Fuller house on Dudley Avenue after her long bus ride from Alabama. "I'll never forget it," she said. "I thought, 'Where the hell am I going?' When I got out where I was, I thought, geez, I don't see any Black people. I'm looking at all these beautiful homes, huge mansions. I thought, 'Wow, I'm riding in a Cadillac.'"

Hicks was shown to her room and given a uniform to wear. Her job was to look after the Fullers' four oldest children. A nurse cared for their three youngest kids. The family also had a cook. They had maids who cleaned the house. They had gardeners to maintain the lawn and flowers. She was the only Black employee. She sent money home regularly to help her family.

She made friends with other Black domestics hired through the same personnel agency. They would go out on Thursdays, their day off. The Fuller family allowed Hicks to use one of their cars. She and her friends would go shopping or dancing in the evening. One day, Barbra accompanied one of her friends to pick up her car that was being repaired at a service station on Warren Street in Roxbury. She met her future husband, Willie Hicks, at the shop, where he was a mechanic. She went back to the service station a second time with her friend. She and Hicks talked. They began dating. "That's how I met my husband— underneath a car," she said. "He said to the owner of the business, 'I want her.' " Willie Hicks also migrated to Boston from the South. He grew up in Aiken, South Carolina, where he learned to be a mechanic by working on tractors. In the 1950s, he moved to upstate New York, where he trained in auto body repair. In 1958, he moved to Boston, where he worked at two car dealerships.

Hicks's career as a domestic was short-lived because, contrary to every- thing her parents taught her growing up, she got pregnant. It was not planned. Complicating matters, her future husband was married to someone else at the time. But he got a divorce and they married in 1965. Their daughter, Tiffany, was born in March 1966. "That stunted my growth," she said. "I wanted to travel. I wanted to go places. I knew nothing about protection. My mother kept everything quiet."

Hicks quit working for the Fuller family after two and a half years. She left her job at the same time many other Black women in the Boston area were abandoning domestic work as new jobs opened to them. The share of Black women in Boston who worked in private domestic service had declined from 54 percent in 1940 to just 14 percent in 1960.[6] She and her husband got an apartment on Seaver Street in Roxbury. She did not get another job right away because her husband wanted her to stay home and raise their children. They had a second child, Willie Jr., in 1968. That year they moved into a two- family house in Mattapan. After their home was burglarized, they bought a house in a better area of Mattapan, where Barbra still lives.

Willie continued to work at the service station, working his way up to be manager. Then he and a friend took out a small business loan and opened an auto body shop on Columbus Avenue in Roxbury. Several years later, Hicks bought out his partner. In 1970, he moved Hicks Auto Body to its current location, at the corner of Talbot and Blue Hill Avenues in Dorchester.[7] Her husband's business prospered. They had plenty of money. They had a piano at home and their children took private lessons. They played tennis. Their kids had a very different upbringing than she did in Alabama. Hicks Auto Body has now been in operation for more than fifty years, so it is one of the most stable and successful businesses in Boston's

Black community. For a time, she and her husband also owned a taxi-cab company.

"We did very well," she said. "My husband is a very smart man."

When Hicks was still working as a governess for the Fuller family, the kids she cared for all went to private schools. She saw firsthand the benefits of that and wanted the same opportunity for her children. "I admired the Fuller family," she said. "So I said, 'If I have children, they will get the best.'" Hicks and her husband were able to send both their children to private Chestnut Hill School in Brookline for elementary school. They then attended the elite Beaver Country Day School in Newton, which offers education from grades 6 to 12.

Both Chestnut Hill School and Beaver Country Day were overwhelmingly White. Because of that, Hicks's daughter told her parents that she wanted to go to school with more Black kids. But they were wary of sending their children to Boston city schools, particularly those in the Black part of town, which were known to be inferior.

Instead, they became involved in an innovative voluntary busing program begun in 1966. The Metropolitan Council for Educational Opportunity has enabled Boston students of color to go to schools in predominantly White school districts in the suburbs. Tiffany attended Swampscott High School, thirty miles northeast of Boston, through the METCO program. Although she did not attend school with many Black students, she did ride the bus with them. Willie Jr. attended Concord-Carlisle Regional High School, northwest of the city, where he became a star athlete, playing football and basketball.

Willie Jr. was the quarterback for the Concord-Carlisle football team. After his senior season, he was chosen as eastern Massachusetts player of the year by both the *Boston Globe* and *Boston Herald*. He then went to Boston College on a football scholarship. He became the first Black quarterback there and was a starter for parts of two seasons. In 1992, he graduated, earning a bachelor's degree in communications.[8] After pursuing a career in sports as a sideline announcer for ABC television and working for the Big East Conference, Hicks in 1994 went to work for his father at Hicks Auto Body. The younger Hicks now manages the business. Although the daughter of another migrant profiled for this project was critical of her METCO experience, Willie Jr. had a more positive view.

"I was really fortunate," he told a reporter in 2008. "METCO doesn't work for everybody. I had friends who became drug addicted and ended up in jail.

Barbra Hicks's son, Willie Hicks, playing quarterback for Boston College about 1989. He was the first Black quarterback at Boston College and was the team's starting quarterback for parts of two seasons. Photograph by Rudy Winston; used with permission.

I'm forever grateful for the help I got. It was about having access to all those resources. It was about an innocent kid being given an opportunity."[9]

While Black people who left the South moved north in hopes of improving their lives, often their children gained even more. Willie Jr., for one, recognizes that the decisions of his parents to move to Boston benefited him. "They sacrificed their whole life so I could have the opportunities I had in my life," he said. "They both grew up in the South and certainly weren't afforded the same opportunities I was."

Once her children reached high school, Barbra Hicks went back to work. She got a job with a company called ROLM that provided telephone systems for businesses. She worked for the company for twenty-seven years through multiple ownership changes. The company was later acquired by IBM and ultimately Siemens AG. She worked at offices in Watertown, Lexington, and Lowell. She started in the accounting department, but later worked in customer service, providing on-site customer training in the use of the company's phones.

Over the years, Hicks's marriage deteriorated. Partly to enable her to get away from an unhappy situation, she began to do volunteer work, organizing a college scholarship program for inner-city kids, working for a cancer organization, and helping at nursing homes. In the early 1990s, she and her husband divorced after twenty-seven years of marriage. "I couldn't live with him," she said. "He likes his cake and ice cream, and wants to eat it, too. There were times it became unbearable. He was very good to my parents. He was wonderful to the children. We moved on."

After she was laid off by Siemens, she trained to become a certified nursing assistant and worked as a CNA in a variety of settings, including hospitals, convalescent facilities, and private homes. As her parents and siblings aged, she also became actively involved in caring for them, traveling around the country to do that. All but one of her siblings are now dead.

She traveled to Alabama to help her mother and father. Her mom required back surgery. Her dad suffered from dementia and died in 2007. She traveled to Detroit to donate one of her kidneys to one of her sisters. She later traveled to St. Louis to help another sister, who had colon cancer. Soon after her father died, her mother had a stroke while Barbra was talking to her on the phone. She brought her mom to Boston to live. Her sister Maxine also moved to Boston to live with her. Hicks stayed home for three years to care for her mother, who died in 2013. She is now caring for Maxine, who is in bad health. Maxine was the last of the nine Davis children to leave Alabama. All nine fled the South and moved to northern states or California. "Everybody," Hicks said. "There was no freedom there."

Hicks has come a long way from the dirt road mining camp in Alabama where she grew up. She obtained the freedom she sought when she moved to Boston. She has been free to do what she wants, say whatever is on her mind, and be the person she wants to be, without fear. She does not believe Boston is a racist city, despite its reputation. She acknowledged there are racist people in Boston. She has occasionally encountered them. One of her supervisors at the telephone company, she said, was racist. Working as a home health aide, she occasionally encountered family members of the sick she was helping who would "look at you" with contempt, she said. But she dismisses such examples as atypical. She is convinced Boston is less prejudiced, less segregated than Alabama. "Most definitely," she said.

Hicks knows that she and her family benefited in innumerable ways because she left Alabama and moved to Boston. Nobody calls her names, pushes her, or spits on her because of her race. She married a successful man and they raised a good family, earned plenty of money, and bought a nice house. She had a fruitful career. Her kids went to private schools and were given opportunities she never had growing up in the South. They did not have to endure the racism that was an everyday occurrence for her in Alabama.

"I love Boston," she said. "I love the people. Boston has been good to me. I made my family here. I made my life here."

Eleven hundred miles away, in a country cemetery in Alabama, the Hicks family owns a family burial plot. There are two gravesites left beside the graves of her parents. One is reserved for her sister Maxine. The other is for her. But Hicks is trying to sell them both.

"I'm not going back," she said.

10

Al Kinnitt Jr.

Brunswick, Georgia, 1964

When Al Kinnitt joined the air force in May 1961, he intended to return to his hometown of Brunswick, Georgia, when his tour of duty ended. He loved Brunswick, had many friends in the city, and his high school sweetheart was waiting there for him. He thought he would coach sports or make a living doing something related to recreation. He spent most of his free time growing up playing sports and figured he would follow in the footsteps of his own athletic mentors.

But Kinnitt never returned to Brunswick except to visit. His mother suffered a stroke while he was in the military and relocated to Boston, where several of her children lived, to recuperate. When Kinnitt was discharged from the air force in 1964, he went to Boston, too, so he could be near his mother.

He has lived there ever since.

Kinnitt is the only person featured in this project who never really chose to leave the South or migrate to Boston. He also differs from most of them in that he has no negative feelings about the South or the place where he was raised, although that may say more about Kinnitt's personality than anything else.

The reasons Kinnitt moved were familial, not racial. His story demonstrates that not all Black people who moved north as part of the Great Migration did so because of racial animus. His life history also shows that migration is not always the result of a carefully considered decision-making process, but is sometimes the product of circumstances, often unexpected. People make major moves that permanently alter their lives without thinking much about them.

In Kinnitt's mind, he gave up as much as he gained when he left Brunswick. "I miss it," he said.[1]

Albert Kinnitt Jr. was the eighth of nine children born to Lue Ida Kinnitt. She had seven kids with her first husband and two with Al's father. Al Jr. was born in 1939 in Meridian, Georgia, a small, unincorporated community near the coast that is one half hour north of Brunswick. By the time Al was born, two of his siblings had already grown and left home. One moved to

North to Boston. Blake Gumprecht, Oxford University Press. © Blake Gumprecht 2023.
DOI: 10.1093/oso/9780197614440.003.0010

Al Kinnitt Jr. in 2016. Photograph by Blake Gumprecht.

Boston, helping to establish what became a well-worn path that he eventually followed.

Meridian was his mother's hometown. His family lived during his infant years in nearby Carnigan, two miles south of Meridian. But his parents broke up soon after that and his mother moved the family to Brunswick, one of Georgia's sea island communities, where one of her sisters lived. Kinnitt's father "did a lot of things," Al said, to scrape together a living. He cut pulpwood and hauled it to nearby paper mills. He worked on road crews. He was a blues musician, playing in area nightclubs on weekends. But Al interacted little with his father until he was a teenager. "He didn't have a lot to do with my life," he said.

Lue Ida Kinnitt raised twelve kids in all because one of her sisters, who had three children, died giving birth. She never remarried after she and Al's father split. The Kinnitt family moved into a public housing project in Brunswick. When Al was ready to enter kindergarten, they moved into a larger, two-story, three-bedroom apartment in another housing project, McIntyre Court, northeast of downtown. That is where he lived most of the rest of his time growing up.

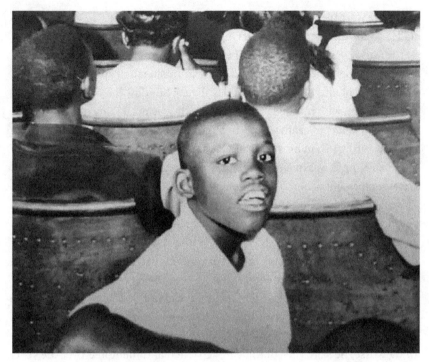

Al Kinnitt, age twelve, about 1951. Used with permission, Stephanie Denise Castro.

Kinnitt shared one of the bedrooms with three other children. It contained only one bed. He slept on the hard floor on blankets. "It was comfortable," he said. Like many Black women who were single mothers and had more children than they could handle, Kinnitt's mom occasionally sent some of her kids to live with relatives. Sometimes they would stay at her sister's home. At other times they would stay with a great-aunt. Some relocated to Boston while in high school.

"Not everybody was there all the time," Kinnitt said. But he was. He always stayed in Brunswick and always lived with his mom.

With so many kids to support, his mother worked two jobs. She cooked for many years for a White woman Al remembered as "Miz Atwood," showing typical Black deference to White people that was expected during the Jim Crow era. She also worked at a shipyard. Kinnitt insisted they were not poor. In addition to working two jobs, his mom cooked, cleaned, and was an expert seamstress, making dresses for his sisters. They always had plenty to eat, he said. "We were blessed to be able to eat all the time," he said. "My mom always had food for us. I never went starving. We ate wholeheartedly."

Kinnitt's eyes sparkled when he reminisced about his mom's cooking. Families in the housing project had gardens outside their apartments, so they always had plenty of fresh vegetables. Every Sunday, his mom made pan-fried chicken, with mashed potatoes and string beans. Living near the ocean, they also ate lots of seafood and freshwater fish—crabs and catfish. Kinnitt stopped eating fish in his youth after getting a bone stuck in his throat.

When Kinnitt was in high school, his mother got a job as a cook at a drive-in restaurant, enabling her to quit her shipyard job. Told that his mother sounded like a good cook, Kinnitt replied, "Not good—she was great. Anything you could name, she could do it." He struggled to identify his favorite foods that his mom made. "My favorite dish," he said, "was whatever she made."

Nobody exerted a greater influence on Kinnitt's life than his mom, and that impact is readily apparent still today.

Kinnitt has never smoked or consumed alcohol, just like his mother. He will not swear, just like his mother. He never has, not even once, he insisted. The closest he comes is to say "God doggit." Because he does not say anything worse, he said, the youth he has coached and mentored over the years know that when he says "God doggit," they better take him seriously. He is deeply religious, just like his mother. He has been a member of Charles Street African Methodist Episcopal Church since 1982. Kinnitt is so adamant about his refusal to swear that he won't say "hell" even in a religious context. He says the "h-word" instead. Rev. Gregory Groover, pastor of Charles Street AME, says that when his congregation recites the Ten Commandments, which include the word "ass," Kinnitt instead blurts out "donkey."[2]

He credits his mom with teaching him manners and respect for others. She also instilled in him a positive attitude about virtually everything. "My mother was number one," he said. "I'm just like my mother. I never complain. I don't complain because [if] I look right or left, somebody's worse than I am."

Kinnitt's memories of his youth revolve around sports. He and his brothers hammered a basketball backboard and net to a light pole at the housing project where they lived. He also played baseball and football on nearby playgrounds and empty lots. As he grew older, he spent much of his time at Selden Park, a Black park and recreation center developed in 1950 on the site of a former Black teachers' college. Located just outside Brunswick's city limits, Selden Park included a gymnasium, swimming pool, tennis courts, a nine-hole golf course, and picnic areas.

Black family picnicking in Selden Park, a Black park and recreation center in Brunswick, Georgia, 1952. Al Kinnitt Jr. spent much of his youth at Selden Park, playing a variety of sports, and his experiences there largely influenced his future life. Used with permission, Al Martin.

Selden Park became a center of Black life in Brunswick during a time when Blacks were forbidden from using White parks, swimming pools, public beaches, and other facilities. Its gym was a regular stop on the so-called Chitlin' Circuit, a network of venues where Black entertainers performed during the Jim Crow era. James Brown, Otis Redding, Al Green, and many other well-known entertainers performed there.

Kinnitt spent so much time at Selden Park that, decades later, he still remembers exactly how far it was from his family's home—twenty-eight blocks. He usually walked there, but sometimes took a city bus. He worked there in high school. At Selden Park, Kinnitt came under the tutelage of Genoa Martin, who was the park's director for thirty-three years. A street in the park is named for him. Martin helped book touring performers at the park. He was reportedly the first Black person to have his own radio show in Brunswick. He also broadcast high school football games featuring Risley High School, Brunswick's Black high school.[3]

Martin became Kinnitt's godfather when he was eleven or twelve years old. He was a leader in Brunswick's Black community, respected by White residents as well as Black ones. In fact, when Kinnitt was a teenager, he said, if he was stopped by White police officers for some reason, as Black people often were throughout the South, all he had to do was tell them that Martin was his godfather, and they would turn friendly and let him go. Martin's name was enough to assure them that Kinnitt had done nothing wrong. Without a father at home, Kinnitt said, "My godfather really raised me."

In addition to playing basketball, football, and baseball at Selden Park, Kinnitt also learned to play tennis and went on to win "the first trophy I ever received" in the sport, he said. A lifeguard at the Selden Park swimming pool, Homer Lee Knight, who taught thousands of Black Brunswick youngsters how to swim, taught Kinnitt to do so "in one day," Al recalled. He taught him how to dive from a diving board and, within five days, Kinnitt said, he was doing flips. In high school, Kinnitt himself taught swimming at the park. Owing to Knight's influence, Kinnitt is fond of saying that he would have become an Olympic swimmer if he had not grown up in the segregated South. "He was like a big brother to me," Al said.

Kinnitt struggled in school, though. He still seems baffled by his difficulties, which began early. His greatest difficulty was in English and reading. He had to repeat second grade. But his problems continued, and, frustrated, he quit Risley High School in tenth grade. Schools in Brunswick were segregated, and Black schools throughout the South received much less funding per pupil than White schools, but Kinnitt does not blame his difficulties on racism. "They were great schools," he said. "If I wanted to get a good education, I could have gotten a good education."

Because Kinnitt was an athlete, he was pressured to return to school, especially by his football and basketball coach, L. J. "Stan" Lomax, who coached at Risley for fifteen years before going on to a successful career at Fort Valley State University, a historically Black college near Macon, Georgia. Lomax was a Boston University graduate. It was Kinnitt's godfather, Genoa Martin, who convinced him to return to school. He was a two-way starter in football, playing tight end and linebacker. When he was a sophomore in 1957, he helped Risley win the state championship for Black schools in its size class. In his senior season, the Tigers went 10-2 but lost in the state semifinals.

Although Brunswick was segregated, Kinnitt insisted that race relations in the Georgia city were better than they were elsewhere in the
South. It might seem easy to dismiss such claims as but one more example of Kinnitt's positive outlook, but the historical record supports
his view. Brunswick attracted national attention in 1963 when its school
board attempted to implement a voluntary desegregation program (it
later succeeded after overcoming court challenges). National Educational
Television, a predecessor to the Public Broadcasting Service, sent a crew
to Brunswick to produce an hour-long documentary about race relations
in the city, entitled *Quiet Conflict*, though it was not aired at the time (it is
now available online).[4]

The *New York Times* also sent a reporter to the city. The *Times* wrote in
September 1963, "Brunswick has the special distinction in the Deep South
of seeking an accommodation with the Negro population without pressure
of court actions or demonstrations." The newspaper reported that White
and Black people lived next door to one another in parts of Brunswick,
most Black people owned their own homes, and Black residents had little
trouble obtaining mortgages and other bank loans. Brunswick had already
desegregated its library, parks, and lunch counters. The local chapter of the
National Association for the Advancement of Colored People had registered
four thousand Black voters, a much higher percentage of the Black population than in most southern cities before Congress enacted the Voting Rights
Act of 1965.[5]

Community leaders said that Brunswick was able to achieve such progress because White and Black leaders communicated openly and worked together to implement changes. Some observers suggested that Brunswick was
more progressive than other cities in the South in part because it was a port.
With ships bringing sailors from all over the world, port cities have long been
comparatively cosmopolitan places and perhaps more tolerant of racial and
ethnic differences as a result.

All of that took place after Kinnitt left town in 1961 to join the air force. But
he said that even before that, Brunswick was "less racist" than other southern
cities. He said he "never felt" that he got less than White people because of
his race. Kinnitt said Black and White kids regularly played sports together,
pickup games on playgrounds and basketball courts, even when school
sports were still segregated. He said he had White friends, including one
named Lonzo whom he met when he sold ice cream by bicycle in Kinnitt's

neighborhood. Kinnitt said he regularly went to Lonzo's house and played with him and his sister in their backyard.

"His parents never said anything," Kinnitt said. "They didn't mind. We were having fun."

Kinnitt certainly knew racism and segregation growing up. When he rode the bus to Selden Park, he had to ride in the back of the bus, as Black bus riders were legally required to do throughout the South. When he was in high school, lunch counters in Brunswick had not yet been integrated. Blacks moviegoers had to sit upstairs and apart from White people in local movie theaters. Kinnitt said race relations in the city did not advance significantly until after he joined the air force. He saw those changes when he came home on leave.

Kinnitt said that once when he was growing up, the Ku Klux Klan came to McIntyre Court and tried to burn a cross on the lawn. "We bombarded them with bricks," he said, "and they never came back." Brunswick still has racial conflicts today, as evidenced by the 2020 killing of Ahmaud Arbery, an unarmed twenty-five-year old Black man who was shot by White residents while jogging through a suburban subdivision.[6]

When Kinnitt was in high school, he said that he and some of his buddies sat at a Whites-only lunch counter in Brunswick, a few years before the lunch counter protests in Greensboro, North Carolina, that were pivotal to the civil rights movement. He and his friends were not served, he said, but the restaurant's owners did not call the police either. Eventually, they got up and left. Kinnitt said he and his friends also occasionally tried to test Jim Crow laws that required Blacks to sit in the back of city buses. They would board a bus but refuse to go to the back. They did not push those protests as far as Rosa Parks did in Montgomery, Alabama. They eventually chose to get off the bus rather than move to the rear.

Kinnitt believes those incidents never gained national attention because White people in Brunswick were less likely to react angrily or violently. They did not call the police, he said, so the media never found out about them. It is impossible to know whether those incidents happened or are apocryphal. "Brunswick was totally different from a lot of other segregated cities," Kinnitt said. "I tell people, all Whites aren't the same."

Kinnitt graduated from high school in 1960. He moved for the summer to Peekskill, New York, where his youngest sister, Evelyn, lived. She was married with three kids. Kinnitt took care of her children during the day while their parents were at work. He visited Boston that August. By then, four of his siblings lived in the city. His half-sister, Jane, moved to Boston during high school and lived with an aunt. Later, his youngest brother, Lloyd, moved to Boston to finish high school, and lived with Jane. Two of Kinnitt's half-sisters, Marie and Marion, twins, had moved to Boston during the 1950s. All four siblings remained in Boston for the rest of their lives. Kinnitt does not know who the first family member was who migrated to Boston or what inspired the move.

By the time Kinnitt visited the city, his brother had graduated from high school and was living on his own in an apartment in the South End. Al stayed with him. Initially, he only planned to visit for a few weeks. But he tried out for an adult Park League football team, made the team, played quarterback, and stayed in Boston until the season was over that fall.

He never considered staying in Boston because his mother was still in Brunswick. He returned to Georgia after football season ended

In May 1961, Kinnitt enlisted in the air force. After basic training in Texas, he became an air force police officer and went overseas to England and Germany. Even though the United States was just becoming involved in the Vietnam War, he never got close to combat. Kinnitt intended to return to Brunswick after he was discharged from the military in 1964, but his mother's stroke changed his plans. She relocated to Boston to undergo therapy, living with one of his sisters. She lost the use of one hand and was never able to work again.

By that time, Kinnitt had no other immediate family in Brunswick. So he went to Boston to help care for his mom. He was twenty-five years old. He is convinced that if his mother had not gone to Boston he would have returned to Georgia permanently. "I stayed here because of my mom," he said. "That's the only reason why I stayed here. If my mom was down south, that's where I [would have] ended up. I would have ended up down in Georgia."

Kinnitt stayed initially with his sister, Marie, who lived in a public housing project in the South End. He got a job as an orderly at a Veterans Administration hospital in West Roxbury. Several months later, he "sent for" his high school sweetheart in Brunswick, Shirley Dean Coley. Kinnitt and Coley met at Selden Park in Brunswick when they were in high school. Like Kinnitt, she was an athlete. She played basketball and ran track. They

Al Kinnitt with his niece, Mary Hazel Fulks, left, and the mother of a different niece, Bobbie Hudson, right, circa 1965, Boston. Used with permission, Stephanie Denise Castro.

married and moved into an apartment in the same complex where Kinnitt's mother lived.

About 1966, Kinnitt got a job as a youth worker for the Urban League, organizing its recreation programs. He eventually became its youth director. That began Kinnitt's long career of working with kids in Boston and coaching sports. He also coached youth sports for the YMCA. He was coaching youth football at a Mission Hill housing project when he met Alfreda Harris, who became a leader in Boston's Black community. Harris would become the longest serving member of the Boston School Committee and a successful women's basketball coach. She lived in the housing project and Kinnitt coached her nephew.

In 1968, Harris became the founding director of the Shelburne Community Center, a city-owned facility in Washington Park, which was called "an oasis" in the city's Roxbury neighborhood. A few years after the Shelburne Center opened, Harris hired Kinnitt as a recreation instructor there. She remembered him from his days coaching youth football at her housing project. "I knew he was sincere when he came to young people," Harris said. "I knew he was hard-working. Whatever people asked him to do, he did."[7]

Kinnitt worked for the city of Boston off and on for two decades and touched the lives of thousands of young people in the process. Although he was originally hired as a recreation instructor, Harris said titles were meaningless at the Shelburne Center. Located in a poor Black neighborhood, where many children were raised by single parents, the Shelburne had a reach that went beyond its official mission. Staff members mentored young people. If they were having trouble in school, staff would go speak to their teachers. If they got in trouble with the law, staff would accompany them to court.

"We were the mothers, we were the fathers, we were the teachers—we did it all," Harris said. "Al did more than anybody else, to tell you the truth."[8]

Kinnitt even started an ice hockey program in Roxbury, as far from his Georgia experience as imaginable. It influenced a future Boston police superintendent, Bruce Holloway, who later helped launch a hockey program for inner-city youth. Holloway told the *Boston Globe* in 2009 that one day Kinnitt told kids at the community center that they were going to play hockey. "We all said, 'Well, yeah, that's gonna happen,'" Holloway later recalled. But, the *Globe* reported, "Kinnitt somehow cobbled together equipment and got Holloway up on skates." He became a goalie, continued to play into adulthood, and that experience inspired him to launch SCORE Boston Hockey, a program that seeks to expose urban kids to a game they seldom play because of the high costs.[9]

Kinnitt's wife gave birth to their only child, Stephanie, in 1969. They divorced three years later, and Stephanie lived with her mom. But Kinnitt continued to play an active role in her life and they remain close today. His daughter is an administrator in the Boston school system and a part-time minister. He met his second wife, Shirley Campbell, in 1978 at the Shelburne Center. She worked for Boston mayor Kevin White and was manager of a "little city hall" that served the Mattapan–Franklin Park area of Boston. They met during the infamous blizzard of 1978, when the Shelburne Center was turned into a shelter.

Kinnitt and Campbell married in 1981 and eventually bought a house in Mattapan. She had three children from a previous marriage and Kinnitt helped raise them. "They all called me 'Papa Al,'" he said. Soon after they married, they moved for two years to Tampa to help care for Campbell's aunt, who was in poor health. Kinnitt managed a convenience store there but also coached high school football. When they returned to Boston, Kinnitt went back to work for the Shelburne Center, working there until about 1995. He then took a job as athletic director at the Roxbury Boys and Girls Club. Three years later, he was again hired by the city of Boston, working for his first wife at the Madison Park Community Center.

Kinnitt has coached countless sports teams over the years—different sports at different levels. He coached basketball at Roxbury Community College. He coached high school football at Cathedral High School and Catholic Memorial in Boston. He coached youth and AAU basketball teams at the Shelburne Center. Once, he even coached a basketball team composed of Taiwanese immigrants and traveled with them to Taiwan to play in a tournament.

He helped re-establish the Shelburne Cobras, an adult football team then went on to win two Park League titles in the 1980s. He helped found a youth baseball program, the Roxbury Rookie League. He coached church teams and all-star teams that went to state and regional tournaments. He also officiated high school football and basketball games.

"Al was everywhere," Harris said. "I'm not fooling."

People who know Kinnitt will tell you that he has influenced the lives of countless Boston young people over the years, particularly Black kids in low-income neighborhoods who were often most in need of help. One such person was Karl Hobbs, who grew up in Roxbury, went on to become a four-year starter for the University of Connecticut basketball team, and has had a long career as a college coach. He is currently an associate head coach at Rutgers University.

The youngest of six children, Hobbs moved to Boston from Florida after his parents divorced when he was in elementary school. One day, he went with a friend to the Shelburne Center, where he came under the wing of Kinnitt. Before long, he was going there every chance he got. When school was not in session, he was at the Shelburne Center every day, from the time it opened in the morning until it closed at night. Kinnitt often drove him home.

Kinnitt became a mentor for Hobbs. He taught him how to play basketball. He took him to his first Boston Celtics game and on his first out-of-town trip to play basketball. Kinnitt pushed him to play against older kids so that he would improve. He was the first person to tell Hobbs he could play at a higher level. Hobbs came to call Kinnitt his godfather, just like Al had done in Georgia with Genoa Martin. But Hobbs said that the greatest influence Kinnitt had on him was off the basketball court. He taught Hobbs the same lessons Kinnitt learned from his mother about character and treating people with respect. Hobbs says Kinnitt strongly shaped the person he is today.

"Al gave me what I needed at that time," he said. "I needed a father figure. I needed a coach. I needed someone to believe in me. I needed someone to instill confidence in me. When you're the youngest of six kids, there's not a lot of attention being given to you."[10]

Kinnitt's second wife died due to complications from diabetes in 1998. He sold their house and moved into an apartment. In 2004, he remarried. Fittingly, he met his third wife, June Robinson, while coaching. She coached basketball and softball at Snowden International High School. Kinnitt also coached there. She is nine years younger than he is.

He retired from Madison Park Community Center in 2011. As his physical ability diminished with age, he remained involved in youth sports as an organizer and in other ways. Instead of officiating basketball and football games, he began running the scoreboard clock for high school football games at White Stadium in Franklin Park.

Until his health deteriorated recently, he was a daily presence at Charles Street AME Church. He served on the church's board of trustees, sang in its men's choir, and helped run a food pantry. He volunteered to pick up groceries for older church members who were unable to do so. He transported senior citizens to doctor's appointments. He stopped by the church every Friday to fold church bulletins.

"Al and Charles Street are inseparable," the church's pastor, Rev. Gregory Groover, said. "The church really became the center of his life. When Al was not working he was at the church. He never-never-never said no to anything that he was asked to do by anyone. Al has an amazing way. He's just so well loved by so many people. He's touched so many lives. Everyone has an Uncle Al story."

In 2019, Kinnitt developed a brain tumor, which slowed him considerably and took away his ability to speak. The following year he underwent brain surgery, and the tumor was successfully removed. Afterward, he underwent physical and speech therapy and was able to partially regain his speaking ability. He continued to improve and by 2022 was "doing well," according to his daughter, though he had not completely regained all his cognitive abilities. Despite that, she said, "he is still full of life, especially when he goes to church."[11]

Looking back on his life a few years before that, Kinnitt struggled to respond when asked whether he benefited by leaving the South and moving to Boston. He is less sure of that than every other person profiled for this project.

He said he has experienced little animosity because of his race in Boston, except occasionally related to his sports activities, which took him outside of the Black community. In 1979, when he was coaching a Park League football team, the Shelburne Cobras, he pulled his team from the field in a game against the South Boston Chippewas because he feared there would be a racial conflict if he did not. The Cobras went to court over the issue because they forfeited the game and the forfeit threatened to keep them out of the league playoffs.[12]

On another occasion, after officiating a basketball game in Charlestown, an elderly White man threw a walker at Kinnitt's van and yelled, "Get out of here, nigger." He also recalled playing a Park League football game in Charlestown when a White player on the opposing team, he believes, deliberately tried to injure his knee. While many Black people will not go to South Boston because it is perceived as racist, Kinnitt feels the same way about Charlestown, which, like South Boston, has traditionally been an Irish neighborhood. But he thinks such incidents were anomalies. He doesn't believe Boston's reputation for racism is deserved.

"I don't think the color of my skin hurt me," he said.

Kinnitt likes how his life turned out. He never considered returning to Georgia, even after his mother died in 1970. He said he believed he was given leadership opportunities in Boston that he might not have gotten in Brunswick, perhaps because Boston was more tolerant about race. But then he hesitated and seemed to change his mind. He said he knew more people in Brunswick when he was entering adulthood than he did in Boston, which may have enabled him to achieve more there. He still considers himself a Georgian, not a Bostonian. He cannot help but wonder what his life would have been like if he had remained in his hometown.

Most Black people who left the South did so because they believed their lives would be better if they moved north. Nearly all those featured in this project judged later in life that they made the right choice. But Kinnitt's story is different. It demonstrates that such a calculation is not the same for everyone. It also shows that the reasons behind the individual moves that made up the Great Migration were diverse. The exodus of Black people from the South was not as straightforward as it is often portrayed.

"I would have gladly stayed in Brunswick," he said.

11

Elta Garrett

Sun, Louisiana, 1969

Elta Garrett's life in Louisiana was not horrible. That's not why she left.

In fact, her descriptions of life growing up in the small town of Sun, Louisiana, sound idyllic in many ways, though there was racism all around her. Even after she grew up, became a teacher, and taught first in a segregated school in Louisiana and then in a mostly White high school where the principal had a Confederate flag on his office wall, she adjusted. She did not want to leave Louisiana.

"I loved it there," she said.[1]

Garrett was born in 1942 to Willie and Mary Sibley, and was raised an only child. Her mother twice gave birth to twins, but she was the only one of the four children to survive past infancy. Garrett's twin sister, Alta, lived but two months. Elta is diabetic, and her doctors at Joslin Diabetes Center in Boston suspect that her twin may have been diabetic, too, and that may have contributed to her death. She died after her lungs filled with fluid. Elta also has a half-sister, her father's daughter from a previous relationship, though she says, "We don't like to use that word because we love each other so much." Her half-sister lives in Jackson, Mississippi, and they "visit and talk" by phone every other day.

The Sibley family was better off than many Black households in Sun, which was a typically segregated southern town. White residents lived on one side of the railroad tracks and Black families lived on the other, she said, in a section called "The Backwoods." Sun was unincorporated, too small for its population to be included in census data until 1960, when it had 224 residents. It was settled in the late 1800s on the high ground north of the Bogue Chitto River, two miles west of the Pearl River, which forms the boundary between Louisiana and Mississippi. Sun is about an hour north of New Orleans.[2] When Garrett was a girl, the town had a post office, a store, and four churches, two for White residents and two for Black residents.

North to Boston. Blake Gumprecht, Oxford University Press. © Blake Gumprecht 2023.
DOI: 10.1093/oso/9780197614440.003.0011

Elta Garrett in 2016. Photograph by Blake Gumprecht.

The Sibley family lived apart from most Black families in Sun, Garrett said, because her great-grandfather, who had been a slave to a large landowner in Sun, was bequeathed more than two hundred acres of land by his master. Her family still owns much of that land. Garrett owns a small parcel, as do relatives, but most have left the area.

According to stories passed down in Garrett's family, the mother of her great-grandfather gave birth to him in a field while she was working as a slave on a plantation owned by a man named William Ellis. She tried to hide the child from her owner because she feared the consequences, but Ellis heard a child crying and asked if the baby belonged to her. She confessed that it did. She later worked as a servant in Ellis's house and Ellis permitted her to raise her son in "the big house," alongside his son. As he grew older, Garrett's great-grandfather learned to farm and worked in the fields with other slaves. But he became a favorite of Ellis, Garrett said. "The master didn't call them slaves," she said. "He was a good master, as it is recorded. That's what my grandmother and them, they wrote down."

Ellis saw his own son as a disappointment, Garrett said, but her great-grandfather became like a son to him, and he was treated like one. Ellis ultimately bequeathed his entire property to her great-grandfather, she said. Ellis was not his father, Garrett said. His father was another enslaved person. Her great-grandfather's family name was Wrightout. But he eventually took the name of his owner, William Ellis. "The master said to his son, 'You have done nothing for me. You won't work. You don't want to do anything. But William does everything,'" Garrett said.

When Elta was born, her family lived with her maternal grandparents on Ellis land in "the big house," the plantation house inherited by her great-grandfather from his owner. It was "huge," she said. It contained six bedrooms. Her father then built the family a small, four-room house on family land. It was a nice house by Black standards in rural Louisiana at the time. It had a big front porch, where the family sat in white rocking chairs. There was a large oak tree in the front yard, where her father hung a swing for her. "It was nice back in the day," Garrett said of the house. "I wouldn't want it now."

The house was covered on the outside by tar paper. It did not have electricity or running water initially. When Garrett was young, she had to wash the globes for the kerosene lamps that provided the only light. Her family obtained electricity when she was in about the sixth grade. The house was heated by a fireplace and a pot-bellied wood stove. There was another wood stove in the kitchen. Her father cut the wood for the stoves and fireplace, but, as the only child, it was Garrett's job to stack the wood neatly on the front porch.

Garrett's father was about fifteen years older than her mother. He was working on the railroad near where her mother lived when he first encountered her. "He liked what he saw," Elta said. They married when Garrett's mother was fifteen years old. She gave birth to her first set of twins a year later. Her father cut pulpwood for paper manufacturing. He was also a part-time musician, playing guitar in house bands that would perform behind touring musicians in small cities in the area, such as Bogalusa, eleven miles north of Sun. She said he played with Fats Domino, B.B. King, Ike and Tina Turner, and others. Her mother "did housework" in White homes, cleaning and cooking, typically the only non-farm work available for uneducated Black women in the segregated South, though she later went to school to become a beautician.

Garrett's parents did not farm commercially, but they had extensive vegetable gardens at their home. Both came from farming families. Her mother's

Elta Garrett on her fifth birthday, 1947. Used with permission, Elta Garrett.

family still farmed some of the Ellis land, and leased the rest to other farmers. Her father's family were sharecroppers in the area. Her family raised peas, string beans, corn, tomatoes, turnip and mustard greens, cucumbers, watermelon, and strawberries. Behind their house was a small pond, where Elta's parents taught her how to fish. She caught catfish and perch that the family ate.

"We had plenty food," she said. "It was country food, like ham hocks, ribs, salt pork, chitlins, chicken, plenty fish."

Garrett's life growing up revolved around school, church, and music, all of which involved her family. Her aunt was the principal of the Black elementary school in Sun, which was a mile and half walk through the woods from her home. Elta excelled as a student, skipping the second and fifth grades. Her maternal grandfather was a minister. He was pastor of the St. Paul African Methodist Episcopal Church in nearby Bogalusa and preached at other churches in the area. She spent all day every Sunday in church, attending Sunday school and church services, singing in the choir, and helping clean the church. She served as secretary of the Sunday school. She often had choir practice during the week.

Garrett's maternal grandmother was a singer and voice teacher. She studied music at New Orleans University, now Dillard University. She led the choirs at her husband's church, but also gave individual voice lessons to children, mostly using the AME hymnal. They sang spirituals, solo voice music based on slave songs, not gospel music. She began to teach Elta to sing as soon as she started to talk. In fact, Elta sang her first solo at age three in church, a spiritual entitled "My Task." Every night after dinner growing up, Garrett's mother would walk Elta to her grandmother's house for voice lessons. She joined the church choir at age five.

"She drilled me and drilled me every night," Garrett said. "We would sing and sing and sing. I had an unusual, mature voice. They used to ask my mother, 'Is that voice coming out of that little girl?' I was such a puny little thing."

Garrett's parents had high expectations for their daughter, perhaps because they had three other children who died. With an aunt who was a teacher, they expected her to do well in school. She had chores around the house. She stacked the firewood whenever her father cut wood, made her bed every day, and on Fridays had to iron five dresses, one for each day of school the following week. Educated and deeply religious, her parents and grandparents were strict, all except her paternal grandmother. They closely monitored her behavior, and dictated what she could do and where she could go. They would not allow her to play with certain children. She was not allowed to eat dinner at her best friend's house. She was not even allowed to sit on her own bed.

If she misbehaved at school, her parents would sit her down and make her read a Bible verse. The family always prayed before meals. "Heaven forbid if you were real hungry and forgot to say your blessing," she said. "My grandmother prayed so long you wondered, 'Are we ever going to get to eat?'"

Garrett thought her parents were too demanding. "As I got older, I felt that the expectations were a bit too tough for me," she said. "But I was afraid to rebel."

Her best friend growing up was Lena Johnson, who moved to Sun when she was ten. They remain close. Lena still lives in Sun and married Garrett's cousin. Growing up, they sang in the church choir together. Both liked to play with dolls. Lena knew how to sew and made clothes for their dolls. They liked to jump rope, fish at the pond behind the Sibley house, and go swimming at a large lake near Sun. Once they saw five alligators in the lake, and never went back to that area. On weekends, they sometimes took a bus to Bogalusa to shop, eat hamburgers, or go to a movie at the Ritz Theater there. The theater was segregated, but that did not seem to bother Garrett much at the time. That is just the way life was in the South.

Garrett recalls her childhood with affection. In her view, she had a good life. "I did," she said. "If we were poor, I didn't know it. I was a happy kid."

But Garrett was not oblivious to how Black people were treated in Louisiana at the time. To White people in Sun, Black residents were largely invisible. Black people may have washed their clothes or cooked for them, but they otherwise acted like they did not exist, Garrett said. A twenty-seven-page online history of Sun (there is little else written about such a small town) does not mention Black people even once. It includes forty-three illustrations but not one shows a Black person.[3]

Garrett's parents taught her from a young age about the racial codes, unwritten but inflexible, that all Black people were expected to follow—where they could go, how they should behave, the ways in which they were required to speak to White people. Her parents never questioned the social order. She is outspoken and that concerned her parents when she was growing up. "They warned us, being little Black girls, you have to be very careful," she said. "They taught us what prejudice was and to be aware. My mother used to always tell me, 'You watch your mouth, because sometimes you can open it when it should be shut.'"

She recalled that once when she went to the store in Sun, she approached the counter to pay, but the clerk scolded her and told her to "get to the back of the line," even though she said there was no line, just customers milling about. Sometimes when she went to the store, the clerk would say to her loudly, so everyone else in the store could hear, "Tell your mama to come pay her bill." She found that humiliating.

Garrett attended a one-room Black school in Sun through the eighth grade. It had a single teacher, her aunt, who was also the principal. Each grade occupied one row of desks. It was heated by a pot-bellied stove. The school had been built about 1921 with money provided by the Rosenwald Fund, a philanthropy created by Julius Rosenwald, president of Sears, Roebuck and Co. It helped build more than fifty-three hundred schools, shops, and teachers' homes in the South and Southwest between 1917 and 1932, primarily to help educate Black children.[4] Garrett recognized even as a youngster that she was receiving an inferior education at the school. "We got secondhand books, pages missing, no back on the book," she said. "I thought, 'One day, I will be out of this.'" Sun was too small to have a Black high school, so Garrett attended Central Memorial High School, an all-Black school in Bogalusa. She took the bus there every day. She said it was an improvement over the Sun school.

When Garrett was in high school, her parents experienced financial difficulties, so she went to work for a man who owned a nightclub in Sun, washing clothes at his home. One of her cousins cooked for the family. She washed clothes in a shack behind the family's house. When it was lunchtime, her cousin brought her food to the wash shack. Neither of them was allowed to eat at the house. Garrett never entered the family's house in all the time she worked for them. She did not understand that.

There were three nightclubs in Sun, but Black people were forbidden from entering the front of those clubs. She had another cousin who worked at one of them, the Plantation Club. The clubs had small back rooms, with separate entrances, where Black patrons were permitted. The clubs served food, but Black customers were served only after all Whites had been served. Her cousin told her that Black diners were given food that was inferior to that served to White customers. "The front of the nightclub was beautiful," she said. "But the back was a broken-down looking place. When I got old enough to go in those nightclubs, I never went."

The Ku Klux Klan was active in St. Tammany Parish, where Sun is located, and its presence created a climate of fear among Black residents, who knew even minor violations of social codes could be punished violently.[5] Although

Garrett said her family never encountered the Klan, she knew families who had crosses burned in their yards.

Most Black families in Sun were poor. There were few employment options for uneducated Black people who were not sharecroppers. Most Black women worked as maids in White homes. Most Black men worked at a sawmill or a glass factory in Sun, difficult jobs and hazardous workplaces. Garrett said that the glass factory emitted smoke that contained silica that would cover the town in white dust. She had to walk past the plant on the way to school and her clothes often became coated with the dust. Silica has since been found to cause cancer, though the glass factory likely employed few health precautions at the time.

"All the Black people there have some sort of cancer, mostly lung cancer," she said. "That plant caused so many people to die from lung disease. Everybody just about in that town, including my mom and dad, they had lung problems. I have chronic bronchitis, too."

Garrett graduated from Central Memorial High School in Bogalusa in 1958 at age sixteen, because she had skipped two grades. She was a soprano in the high school choir and also participated in theater. She was a majorette in the marching band until her voice teacher made her quit because she did not want her to be outside during cold or wet weather, fearing she might get sick and hurt her voice.

She intended to enroll at Grambling State College, but delayed her entrance one year because her maternal grandmother, her first voice teacher, had contracted colon cancer. Her grandmother died in 1959. Garrett enrolled at Grambling that fall, planning to study to be a nurse. But her plans changed after she participated in a talent show that began the school year. Students represented the towns from which they came. Friends of hers from high school persuaded her to represent Bogalusa as a singer.

"By the time the talent show was over, there was six music teachers at the foot of the stage that wanted to talk to me," she remembered.

They asked what her major was, and she told them. They tried to persuade her to change her major to music. They convinced her to come to the music department the next day to meet with them and discuss it. She agreed to try music for one semester. She ended up liking it and majored in music education.

She joined the Grambling Concert Choir, which was highly regarded and traveled all over the country and beyond to perform. Choir director Robert Williams had attended Morehouse College with Martin Luther King Jr. and later served as one of his bodyguards. Garrett said that the choir traveled to Birmingham, Alabama, to perform for King at Ebenezer Baptist Church after he was released from the Birmingham jail. It traveled to the Caribbean to perform for members of the US military serving there.

Garrett graduated from Grambling in 1963. She said she turned down a scholarship to continue her studies at the renowned Juilliard School in New York City because her mother was sick. Instead, she took a job teaching at a rural, all-Black middle school, another Rosenwald school, in Folsom, Louisiana, about thirty miles west of Sun. Because the school was small, she taught a diverse curriculum to sixth graders—music, but also science, English, and math. She stayed at the school for five years. Elta met her husband, Floyd Garrett, in Folsom. He knew the school principal and they met at an end-of-school-year party. He lived in Covington, the parish seat. He worked as an orderly at a hospital. They married in 1966.

In 1968, Elta was transferred to Covington High School as part of efforts to integrate schools in St. Tammany Parish. The high school at the time was almost completely White. In 1954, the US Supreme Court, in *Brown v. Board of Education*, had ruled that school segregation was unconstitutional, but many school districts in the South ignored the decision for years and only integrated in response to lawsuits.

St. Tammany Parish schools, like many school districts in the region, adopted "school choice" as a way to incrementally integrate its schools, allowing White and Black students to attend the school of their choice. But that approach did not significantly change the racial composition of schools. In 1968–69, when Garrett transferred to Covington High School, eleven of thirty-five schools in the parish were still composed entirely of students of one race.[6]

Garrett said she was one of five Black teachers assigned to Covington High School when the school year began in August 1968. Only a handful of Black students had chosen to attend the school. Her memories of what happened differ somewhat from historical accounts. Sheriff's deputies escorted the Black teachers into school on the first day, according to Garrett. She said that her first class was chorus and that all students in the class were White. She began the class by encouraging her students to set an example.

"I'm new to you, you're new to me," she told the class. "But let's fool the world and teach them a lesson that we can work together."

The class, she said, applauded in response. "That's a good sign," she thought.

Garrett said that the school's principal, Louis Wagner, called her to his office during the second week of school to ask how she was doing. He asked her to act as liaison to the school's Black female students. She said Wagner asked her if there were any changes she would like the school to implement to aid the integration process. She had immediately noticed when she entered his office that Wagner had a Confederate flag hanging on his wall.

She recalled saying to Wagner, "Well, maybe this can happen, but first I'm going to ask a favor: Remove that Confederate flag out of your office."

He said, "Oh, you think all . . ."

She said she interrupted him, adding, "I know so, sir. That's just not a good start for what we're trying to do here."

Garrett said that the principal removed the flag from his office the next day. However, a history of Covington High School that quotes newspaper reports from the period said that it was Black students assigned to the school the following year who demanded that the flag be removed. Wagner and the school board refused. It was only removed after a lawsuit was filed and a judge ordered it taken down, according to the history.[7]

Interviewed forty-six years later, Garrett recalled only one negative incident caused by integration during her time in Louisiana, and she described it in a somewhat positive light. She traveled with the Covington marching band to a football game at another school. When they arrived, she said, a White player from the opposing team, noticing her presence, said, "Oh, they got a nigger with them." She said White students from her school defended her. A fight broke out, she said, and had to be broken up by sheriff's deputies.

Garrett escaped the worst conflicts caused by integration in St. Tammany Parish because she moved to Boston in 1969. Integration grew considerably more contentious after she left. As one of a small number of Black teachers in an overwhelmingly White school, she remembered her experience there favorably.

"It turned out so wonderful," she said. "The kids did dearly love me, and I loved them. I learned not to see White and Black. The school was mainly White. Those kids, we learned each other together."

In July 1969, a US district court judge ordered the St. Tammany school district to scrap the "school choice" approach to desegregation and fully integrate its schools. White people protested the decision, but the order was implemented. The result, according to one Covington High teacher, was "chaos." When hundreds of Black teenagers enrolled at Covington High School that fall, "fights broke out in the halls" between White and Black students, according to the school history. In one incident, more than one hundred students were "embroiled in a free-for-all." Sheriff's deputies had to be stationed every forty to fifty feet in the school's hallways to maintain order. White and Black students who caused trouble were arrested. In February 1970, a bomb exploded in a male lavatory. Then in April, 150 Black students protested conditions and 77 were arrested. Integration became more peaceful over time.[8]

Garrett moved to Boston in 1969 with her husband because he had family there. His brother had moved there first and then his sister followed. His brother had been stationed in the Boston area while in the military and stayed there after his discharge, working as a mechanic. His sister went to school in Connecticut to become an airline stewardess.

Although Garrett's husband was the eldest child in his family, she said that his younger brother made major decisions for the family and persuaded him to come to Boston. Her husband was attracted by the many colleges in the Boston area and hoped to go to school there. He also believed that he would have better job opportunities in the city. Garrett's husband moved to Boston before she did. He got an apartment in the South End and stayed there off and on for a year and a half while trying to persuade Elta to relocate. She visited him once in Boston, but was unimpressed.

He said, "I guess you're ready to go back and get your things."

She replied, "I'm not moving here. I don't like Boston."

Garrett continued to resist. She did not want to leave Louisiana. She had no interest in uprooting and moving north. She liked her job and the school where she worked. She said she was being considered to become an assistant principal the following year. She had begun taking graduate classes at Southeastern Louisiana College and intended to eventually earn a doctorate. She wanted to build a house in Louisiana, where the cost of living is considerably less than in Boston.

But it was the 1960s and women were still largely expected to follow their husband's wishes, particularly in the conservative South. Her mother told her, "You need to be with your husband." In March 1969, Garrett submitted her resignation and begrudgingly moved to Boston. She was twenty-seven years old. She moved to the city one month after a nor'easter buried the city under twenty-six inches of snow. Much of that snow remained when she arrived, piled high along city streets but brown and muddy. That only increased her discontent about moving there.

Her husband had rented them an apartment on Hansborough Street in Dorchester. She had only ever lived in houses and did not like the idea of living in an apartment building, separated from neighbors by thin walls. The apartment was not ready when she arrived, but they visited it. She said the apartment was dirty and crawling with cockroaches. That did not help her attitude. "I cried," she said. "Oh my goodness, I cried!"

Garrett's husband got a job as a ramp agent at Logan International Airport. She applied for a teaching job with Boston public schools and was hired to teach at the Martin Luther King Jr. Middle School in Roxbury beginning in September 1969. The school, located in a poor, Black neighborhood and composed almost entirely of Black students, was a stark contrast from the high school where she taught in Louisiana. During the previous school year, students had rioted, assaulted teachers, and set fires in classrooms.[9] Disturbed by the lack of discipline at the school, Garrett quit after her third day on the job.

"It was terrible there," she said. "The kids wouldn't listen. They wouldn't sit down. They were burning up teacher's cars in the parking lot."

Garrett asked the personnel office of the Boston public schools to consider her for future teaching openings. In the meantime, she got a job as a reservation agent for Northeast Airlines, working at Logan Airport like her husband.

In January 1970, Boston schools hired her as a long-term substitute teacher, teaching music at Timilty Middle School in Roxbury in place of a teacher who was on maternity leave. Most students at the school were Black, but nearly all the teachers were White. Her principal, however, was a Black man. She was eventually hired permanently by the school. When the Boston schools implemented court-ordered busing in 1974, she was transferred to the Frank V. Thompson School in Dorchester, where most of the faculty was also White. The principal from Timilty moved there, too. She stayed there eleven years. "I loved it there," she said.

Despite her experiences helping to desegregate a school in Louisiana, Garrett was not active in the movement to integrate Boston's schools. Still, she supported busing and said it improved the education that Black children received. Although she considers herself politically "interested," she never became involved in civil rights efforts in Boston because, she said, teachers were told they should not be "on the front lines." She did attend meetings of

the Black Educators Alliance of Massachusetts, which worked for desegregation and pushed Boston public schools to hire more Black teachers.

"We had to be careful being a teacher of what you were saying and what
you were participating in," she said. "We couldn't get involved."

Garrett struggled to adjust to living in Boston. She is a quintessential
southerner, friendly and upbeat. But Boston was a big city in the Northeast,
where attitudes and social norms were vastly different from Louisiana. She
found Bostonians, including Boston-born Black people, "cold" and "cliquish."
Her husband scolded her for speaking to strangers. When they walked down
the street, if someone was sitting on their porch, she would greet them. Her
natural inclination was to say "Hello" and ask, 'How y'all doing?" just as she
would have done in the South. Her husband implored her to stop. She did,
she said, but "I didn't like that."

Even her church was unsatisfying. Although she was raised in the
AME Church in Louisiana, her husband was Catholic, and initially they
attended the Cathedral of the Holy Cross Church in the South End, the
largest Catholic church in New England. Nearly all the parishioners there
were White. She could not tolerate that church, with its elaborate ritual and
formal music. At the time, she and her husband were staying with her in-
laws in an apartment in Roxbury before they could move into their apartment. One day she was walking down Elm Hill Avenue in Roxbury and told
herself, "The first church that I hear some Black music coming out of, I'm
going in."

That church was Charles Street African Methodist Episcopal Church,
which sits at the corner of Elm Hill Avenue and Warren Street. She joined the
church in April 1969 and has been a member ever since. But even though she
was raised in the AME church, she found Charles Street unlike her church in
Louisiana. Many of its members were native-born Bostonians, she said, and
she found that Black people who were born in Boston often looked down on
Black people from the South.

"The Black people in Boston who were born here, they are just very different," she said. "All the ladies with the big hats and could dress real nice,
they all sat together. I used to look at them and I said, 'Mmm, they aren't that
friendly.' "

Garrett struggled to fit in wherever she went. Most of her fellow teachers,
at first, were White. Many of the members of her church were Boston-born
and she found them arrogant. Her worst fears about Boston were all coming

true. "I told my husband every day I wanted to go back home," she said. "I hated Boston."

Garrett also experienced trouble in her personal life. She and her husband moved to a better apartment, on Oldfields Road in Dorchester. Their only child, Denton, was born in 1971. But two and half months later, Elta's husband left her without saying a word. She arrived home one day from work and he had moved out. She did not realize that until late in the evening when she opened a closet and all his clothes were gone, only the hangers remaining.

They divorced in 1975. He eventually remarried and moved to California. He had nothing to do with their son until the boy was nine years old, Garrett said, and never paid child support. Their divorce was "bitter," she said, and soured her on marriage. She vowed that she would never marry again, and she has not.

"He just walked out of our lives and that was that," she said. "It worked out well for me in the end, I guess. I only wish my son could have been with his father more."

Despite her initial concerns about Charles Street AME, Garrett grew to like the church and credits it with helping her survive the difficult times she experienced after her husband abandoned her and her son. She had lived in Boston for less than two years when her husband left. She had no other family in the city, except a sister-in-law, who, she said, "stuck by me." She knew few people and had no close friends.

But Charles Street's minister showed concern for her situation and told her, "Trust God, it's going to get better." When mothers in the church learned what happened, they offered to help Garrett whenever she needed it. Men in the church provided her young son the male guidance he lacked after his father disappeared from his life. Garrett became active in the church right away, directing two choirs. She became involved in the church's educators' alliance, which helped students who want to attend college to prepare and seek scholarships. She was a member of the church's missionary group, once serving as its vice president.

"My faith really brought me through that ordeal," she said. "The church was my family. They were very good to me. I could have crumbled, but I prayed a lot. I thank God for keeping me safe. We were never hungry and that's a blessing. I feel like I've really been blessed by God."

After her marriage ended, Garrett contemplated returning to Louisiana, but her mother talked her out of it. That proved fortuitous because in 1976 her mother was seriously injured in a car accident in New Orleans, breaking her hip and both of her arms. Garrett brought her mother to Boston for medical treatment and rehabilitation. She was treated at Beth Israel Hospital and Boston University Medical Center, and she remained in Boston until her death in 1988. Garrett's father died in Louisiana in 1980.

"These hospitals here, they literally put her back together," Garrett said. "For medical care and for the services she could get, I said this is my best bet—to stay here."

Garrett never again thought seriously about leaving Boston. She moved into an apartment complex in Roxbury then owned by her church, where she still lives today (the church later sold it). Her teaching career improved, though not without some difficulties along the way. She also began to realize other benefits of living in Boston. She earned a master's degree in secondary education and administration from the University of Massachusetts, Boston. She was able to do that as a single parent because her mother took care of her son when she was working or taking classes. Later, she earned a master's degree in special education from Boston College.

She taught at the Thompson School from 1974 to 1985. The principal she followed from Timilty Middle School was transferred to another school, and the new principal, Garrett said, "didn't like me." He would not let her lead a chorus. He changed her homeroom, giving her twelve students who had a history of disciplinary problems and trouble with the law. They had been in and out of school.

But, as in Louisiana, Garrett welcomed the challenge. She nicknamed the group "The Dirty Dozen," which she said they liked. She asked their parents to help make sure they attended school every day. She pleaded with the students to work harder and do their schoolwork. Frustrated at first, she told them one day, "Look, I need something more from you. You're all smart kids. If you're smart enough to steal a car, you're smart enough to do this work that you have in front of you."

She said the students passed all their classes that year and were promoted. At graduation, she said, the principal recognized them for their improvements. She said she was able to change their attitudes and that they came to appreciate her efforts. "Do you know that until this day some of those students still call me?" she said. "They do. They are so happy to tell me that they have a job."

After teaching for a year at the Woodrow Wilson School, she returned to the Martin Luther King Jr. Middle School, the school she quit after three days when she first arrived in Boston. She taught music there from 1986 until her retirement in 2005. Teaching there went much better the second time. Even after she retired, Garrett continued to work at the King school as a volunteer, helping keep attendance and calling parents of students who were chronically absent. Her great-granddaughter attended the school. "I love that school," she said. "It's just so ironic: the school that I resigned from I ended up retiring from. Isn't that something?"

In addition to teaching and leading school choruses, Garrett also became an admired singer in Boston. She sings in the sacred ensemble at Charles Street AME and has been a frequent soloist there. Over the years, she has performed with the Boston Orchestra and Chorale, at the Boston Public Library as part of a Black history event, and at celebrations honoring Martin Luther King Jr. Garrett said that many people incorrectly assume that because she's a Black singer and performs religious music that she sings gospel, but she is quick to correct that misconception. She is a classically trained soprano and can sing opera.

She has also been recognized in Boston for her musical contributions. In 1994, she was among eleven people honored by Mayor Tom Menino with the city's first African American achievement awards. In 2006, the New England Conservatory gave her its lifetime gospel achievement award for her years of teaching, performing, and community service. The fact that she was recognized for her contributions to gospel music may reflect misperceptions about Black spiritual music, even at a respected music school.[10]

After retiring from full-time teaching, she cofounded the Hamilton-Garrett Center for Music and Arts, which is affiliated with Charles Street AME. It teaches voice, piano, percussion, guitar, and violin to young people aged 5 to 18, alongside classes in music theory, history, and Black identity. It sponsors a youth choir, musical ensemble, and drumline, and offers master classes to area schools.[11]

Five decades after moving to Boston, Garrett has adjusted to life in the city, even if it has never seemed quite like home. Asked when she finally came around to living in Boston, she joked, "Yesterday." She acknowledged that it took a "good while" and that she's "still not like the average Bostonian."

She still has regrets about leaving Louisiana. She never got to build her dream house and still lives in an apartment. Most of her friends in Boston are southerners. They like to shop and cook southern food. She contributes gumbo, jambalaya, and other Louisiana specialties. She is confident that if she had stayed in Louisiana she would have earned a PhD. She thinks she would have eventually become a school principal.

She is still wary of some Boston-born Black people, who she calls the "siddity" Bostonians ("siddity" is Black slang for snobbish). But a few years ago, she resolved to introduce herself to anyone she does not know at her church to overcome those barriers.

Garrett recognizes that moving to Boston has brought her certain advantages—world-class healthcare for her mother, advanced education and a higher standard of living for herself. But she also believes Boston lags its image as an enlightened metropolis when it comes to its treatment of Black people. Now that she is retired, she no longer feels constrained from showing her political inclinations. Three times recently she has shown her support for Black Lives Matter protests in Boston. Once, after George Floyd was killed by a White police officer in Minneapolis, she and some other senior citizens left a computer class they were taking in Nubian Square to watch a Black Lives Matter march that was passing by, "just to give them our support," she said.

She is concerned about the quality of public education in Boston, and particularly about "the education of our Black boys." Only about half of Black males in the city finish high school in four years. "Somebody needs to look into why our Black boys aren't achieving as they should be," she said. She believes Black people are still excluded from some aspects of Boston life, especially elite forms of culture. She criticized the Boston Symphony Orchestra for having too few Black members and for its failure to encourage Black youth in the city to develop a taste for classical music. In 2021, only one of ninety-three orchestra members was Black.[12] She said children who participate in its youth orchestras are more likely to come from New York than inner-city Boston.

But she also recognizes that her ability to speak out about such issues is perhaps one of the greatest benefits she has gained by moving north. She did not feel like she could do that in Louisiana before she left. She isn't convinced she would be able to do that there even today.

"Living down there, I think I still would have been the same person—doing as I was told," she said. "But when I came here, it's like, you better speak up or you're going to get lost in the shuffle. Boston was a place that I could speak my piece. Whether it was liked or not, I did it. I learned to do it more because there was no fear that you were going to have repercussions from it."

Sometimes freedom of mind is the greatest freedom of all.

12

Ten Lives, What They Teach Us, and Why They Matter

Why should you care about the lives of ten Black men and women, all of whom fled racism and mistreatment in the South and moved to Boston, but who led ordinary lives, largely unknown except to family, friends, and other acquaintances?

Because their stories illuminate an important but largely unknown aspect of Boston's history that helped make the city what it is today. They were like tens of thousands of Black people who migrated to Boston from the South and transformed the city in the process. Boston was an overwhelmingly White city before the Great Migration. Today, people of color are the majority and Black people are the largest non-White group, making up one-quarter of the population. Yes, there are other Black groups who have helped to shape Boston, but Black southern migrants and their descendants outnumber them. More than any other group, they changed the complexion of Boston.

The movement to Boston of people like those featured shows that the Great Migration affected cities that have been largely left out of histories on the subject. Telling their stories expands our knowledge of what happened. There is a sizable literature about the Great Migration, but if you read much of that you will conclude that Black southerners stopped in their trek northward before reaching New England. Some Black leaders in Boston likewise believe that southern migration to the city was insignificant. Although Boston received fewer migrants than places such as Chicago and Detroit, the city was the destination for thousands of Black southerners, and the impact of that migration was substantial. You cannot understand contemporary Boston without considering the impact of the Great Migration.

The experiences of these ten people bring to life the story of the Great Migration and help us to understand a major historical event at the individual level. More than six million Black people left the South and moved north, and each of their stories was different. The Great Migration was more complex than is often portrayed, as the lives of these individuals show.

North to Boston. Blake Gumprecht, Oxford University Press. © Blake Gumprecht 2023.
DOI: 10.1093/oso/9780197614440.003.0012

Their experiences growing up in the South were different. The factors that motivated them to leave the region were different. Many enjoyed their lives there. Most were not driven from the South by oppression, as is commonly assumed, but instead were drawn north by the hope of something better. They didn't plot for years and often acted impulsively. Their experiences in Boston varied, too. All were subject to racism, just as they were in the South. None underwent any sort of dramatic personal transformation because they moved north. The benefits of migration were relative.

The details of their lives make the Great Migration seem more real, more remarkable, more meaningful. We shudder when we hear Geraldine Walker talk about being raped as a thirteen-year-old girl by her White employer in rural Alabama. We feel the world closing in around Ollie Sumrall as he grew up amid lynchings and a climate of racial violence in small town Mississippi. We share Lucy Parham's aggravation when she is told by a North Carolina employment agency that the only jobs available for Black women like her were for domestic servants working in the homes of White people. Our muscles tense when we hear Willie Pittman describe being threatened by a carload of White teenagers on a bridge in South Boston during the city's busing crisis. But we also sense the great pride Charles Gordon felt when, after working for years as a welder, he was hired as a manager by Harvard University, one of the world's elite higher education institutions. We come to appreciate the benefits all these people gained by moving north.[1]

The lives of the people featured in this book also provide a rare glimpse inside Boston's contemporary Black community, which has been largely ignored by writers and scholars. They were part of waves of change that swept over Black Boston following World War II. The city's Black community grew and grew because of migration, expanding ever further southward and absorbing areas previously inhabited by White people. Block by block, first in Roxbury, then in Dorchester, later in Mattapan, and finally in Hyde Park, Black people moved in and White residents moved out. As that happened, Black-oriented businesses replaced White businesses. Houses of worship changed denominations to serve the new residents, and storefront churches sprang up. The street life changed. The sounds changed. The smells changed. Black culture replaced Jewish and Irish culture.

Finally, I believe you should care about the people whose stories are told in this book because their lives are worth knowing. In learning about each of these ten men and women over the last seven years, I have gained an appreciation for their lives, all they have gone through, and what they have accomplished. They have shown initiative and bravery. All have achieved success as defined by them, which is the most important measure of all. I find their lives inherently interesting, as affecting as the most absorbing novel or motion picture. We learn too little about people like these—Black people, working-class people, regular people leading anonymous lives—and too much about the powerful and famous. We seldom hear voices like these. The experiences of ordinary people teach us far more about America than any number of histories about important events or biographies of politicians and movie stars. These are people like us: Why wouldn't you care about them?

What do we learn from the lives of these ten men and women? Some of what their stories tell us was expected, while other aspects were surprising. Most moved as young adults (median age: twenty), before they married and had children, but that is true of migrants in general. Four came from cities in the South, the rest from small towns and rural areas, which is where most Black people lived before they began migrating, a legacy of slavery's agricultural focus. Most grew up comparatively poor and uneducated, characteristics they shared with Black people throughout the region. Their fathers were sharecroppers, coal miners, loggers, and itinerant musicians. Their mothers, if they were employed outside the home, were domestic workers—cleaning, cooking, and caring for children in White homes. Their parents' jobs reflected the limited range of occupations open to Black workers at the time. Some grew up in extreme poverty, living in dilapidated houses, often without running water or electricity, at least initially. They shared beds with siblings or other relatives.

Their lives before moving to Boston were strongly shaped by racism. All grew up in a South that was segregated by law, though the dimensions of segregation differed between cities and small towns, where there was greater mixing. Public facilities were separated by race. They attended all-Black schools, which were often rundown and received considerably less funding than White schools. They had to sit upstairs in movie theaters and were required to go to the back of public buses. Like all Black people, they were prohibited from swimming pools, parks, libraries, golf courses, and the dining rooms of restaurants. They used separate restrooms and water fountains.

Black lives were also governed by unwritten but well-understood social codes that dictated how they should behave around White people. They were expected to show deference wherever they went, addressing White men as "sir" and women as "ma'am." When Black and White people patronized the same businesses, the people in this book knew to let White customers go before them. They stepped aside on sidewalks to let White pedestrians pass. Even when they adhered to such rules, White people treated them with contempt, pushing them out of the way, spitting on them, and calling them "nigger." The threat of violence was ever-present. All Black people heard stories of individuals punished, even killed, for perceived violations of racial codes.

The ten men and women in this book adapted to the hostile environment as best they could. Their parents taught them at a young age how to act around White people. "You didn't cross that line," Geraldine Walker said. They followed the rules because they knew what could happen if they did not. They stayed away from White people whenever possible. Faced with limits on where they could go, they avoided those situations or created alternatives. Ollie Sumrall Jr. stopped going to movies at the segregated theater in his hometown because he objected to having to enter via a fire escape and sit in the balcony while White patrons sat downstairs. Prohibited from swimming in public pools or golfing on established courses, Thomas Lindsay and his friends swam in a nearby creek and created their own small golf course on the grounds of an abandoned factory.[2]

Somehow in the face of poverty and the daily indignities of being Black in a racist region, most of the individuals in this book found ways to carve out separate lives, beyond the influence of White people, that were happy and enjoyable. Most have surprisingly fond memories of their childhoods, which were full of love and good times. All worked to help their families, laboring in the fields, washing clothes by hand, cooking and cleaning for White families, but they also had free time to spend with friends. They played house and baseball. They fished and climbed trees. They explored woods near their homes. They did what all children everywhere did, regardless of race. "I was a happy kid," Elta Garrett said.[3] Most of the others seemed to be as well. Certainly, they resented how they were treated, but they adjusted, did what they were told, kept their mouths shut, and left the South when they were old enough to do so. To some degree, they seemed oblivious to their inferior status because it was all they had ever known.

What motivated the individuals featured to leave the South more than overt racism was a lack of opportunity. Without a college degree, Black men had little choice but to do physically demanding labor like their fathers— farming, felling trees, hazardous work in sawmills or glass factories. For women, the options were even more limited, as Lucy Parham discovered when she tried to get a job after high school and was told that the only jobs for Black women were doing domestic work. "I don't want to do that," she said. Other individuals in this book were similarly discouraged by their employment choices in the South, which strongly influenced their decisions to move north. Ollie Sumrall and Willie Pittman grew up farming, but had no interest in doing that as adults. "I didn't want that kind of life," Sumrall explained. "I don't know how we stood it," Pittman said.[4]

All but two of the people followed family who migrated to Boston before them. In this way, they participated in a process known as chain migration, by which migrants follow family or friends to a destination. Probably no factor explains why migrants of all types choose a particular destination more than chain migration. Family and friends who have already migrated are an important source of information to people considering such moves themselves. Sometimes migrant stories exaggerate the merits of a destination, but can exert a persuasive influence even when they do.

Migration is always easier when you know someone on the other end who can provide a temporary place to stay, help you to find work, introduce you to other people, and aid in getting oriented to an unfamiliar place. Thomas Lindsay's aunt wrote him letters telling him about Boston. Elizabeth Hall Davis followed her mother to the city. "She said Boston is a better place," Davis recalled. Two of Willie Pittman's siblings preceded him to Boston, and his brother told Willie he could get him a job at the same rubber factory where he worked. While the migrants in this book were influenced by family members who moved before them, they in turn influenced other family members who came later. Three of Lucy Parham's four siblings followed her to Boston. All of Geraldine Walker's six siblings eventually moved to the city.[5]

The decision to migrate hundreds or thousands of miles is a major life event, but the examples here show that, contrary to common perception, it is not always the result of careful planning and thought, and sometimes is done impulsively or because of circumstances. Most of the migrants in this book knew little about Boston before they came. Four never really intended to move to the city and one resisted it strongly. Lucy Parham had planned to go to college in North Carolina, but traveled to Boston to help her aunt after she gave birth and quickly realized the city's advantages. Willie Pittman went to the city only intending to visit his brother and sister for a short time, but never left. "I liked it," he said, "and seen there was opportunity." Ollie Sumrall had intended to move to Chicago and only decided to go to Boston when his sister changed her mind about moving there at the last minute, which meant his brother had an empty seat in his car. Sumrall decided to go with him and moved to Boston the next day.[6]

When they arrived in Boston, only two individuals possessed college degrees and none of the rest had marketable skills or anything other than entry-level job experience, so it took them time to get established. They found what jobs they could, then moved on when they could find something better. Two went to trade school. One attended Boston State College part time while working full time. Two others earned college degrees after they became established. All found their way and most developed long-lasting careers, working for the same employers for years. Several benefited from programs designed to increase minority hiring. All rose above the class standing of their parents. None became rich or famous, but they did okay. Growing up Black and relatively poor in the South may have reduced their ambitions. Like immigrants, they worked hard so their children could do better than they did. And many of their children did do better.

What they heard about Boston was true, for the most part. Jobs were plentiful and there was a greater variety of careers open to Black workers than in the South. Whether educated or not, they found they could earn more money than was possible where they grew up. Yet Boston was also a disappointment in other ways. Race relations in the city were not as advanced as most expected them to be. Some experienced overt racism, especially during Boston's busing crisis in the 1970s. Lucy Parham had a beer can thrown at her. Willie Pittman was threatened by a carful of White teenagers one Sunday morning while walking home from work. Al Kinnitt had a walker thrown at him and was called "nigger."

They could go where they wanted and do what they chose, but they grew accustomed to White store clerks following them with their eyes as they shopped. Most have avoided certain parts of the city, especially South Boston and Charlestown, predominantly White and Irish, which have reputations for racism. Several noticed on visits home that race relations in the South had advanced more than in Boston, and that interaction and mixing between White and Black people there was greater. They observed that racism is more inconspicuous in Boston than in the South, but is still present. "Down there they let you know they're racist," Ollie Sumrall said. "Here they hide it. They do it in a sneaky way."[7]

Boston has remained one of the most segregated cities in the United States. The city's troubled racial history has shaped where Black people reside and how they live their lives. Eighty percent of Boston's Black residents live in just four neighborhoods—Roxbury, Dorchester, Mattapan, and Hyde Park. Although Black people make up one quarter of the city's population, they make up just 5 percent of residents in the rest of the city. In Beacon Hill, the North End, and East Boston, fewer than one in forty residents is Black. Boston is not the "city on a hill" that its founders imagined it would be.[8]

Seven of ten people featured remained in one of the city's four predominantly Black neighborhoods. Three eventually moved out of Boston, but two moved to suburbs with sizable Black populations. Only one moved to an area that was predominantly White, and she has since moved back to Mattapan. None of the rest has ever sought to integrate or move to White areas. That was intentional. Their friends are Black (and, in many cases, southern migrants). They attend a Black church. They shop mostly in stores in Black areas. They spend most of their lives in Black Boston by choice. If they have interacted with White people, it has primarily been in the workplace or while shopping.

That may seem surprising and disappointing, but perhaps it should not. All grew up in places where they were mistreated because of their race. Living in such antagonistic environments, Black people naturally chose to keep to themselves in an effort to have something resembling normal lives. When they moved to Boston, the people featured in this book discovered that racism also exists there, so they continued to show a preference for living among their own. Who can blame them? Why live someplace where you feel unwanted? Why go somewhere you feel out of place? "We didn't try to blaze any new trails," Charles Gordon said. If anything, growing up in the South may have predisposed migrants to remain within the Black community because their experiences with White people had been so negative. "I can avoid them here," Ollie Sumrall said.

All the individuals portrayed still attend a Black church, Charles Street African Methodist Episcopal Church in Roxbury. All grew up in religious families. Several attended Baptist churches in the South but switched after coming to Boston for different reasons. They all share a deep religious belief that began during childhood, and they are like most Black people in that way. Studies have found that Black people in the United States are more religious than other groups.[9] Several spoke at length about the importance of religion in their lives. For most, church has been the one constant since they moved to Boston. Jobs and residences changed, children grew up and left home, marriages broke up or spouses died, but their church remained. Most have attended Charles Street for more than forty years. Church is family. Church is community. Church is faith. Church is hope. Church is a guiding hand. Church is security in an uncertain and sometimes hostile world.

Despite their experiences in the South and Boston, none of the people who are the focus of this project became active in the civil rights movement or politics in general. Most do not consider themselves apolitical, however. The reasons they never became involved were personal and pragmatic. Three people said they did not participate in politics because family and work responsibilities prevented them from doing that. "I didn't have time," Thomas Lindsay said. "I had a family to take care of." Lucy Parham worked full time and went to school at night. Elta Garrett was a schoolteacher and she said school officials told teachers they should not be "on the front lines" of any political or civil rights activities.[10]

Three people deliberately avoided politics. Charles Gordon chose not to participate because he did not trust himself to remain nonviolent. Ollie Sumrall had a cousin in Mississippi who helped lead civil rights efforts in the county where they grew up, but violence against Black people there discouraged Ollie from doing that. "I didn't think it was worth it," he said. While some Black southerners were motivated by their experiences to combat racism and demand their rights, it is important to remember that most Black people did not actively participate in the civil rights movement. Some made that choice out of fear or the natural human inclination for self-protection. For every John Lewis, the congressman and civil rights leader who grew up in the same Alabama county and in similar circumstances to Willie Pittman, thousands more chose to leave the South rather than stay and fight. "All I wanted to do was try to better myself," Pittman said.[11]

What did the Black migrants featured gain by moving north? Plenty. All advanced economically and most achieved middle-class status. A greater variety of jobs were available to them than in the South. They made more money than was possible where they grew up. Three earned college degrees in Boston. All but two bought houses. Some moved up to nicer homes as their incomes grew. Most met their spouses in the city and all but two remained married to them. Fulfilling the dreams of migrants throughout history, their children may have benefited more from their moves than they did. They received a higher-quality education in Boston than their parents did in the South. Many went to college. Some earned graduate degrees. They became engineers, college professors, school administrators, ministers, police officers, and nurses.

But they gained more than economic success. Above all, they gained a feeling of freedom that they never had in the South. They can do what they want, go wherever they choose, and speak their minds without fear. When you have lacked such freedoms, you appreciate them even more. Most remained in Black neighborhoods, but they knew that they did not have to do that. They could go to Fenway Park. They could go to the symphony or a museum. They could go to the beach. They could eat in any restaurant. They came to value Boston's many advantages—numerous colleges, world-class healthcare, a vibrant arts scene. Boston may still be racist, but every Black person interviewed felt their lives turned out well and that they benefited by moving to the city. Interviewed four decades or longer after leaving the South, all looked back on their lives with contentment.

What did they give up by leaving the South? Less, it seems, than you may think. Migration can be a wrenching experience, severing connections to home, family, friends, and a way of life. Many migrants become nostalgic for the place they leave behind. They wonder if they made the right choice. They worry that they gave up more than they gained. They question whether it was worth it. Some give up and return home.

Moving from the South to Boston certainly required adjustments. Boston, they discovered, was a place quite different from where they grew up. The people were different. The buildings were different. The weather was different. The pace of life and the way people spoke were different. The food was different. Everything was different. Tears were shed, but all adjusted. The presence of family and other Black southerners made that adjustment easier and enabled them to live, in some ways, like they always had.

One of the most surprising aspects about their lives is the degree to which they maintained a Black southern cultural identity even after moving to Boston. They married southerners, they go to a church full of southerners, and many prefer to live around other southerners. They prefer southern food, talk with southern accents, and have southern manners. They possess a friendly and easygoing nature that reflects their southern roots. The South shaped them and helped make them who they are. They chose to leave the South, but the South lives on within them.

Black southerners are not normally considered an ethnic group, but they could be. They do not have any other meaningful group identity beyond their racial status. But they are different from Black people born in the North and different from immigrant Blacks. They consider themselves different. They share a collection of attributes that makes them comparable to other ethnic groups.[12] They have a common geographic origin. They have a shared history that began with enslavement and continued through the Jim Crow era and the Great Migration. They have a common spirituality rooted in the Black church. They have long relied on intergenerational networks of family and friends to protect them from hostility. They share certain traditions, such as a love for Black southern food, better known as soul food, which was born of slavery and poverty, and Black southern music, much of which had to travel north to achieve commercial success. They have a Black and southern way of speaking.[13]

But these Black southerners also display an ambivalence about the South. Most have never wanted to return, except to visit, and they are emphatic about that. Since 1970, there has been a return migration of Black people to the South, particular among retirees but also younger Black people who have discovered that the region has a certain appeal.[14] The cost of living is less than it is in the North. The economy has expanded. Racism has diminished. Black culture there is deeply rooted. Family and friends of people in this book have tried to persuade them to return home. But not one of them has seriously considered going back. Most reject such suggestions without hesitation. "I couldn't live down there," Lucy Parham said.[15] Boston has become home for all of them. Most now feel like Bostonians.

The lives of the individuals featured in these pages are powerful proof of the value of the Great Migration. They show it was possible to leave behind hate and deprivation, and achieve something better. They are but a few of the thousands of Black people who migrated to Boston from the South, but their stories show that for them the move north was worth it.

How many Black people living in the city of Boston today have southern roots? How many Black Bostonians were born in the South, or have parents or grandparents who were born in the South? It is impossible to know for sure. Although the US government compiles data on the place of birth of residents within the United States, it does not collect statistics on Black people who trace their origins to the South. The math must, therefore, be imprecise.

The number of Black people in Boston who were born in the South has diminished significantly since 1980 because many have died. A Black person born in the South who migrated to Boston in 1955 at the age of twenty-five would have been ninety years old in 2020, an age few people reach. Others have no doubt left the city, moving to the suburbs (as did three of people featured in this book) or out of state. For a five-year period ending in 2019, there were just under sixteen thousand southern-born Black people who lived in the city. There were more than forty-four thousand in Massachusetts.[16]

In 1980, there were about thirty-five thousand southern-born Black people in Boston. Using that number, I estimated the number of children that had been born to Black female southern migrants. If female migrants had children at the same rate as other Black women in Massachusetts, they probably had about twenty-five thousand children in 1980. Male migrants who mated with nonsoutherners had children, too, but the number is impossible to calculate. These are very rough estimates, it must be acknowledged.[17]

The children of Black southern migrants had children of their own, the grandchildren of the migrants. The grandchildren, too, had children, the great-grandchildren of migrants. With each generation, the size of the Black southern community in Boston grew. Like members of all ethnic groups, Black southerners carry some of their heritage with them even if they were not born there—maybe a favorite food, the church they attend, or southern manners—passed down by parents and kin, or experienced on trips to the South.

If we assume that the female children and grandchildren of southern migrants had kids at the average rate for Black women in Massachusetts, that would add more than fifty thousand Black people with southern roots to Boston's population.[18] If we sum the totals for each generation, we wind up with a grand total of about ninety-two thousand Black southerners—people born in the South or the descendants of people who were. But that number is clearly too large; it would mean southerners constitute 54 percent of Black residents in the city. Immigrants alone make up one-third of the city's Black population.

But it seems safe to say that at least seventy thousand Black Bostonians have southern roots. That would mean they make up about 40 percent of the city's Black population, which seems reasonable. That would make Black southerners the second largest ethnic group in Boston, after the Irish. There are about ninety thousand people in the city who claim Irish ancestry. That would also mean that there are more Black southerners in Boston than there are Italians, English, or Jews, groups long associated with the city who have received far more attention from writers and researchers over the years than Black southerners.[19]

These estimates demonstrate that Black people born in the South and their descendants are a major group in the city, who by their numbers alone have played a significant role in making Boston. Yet they have been almost completely ignored. They are seldom discussed, seldom written about, seldom acknowledged as even being present. The lack of interest in Black southern migrants in the city reflects a general indifference toward Black people in today's Boston.

Books about contemporary Black Boston are rare, even though the city has long been a center for both trade and academic publishing. Boston-area publishers have shown greater interest in Black people elsewhere or the history of Black people in the city than they have about Black people who live in Boston today. Yet numerous publishers have produced books about other ethnic groups in the city, most of which are smaller in size.

To read about Boston is to encounter a city that was settled by the English, remade by the Irish, Italians, Jews, and other European groups, and is being transformed today by Latinos, Asians, and other recent immigrants. US-born Black people are seldom mentioned, except in passing. There have been multiple books written about the Irish, Italians, and Jews in Boston. There have been books published recently about the Chinese, Dominicans, Puerto Ricans, Vietnamese, and other groups in the city.[20] But most books that have been written about Black Boston were written long ago or focus on time periods before World War II.

Despite a growth in the number of books published about recent immigrants, Boston is still almost always portrayed as a White city because White people have dominated its history, its government, its leading businesses, its colleges and universities, and its cultural life.

The absence of books about contemporary Black Boston reflects a general lack of awareness by White people of the city's Black community. How many White residents ever venture into the city's predominantly Black neighborhoods? How many would consider living in one of them? How many people who live on Beacon Hill or in Back Bay ever think about Roxbury or Mattapan, except as places to avoid? White people and Black people in Boston live in parallel worlds that seldom overlap, except in superficial ways.

That likely also reflects persistent racism in Boston. Why else do US-born Black people in the city continue to lag shockingly far behind White people in income, assets, and most other social indicators? One recent study found that the median net worth of US-born Black families in Boston was a mere $8, compared to $247,500 for White families. Why did three Black candidates for mayor in 2021, including incumbent Kim Janey, fail to advance beyond the primary or generate much support in predominantly White districts? White people participated in Black Lives Matter protests in the city immediately following the killing of George Floyd, as they did nationwide, but why did that interest so quickly diminish in Boston?[21] The problems of Black people are not, by and large, the concerns of White people in New England's largest urban area.

Black people from the South transformed Boston in the decades following World War II, but they did so quietly. Few became famous. Few were elected to public office. Most were content to live ordinary lives, unexceptional perhaps but usually preferable to the lives they left behind in the South. They were comparatively uneducated, so they did not seek to tell their stories beyond their own social groups. They did not write about the Great Migration and its impacts.

But their importance and the significance of the Great Migration in Boston are undeniable. Isn't it time that Boston and Bostonians, particularly White Bostonians, acknowledged the contributions of its Black citizens to making the twenty-first-century city, especially Black people born in the South and their kin? It is past time. It's overdue.

Notes

Chapter 1

1. James N. Gregory, "The Second Great Migration: A Historical Overview," in *African American Urban History since World War II*, ed. Kenneth L. Kusmer and Joe W. Trotter (Chicago: University of Chicago Press, 2009), 21. For statistical purposes, the South in this book is defined as the US Bureau of the Census defines it. It includes sixteen states, plus Washington, DC. The states are Alabama, Arkansas, Delaware, Florida, Georgia, Kentucky, Louisiana, Maryland, Mississippi, North Carolina, Oklahoma, South Carolina, Tennessee, Texas, Virginia, and West Virginia.

2. Campbell Gibson and Kay Jung, *Historical Census Statistics on Population Totals by Race, 1790 to 1990, and by Hispanic Origin, 1970 to 1990, for Large Cities and Other Urban Places in the United States*, Population Division Working Paper 76 (Washington, DC: US Bureau of the Census, 2005), https://www.census.gov/content/dam/Census/library/working-papers/2005/demo/POP-twps0076.pdf.

3. Gibson and Jung, *Historical Census Statistics*.

4. New England historians have not only mostly ignored the Black Great Migration, but when they refer to the Great Migration they are typically referring to a different event. In New England, the Great Migration usually refers to the arrival of Puritans in the region beginning in 1630. "Black" was included in the title of this book to distinguish the migration that is the focus here from that event. See, for example, Virginia Dejohn Anderson, *New England's Generation: The Great Migration and the Formation of Society and Culture in the Seventeenth Century* (Cambridge: Cambridge University Press, 1991).

5. Stacey K. Close, "Black Southern Migration, Black Immigrants, Garveyism, and the Transformation of Black Hartford, 1917–1922," *Griot* 22:1 (Spring 2003): 55–68; Stacey Close, "Black Southern Migration and the Transformation of Connecticut," in *African American Connecticut Explored*, ed. Elizabeth J. Normen (Middletown, CT: Wesleyan University Press, 2013), 239–52; Kurt Schlichting, Peter Tuckel, and Richard Maisel, "Residential Segregation and the Beginning of the Great Migration of African Americans to Hartford, Connecticut: A GIS-Based Analysis," *Historical Methods* 39:3 (Summer 2006): 132–42.

6. Gibson and Jung, *Historical Census Statistics*.

7. There is no single published source that provides data on the states of birth of Black residents in Boston over time. John Daniels includes such data for the period from 1860 to 1900 in his book *In Freedom's Birthplace* (Boston: Houghton Mifflin, 1914), 468–69. Published volumes of the decennial US Census of Population provide birthplace data for 1940 and 1970, but not for other years. However, the Integrated Public

Use Microdata Series, a website and database housed at the University of Minnesota, provides access to samples of census data from 1790 to present. Birthplace data for cities, metro areas, and states can be compiled from that source. Steven Ruggles, Sarah Flood, Ronald Goeken, Josiah Grover, Erin Meyer, Jose Pacas, and Matthew Sobek, IPUMS USA: Version 10.0 (data set) (Minneapolis, MN: IPUMS, 2020), https://doi. org/10.18128/D010.V10.0.

8. Ruggles et al., IPUMS USA.

9. Gibson and Jung, *Historical Census Statistics*.

10. Pete Saunders, "Thoughts on Boston and Northern Exclusion," January 8, 2018, Newgeography.com.

11. Samuel A. Stouffer, "Intervening Opportunities: A Theory Relating Mobility and Distance," *American Sociological Review* 5:6 (December 1940): 845–67.

12. Ruggles et al., IPUMS USA.

13. Kathryn Grover and Janine V. da Silva, "Historic Resource Study: Boston African American National Historic Site" (Boston: National Park Service, 2002), 118–19; National Park Service, "African American Churches of Beacon Hill," February 26, 2015, https://www.nps.gov/boaf/learn/historyculture/churches.htm; National Park Service, "Charles Street Meeting House," March 9, 2021, https://www.nps.gov/boaf/ learn/historyculture/charles-street-meeting-house.htm; Charles Street African Methodist Episcopal Church, "More History," accessed March 27, 2021, https://www. csamechurch.org/.

14. Lorenzo Johnston Greene, *The Negro in Colonial New England* (New York: Atheneum, 1971), 16–17; Matthew Johnson, "Timeline of Events Related to the End of Slavery," Massachusetts Historical Society, accessed March 28, 2021, http://www.masshist. org/teaching-history/loc-slavery/essay.php?entry_id=504 (no longer accessible); Oscar Handlin, *Boston's Immigrants, 1790–1880: A Study in Acculturation*, rev. ed. (Cambridge, MA: Belknap Press of Harvard University Press, 1991), 53; Gibson and Jung, *Historical Census Statistics*.

15. Handlin, *Boston's Immigrants*, 96–97; Daniels, *In Freedom's Birthplace*, 143; Elizabeth Hafkin Pleck, *Black Migration and Poverty: Boston, 1865–1900* (New York: Academic Press, 1979), 31; Walter Firey, *Land Use in Central Boston* (Cambridge, MA: Harvard University Press, 1947), 47; "Boston as a Paradise for Negroes," *Boston Sunday Herald*, March 26, 1904, magazine section, 22.

16. Gibson and Jung, *Historical Census Statistics*, 85, 468–69.

17. Pleck, *Black Migration and Poverty*, 25–28.

18. Daniels, *In Freedom's Birthplace*, 468–69; Pleck, *Black Migration and Poverty*, 45–47, 51.

19. Handlin, *Boston's Immigrants*, 179, 212; Pleck, *Black Migration and Poverty*, 19, 29; Daniels, *In Freedom's Birthplace*, 99; Robert C. Hayden, *African-Americans in Boston: More Than 350 Years* (Boston: Trustees of the Public Library of the City of Boston, 1991), 40, 48, 92–93.

20. "Boston as a Paradise for Negroes"; "Boston as the Paradise of the Negro," *The Colored American Magazine*, May 1904, 309–17.

21. Pleck, *Black Migration and Poverty*, 77–82; Daniels, *In Freedom's Birthplace*, 149.

22. US Bureau of the Census, *Thirteenth Census of the United States Taken in the Year 1910*, vol. 2, *Population* (Washington, DC: Government Printing Office, 1913); Daniels, *In Freedom's Birthplace*, 152; Pleck, *Black Migration and Poverty*, 79–80; Robert A. Woods, ed., *The City Wilderness: A Settlement Study* (Boston: Houghton, Mifflin, 1898), 37.

23. National Negro Business League, *Official Souvenir Program*, Sixteenth convention, Boston, August 18–20, 1915 (Boston: Boston Negro Business League No. 1, 1915); Hayden, *African-Americans in Boston*, 79.

24. Pleck, *Black Migration and Poverty*, 83, 152; Daniels, *In Freedom's Birthplace*, 122, 242, 258–59; Hayden, *African-Americans in Boston*, 20.

25. "Boston as a Paradise for Negroes."

26. For an interesting perspective about Irish-Black relations in Boston from someone who is both and grew up in Irish South Boston, see Jennifer J. Roberts, "One of Us," *Boston*, October 2014, https://www.bostonmagazine.com/news/2014/10/28/jennifer-roberts-irish-black-race-southie/

27. Stephan Thernstrom, *The Other Bostonians: Poverty and Progress in the American Metropolis, 1880–1970* (Cambridge, MA: Harvard University Press, 1973), 184; Pleck, *Black Migration and Poverty*, 33, 35, 128.

28. Daniels, *In Freedom's Birthplace*, 102, 261–75; Mel King, *Chain of Change: Struggles for Boston Community Development* (Boston: South End Press, 1981), 4; "Banks Finally Seated in City Council after 21-Month Contest," *Boston Globe*, August 7, 1951, 1; State Library of Massachusetts, "Black and Latino Legislators in the Massachusetts General Court: 1867–Present," February 28, 2017, http://archives.lib.state.ma.us/handle/2452/625361.

29. Daniels, *In Freedom's Birthplace*, 314.

30. Daniels, *In Freedom's Birthplace*, 407; Pleck, *Black Migration and Poverty*, 33–34, 114; Ray Stannard Baker, *Following the Color Line: An Account of Negro Citizenship in the American Democracy* (New York: Doubleday, Page, 1908), 120–22; Richard Alan Ballou, "Even in 'Freedom's Birthplace': The Development of Boston's Black Ghetto, 1900–1940" (PhD diss., University of Michigan, 1984), 318, 342, 354–56; Zion's Herald, "The Race Problem in Boston," *Liberia Bulletin* 9 (November 1896): 7–16.

31. Daniels, *In Freedom's Birthplace*, 113–14; "Boston as a Paradise for Negroes."

32. Pleck, *Black Migration and* Poverty, 91–119; W. E. Burghardt Du Bois, *The Black North in 1901: A Social Study* (New York: Arno Press, 1969), 31, 39; W. E. B. Du Bois, *The Philadelphia Negro: A Social Study*, Publications of the University of Pennsylvania, Series in Political Economy and Public Law No. 14 (Philadelphia, 1899), 80.

33. James N. Gregory, *The Southern Diaspora: How the Great Migrations of Black and White Southerners Transformed America* (Chapel Hill: University of North Carolina Press, 2005), 330.

34. Gregory, *Southern Diaspora*, 330; Gibson and Jung, *Historical Census Statistics*.

35. Ruggles et al., IPUMS USA; Violet M. Johnson, *The Other Black Bostonians: West Indians in Boston, 1900–1950* (Bloomington: Indiana University Press, 2006), 6–8.

36. James N. Gregory discusses the difficulties of measuring the volume of internal migration flows, and explains one strategy for addressing them, in his book *Southern Diaspora*, 355–58.

37. Blake Harrison, "Mobility, Farmworkers, and Connecticut's Tobacco Valley, 1900–1950," *Journal of Historical Geography* 36 (2010): 166–67; Emmett J. Scott, *Negro Migration during the War*, Carnegie Endowment for International Peace, Preliminary Economic Studies of the War 16 (New York: Oxford University Press, 1920), 56; Schlichting, Tuckel, and Maisel, "Residential Segregation," 140.

38. Scott, *Negro Migration*, 56.

39. Pleck, *Black Migration and Poverty*, 136.

40. Gregory, *Southern Diaspora*, 330; Ruggles et al., IPUMS USA.

41. Gregory, *Southern Diaspora*, 37.

42. Gregory, *Southern Diaspora*, 330; Ruggles et al., IPUMS USA.

43. National Park Service, "The Boston Navy Yard during World War II," last modified March 27, 2020, https://www.nps.gov/articles/the-boston-navy-yard-during-world-war-ii.htm; Gordon McKibben, *Cutting Edge: Gillette's Journey to Global Leadership* (Boston: Harvard Business School Press, 1998), 39–40.

44. Leonard Lerner, "Negro Masses Move North," *Boston Globe*, March 18, 1956, A43.

45. Lerner, "Negro Masses Move North"; Gregory, "Second Great Migration," 30; US Army Environmental Center, "Base Realignment and Closure Plan: Fort Devens," August 1995, 1–7.

46. Omar M. McRoberts, *Streets of Glory: Church and Community in a Black Urban Neighborhood* (Chicago: University of Chicago Press, 2003), 25; Ronald Bailey, *Lower Roxbury: A Community of Treasures in the City of Boston* (Boston: Lower Roxbury Community Corp. / Afro Scholar Press, 1993), 15–18; Hayden, *African-Americans in Boston*, 81, 85–87; William Buchanan, "The Pioneer Club: An Obituary," *Boston Globe Magazine*, September 15, 1974, 12–16.

47. Malcom X, with Alex Haley, *The Autobiography of Malcolm X* (New York: Grove Press, 1964), 35, 38. Malcolm X returned to Boston in 1954 to help found Temple No. 11 of the Nation of Islam in Roxbury.

48. "Plan A Wins; Boston Gets New Charter," *Boston Globe*, November 9, 1949, 1; Gibson and Jung, *Historical Census Statistics*.

49. Lance Carden, *Witness: An Oral History of Black Politics in Boston, 1920–1960* (Boston: Boston College, 1989), 49.

50. Peter Temin, ed., *Engines of Enterprise: The Economic History of New England* (Cambridge, MA: Harvard University Press, 2000).

51. Gibson and Jung, *Historical Census Statistics*; US Bureau of the Census, *1980 Census of Population*, General Social and Economic Characteristics (Washington, DC: US Government Printing Office, 1983).

52. Ruggles et al., IPUMS USA.

53. Boston Planning & Development Agency, *Historical Boston in Context: Neighborhood Comparisons by Decade, 1950 to 2015* (Boston, 2017).

54. Gerald Gamm, *Urban Exodus: Why the Jews Left Boston and the Catholics Stayed* (Cambridge, MA: Harvard University Press, 1999); Boston Planning & Development Agency, *Historical Boston in Context*.

55. Phillip Clay, "Housing, Neighborhoods, and Development," in *The Emerging Black Community of Boston*, ed. Phillip Clay and James Edward Blackwell (Boston: Institute for the Study of Black Culture, University of Massachusetts at Boston, 1985), 209; Gamm, *Urban Exodus*, 37, 225-26, 242; Sam B. Warner Jr., *Streetcar Suburbs: The Process of Growth in Greater Boston, 1870-1900* (Cambridge, MA: Harvard University Press and MIT Press, 1962), 22, 35, 41; Rheable M. Edwards and Laura B. Morris, *The Negro in Boston* (Boston: Action for Boston Community Development, 1961), 48.

56. Hillel Levine and Lawrence Harmon, *The Death of an American Jewish Community: A Tragedy of Good Intentions* (New York: Free Press, 1992), xiv, 12, 17, 41, 147; Gamm, *Urban Exodus*, 83, 198-99; Alan Lupo, "The Blue Hill Avenue Story," *Boston Sunday Globe Magazine*, May 4, 1969, 36-47.

57. Gamm, *Urban Exodus*, 39-40, 271-72, 277-89; Jim Vrabel, *A People's History of the New Boston* (Amherst: University of Massachusetts Press, 2014), 98-99.

58. BPDA, *Historical Boston in Context*; Gamm, *Urban Exodus*, 241, 273-78; Gibson and Jung, *Historical Census Statistics*; Nathan Kantrowitz, "Racial and Ethnic Residential Segregation in Boston, 1830-1970," *Annals of the American Academy of Political and Social Science* 441 (January 1979): 50; John R. Logan and Brian Stults, *The Persistence of Segregation in the Metropolis: New Findings from the 2010 Census*, brief prepared for Project US2010, March 2011, http://www.s4.brown.edu/us2010.

59. Vrabel, *People's History*, 96-100, 124-25.

60. Vrabel, *People's History*, 42-43, 63-68, 81-88; Anthony Neal and James Jennings, "Strategies for Employment Diversity," in *Boston's Banner Years: 1965-2015; A Saga of Black Success*, ed. Melvin B. Miller (Bloomington, IN: Archway Publishing, 2018), 201-26; Robert C. Hayden, "A Historical Overview of Poverty among Blacks in Boston, 1950-1990," *Trotter Review* 17:1 (2007): 135-38; Tatiana Maria Fernández Cruz, "Boston's Struggle in Black and Brown: Racial Politics, Community Development, and Grassroots Organizing, 1960-1985" (PhD diss., University of Michigan, 2017), 41; Akilah Johnson, "Fury on the Streets," *Boston Globe*, June 2, 2017, A1.

61. Thernstrom, *The Other Bostonians*, 198-201; US Bureau of the Census, *1980 Census of Population*, Detailed Population Characteristics: Massachusetts (Washington, DC: Government Printing Office, 1983); Hayden, "Historical Overview of Poverty," 139; Philip Hart, "A Changing Mosaic: Boston's Racial Diversity, 1950-1990," in *The Emerging Black Community of Boston*, ed. Phillip Clay and James Edward Blackwell (Boston: Institute for the Study of Black Culture, University of Massachusetts at Boston, 1985), 131.

62. Vrabel, *People's History*, 47-61; Ronald Formisano, *Boston against Busing: Race, Class, and Ethnicity in the 1960s and 1970s* (Chapel Hill: University of North Carolina Press, 1991).

63. US Bureau of the Census, *1980 Census of Population*, General Population Characteristics: Massachusetts (Washington, DC: US Government Printing Office, 1982); US Bureau of the Census, *1980 Census of Population*, Detailed Population Characteristics: Massachusetts.

64. William H. Frey, "The New Great Migration: Black Americans' Return to the South, 1965-2000" (Washington, DC: Brookings Institution, 2004); Gregory, *Southern Diaspora*, 39-49.

65. Ruggles et al., IPUMS USA.

66. Gibson and Jung, *Historical Census Statistics*; BPDA, *Historical Boston in Context*; US Bureau of the Census, American Community Survey, "Demographic and Housing Estimates," Five-Year Estimates, 2015–2019, https://data.census.gov/cedsci/.

67. Kim McLarin, "The Great Migration and Me," *Boston Globe Magazine*, October 31, 2010, 6.

Chapter 2

1. All information in this chapter, except where noted, is based on an interview conducted by the author with Charles Gordon on November 19, 2015, in Boston and telephone interviews with him conducted on June 15, 2016; December 10, 2020; and February 7, 2021.

2. National Park Service, "The Boston Navy Yard during World War II," last modified March 27, 2020, https://www.nps.gov/articles/the-boston-navy-yard-during-world-war-ii.htm.

3. Richard Vacca (author, *The Boston Jazz Chronicles*), emails to the author, March 28, 2020 and May 3, 2020.

4. U.S. Bureau of the Census, 1950 Census of Population, population schedules for Boston, enumeration districts 15-536, 15-544, 15-545, and 15-546, https://1950census.archives.gov/, accessed September 3, 2022.

5. Jim Vrabel, *A People's History of the New Boston* (Amherst: University of Massachusetts Press, 2014), 50; Ruth Batson, "The Black Educational Movement in Boston: A Sequence of Historical Events, a Chronology," Northeastern University, 2001, https://repository.library.northeastern.edu/files/neu:cj82p218w, 120, 204.

6. Uncle Dudley, "Key to the Deadlock," *Boston Globe*, August 15, 1963, 16.

7. Ronald Formisano, *Boston against Busing: Race, Class, and Ethnicity in the 1960s and 1970s* (Chapel Hill: University of North Carolina Press, 1991), 77–79.

8. Boston Planning & Development Agency, *Historical Boston in Context: Neighborhood Comparisons by Decades, 1950–2015* (Boston, 2017).

9. Boston Planning & Development Agency, *Historical Boston in Context*.

10. Richard Heath, "Skippy White: 54 Years of Hipping You to the Crossroads of American Music," *Jamaica Plain News*, August 3, 2015, https://www.jamaicaplainnews.com/2015/08/03/skippy-white-54-years-of-hipping-you-to-the-crossroads-of-american-music/12283.

11. Calculated using the US Bureau of Labor Statistics' "CPI Inflation Calculator," accessed August 22, 2022, https://www.bls.gov/data/inflation_calculator.htm.

12. Boston Planning & Development Agency, *Historical Boston in Context*.

13. US Bureau of the Census, American Community Survey, Five-Year Estimates, 2005–19, accessed March 28, 2021, https://data.census.gov/cedsci/.

14. Adelaide M. Cromwell, *The Other Brahmins: Boston's Black Upper Class, 1750–1950* (Fayetteville: University of Arkansas Press, 1994).

Chapter 3

1. Charles E. Connerly, *The Most Segregated City in America: City Planning and Civil Rights in Birmingham* (Charlottesville: University of Virginia Press, 2013).
2. All information in this chapter, except where noted, is based on four telephone interviews conducted by the author with Thomas Lindsay between April 20 and 25, 2020, and additional interviews conducted on December 9, 2020, and February 27, 2021.
3. Judith Rollins, *Between Women: Domestics and Their Employers* (Philadelphia: Temple University Press, 1987), 56.
4. Julie Novkov, "Segregation (Jim Crow)," *Encyclopedia of Alabama*, last modified November 14, 2019, http://www.encyclopediaofalabama.org; Connerly, *Most Segregated City*, 37.
5. US Department of the Interior, "National Register of Historic Places Inventory-Nomination Form: Fourth Avenue Historic District," February 11, 1982; Franklin D. Wilson, "Ecology of a Black Business District," *Review of Black Political Economy* 5:4 (1975): 353–75.
6. David Husock, "Discovering the Three-Decker," *Public Interest* 98 (Winter 1990): 49–60.
7. Boston Planning & Development Agency, *Historical Boston in Context: Neighborhood Comparisons by Decade, 1950–2015,* December 2017.
8. Boston.com staff, "History of Polaroid and Edwin Land," October 3, 2012, https://www.boston.com/uncategorized/noprimarytagmatch/2012/10/03/history-of-polaroid-and-edwin-land; Mark Feeney, "Lasting Impression," *Boston Globe*, October 18, 2012, 20G; "Polaroid Changes Its Image," *Boston Globe*, October 14, 2003, 42.
9. Robert B. Hanron, "State Launches Job-Equality Plan," *Boston Globe*, November 30, 1963, 2; Ian Menzies, "A Quiet Plan to Aid Negroes," *Boston Globe*, July 14, 1964, 21; "Companies Note Job Increases for Negroes," *Boston Globe*, December 12, 1966, 25.
10. Chris Nteta, "The Linkage between African Americans and the South African Black Immigrant Community," *Trotter Review* 10:1 (1996): 24–26.
11. Will Haygood, "Partners in Power: Deval Patrick and Reginald Lindsay Took Different Paths to a Top Boston Law Firm," *Boston Globe*, September 23, 1993, 63–68.
12. Boston Planning & Development Agency, *Historical Boston in Context*.
13. David Masci, Besheer Mohamed, and Gregory A. Smith, "Black Americans Are More Likely Than Overall Public to Be Christian, Protestant," Pew Research Center, April 23, 2018, https://www.pewresearch.org/fact-tank/2018/04/23/black-americans-are-more-likely-than-overall-public-to-be-christian-protestant; Pew Research Center, "Attendance at Religious Services by Race/Ethnicity," 2014, accessed July 26, 2022, https://www.pewforum.org/religious-landscape-study/compare/attendance-at-religious-services/by/racial-and-ethnic-composition/. See also Besheer Mohamed, Kiana Cox, Jeff Diamant, and Claire Gecewicz, "Faith among Black Americans," Pew Research Center, February 16, 2021, https://www.pewforum.org/2021/02/16/faith-among-black-americans/.

14. Akilah Johnson et al., "Boston. Racism. Image. Reality.," *Boston Globe*, seven-part series, December 10–16, 2017.

15. Christopher Gavin, "'Women Made History Tonight': For the First Time, the Boston City Council Will Have a Female and Minority Majority," *Boston* Globe, November 6, 2019, https://www.boston.com/news/politics/2019/11/06/boston-city-council-female-and-minority-majority; Ellen Barry, "She Experienced Busing in Boston; Now She's the City's First Black Mayor," *New York Times*, March 23, 2021, https://www.nytimes.com/2021/03/23/us/kim-janey-boston-mayor.html; Ellen Berry, "Boston Mayor's Race Narrows to a Progressive versus a Moderate," *New York Times*, September 15, 2021, https://www.nytimes.com/2021/09/15/us/boston-mayor-election-michelle-wu.html?searchResultPosition=5; Ellen Berry, "For Progressives, Michelle Wu Points to a Way Forward," *New York Times*, November 3, 2021, https://www.nytimes.com/2021/11/03/us/michelle-wu-boston-progressives.html.

Chapter 4

1. All information in this chapter, except where noted, is based on an interview conducted by the author with Lucy Parham on January 19, 2016, in Boston and telephone interviews conducted on June 24, 2020, and December 29, 2020.

2. US Bureau of the Census, *Census of Population: 1950*, vol. 1, *Number of Inhabitants* (Washington, DC: Government Printing Office, 1952).

3. Imari Scarbrough, "Pushing for Equality: 2017 Is 50th Anniversary of Anson County Segregation Lawsuit," *Anson Record*, February 15, 2017.

4. William J. Collins and Robert A. Margo, "Historical Perspectives on Racial Differences in Schooling in the United States," National Bureau of Economic Research Working Paper 9770 (Cambridge, MA: National Bureau of Economic Research, 2003), 50.

5. Isabel Wilkerson, *The Warmth of Other Suns: The Epic Story of America's Great Migration* (New York: Random House, 2010), 145, 178.

6. Darlene Clark Hine and Katherine Thompson, *A Shining Thread of Hope: The History of Black Women in America* (New York: Broadway Books, 1998), 216.

7. Sam B. Warner Jr., *Streetcar Suburbs: The Process of Growth in Greater Boston, 1870–1900* (Cambridge, MA: Harvard University Press and MIT Press, 1962), 22.

8. US Bureau of the Census, *Sixteenth Census of the United States: 1940*, vol. 2, *Population: Characteristics of the Population* (Washington, DC: Government Printing Office, 1943); US Bureau of the Census, *1970 Census of the Population*, vol. 1, *Characteristics of the Population* (Washington, DC: Government Printing Office, 1973).

9. Gordon McKibben, *Cutting Edge: Gillette's Journey to Global Leadership* (Boston: Harvard Business School Press, 1998), 58.

10. Robert B. Hanron, "State Launches Job-Equality Plan," *Boston Globe*, November 30, 1963, 2; Ian Menzies, "A Quiet Plan to Aid Negroes," *Boston Globe*, July 14, 1964, 21; "Freedom House Recruiters," *Boston Globe*, December 10, 1964, 15; John B. Value,

"Hub Firms Open 'Freedom House' Recruitment," *Boston Globe*, December 15, 1964, 27; John B. Value, "170 Firms Study Negro Unemployment," *Boston Globe*, June 19, 1965, 5; "Companies Note Job Increases for Negroes," *Boston Globe*, December 12, 1966, 25.

11. Gerald Gamm, *Urban Exodus: Why the Jews Left Boston and the Catholics Stayed* (Cambridge, MA: Harvard University Press, 1999), 43.

12. Boston Planning & Development Agency, *Historical Boston in Context: Neighborhood Comparisons by Decade, 1950–2015* (Boston, 2017).

13. BPDA, *Historical Boston in Context.*

14. Ronald Formisano, *Boston against Busing: Race, Class, and Ethnicity in the 1960s and 1970s* (Chapel Hill: University of North Carolina Press, 1991), 75–86.

Chapter 5

1. Jason Morgan Ward, *Hanging Bridge: Racial Violence and the Making of America's Civil Rights Century* (New York: Oxford University Press, 2016), 5. The summary of these events is drawn from Ward and contemporary sources: "Lynch Four Negroes; Two of Them Women," *New York Times*, December 21, 1918; "2 Negro Boys Lynched," *New York Times*, October 13, 1942; Walter Atkins, "Shubuta Bridge's Toll Stands at Six Lynch Victims, but Span Is Doomed," *Chicago Defender*, November 7, 1942, 1; Enoc P. Waters, "Two Lynched Boys Were Ace Scrap Iron Collectors in Mississippi Town," *Chicago Defender*, March 6, 1943, 13; Enoc P. Waters, "Ignorance and War Hysteria Found Underlying Causes of 2 Lynchings," *Chicago Defender*, March 13, 1943, 13.

2. All information in this chapter, except where noted, is based on eight telephone interviews conducted by the author with Ollie Sumrall Jr., between June 1 and 11, 2020.

3. US Bureau of the Census, *Census of Population: 1950*, vol. 1, *Number of Inhabitants* (Washington, DC: Government Printing Office, 1952); US Bureau of the Census, *Census of Population: 1950*, vol. 2, *Characteristics of the Population* (Washington, DC: Government Printing Office, 1952).

4. Judith Rollins, *All Is Never Said: The Narrative of Odette Harper Hines* (Philadelphia: Temple University Press, 1995), 91–92.

5. Ward, *Hanging Bridge*, 177.

6. Gerald M. Stern, "Judge William Harold Cox and the Right to Vote in Clarke County, Mississippi," in *Southern Justice*, ed. Leon Friedman (New York: Random House, 1965), 173.

7. Ward, *Hanging Bridge*, 105–11, 132–59; Atkins, "Shubuta Bridge's Toll," Waters, "Two Lynched Boys Were Ace Scrap Iron Collectors"; Waters, "Ignorance and War Hysteria."

8. Stern, "Judge William Harold Cox," 177; Ward, *Hanging Bridge*, 168, 208.

9. Ward, *Hanging Bridge*, 168.

10. Ward, *Hanging Bridge*, 180, 210, 226–27.

11. C. Vann Woodward, *The Strange Career of Jim Crow*, 3rd ed. (New York: Oxford University Press, 1994), 147.

12. William J. Collins and Robert A. Margo, "Historical Perspectives on Racial Differences in Schooling in the United States," National Bureau of Economic Research Working Paper 9770 (Cambridge, MA: National Bureau of Economic Research, 2003), 50.

13. Ward, *Hanging Bridge*, 171–72.

14. Nicholas Lemann, *The Promised Land: The Great Migration and How It Changed America* (New York: Alfred A. Knopf, 1991), 15–16, 41, 43.

15. US Bureau of the Census, *Thirteenth Census of the United States Taken in the Year 1910*, vol. 2, *Population: Composition and Characteristics of the Population* (Washington, DC: Government Printing Office, 1913); US Bureau of the Census, *Sixteenth Census of the United States: 1940*, vol. 2, *Characteristics of the Population* (Washington, DC: Government Printing Office, 1943); US Bureau of the Census, *1970 Census of the Population*, vol. 1: *Characteristics of the Population* (Washington, DC: Government Printing Office, 1973).

16. Jennifer A. Lemak, *Southern Life, Northern City: The History of Albany's Rapp Road Community* (Albany: State University of New York Press, 2008), 1.

17. "2 Injured, 2 Arrested in S. Boston Clash," *Boston Globe*, July 28, 1975, 3; Robert Healy, "Boston's Beach of Shame," *Boston Globe*, July 31, 1977, A7; Ron Hutson and Michael Kenney, "The Beach and the Leaders," *Boston Globe*, August 3, 1977, 1; Timothy Dwyer, "FBI at Carson Beach; 4 More Arrests," *Boston Globe*, August 3, 1977, 8.

Chapter 6

1. All information in this chapter, except where noted, is based on an interview conducted by the author with Elizabeth Hall Davis on November 19, 2015, in Boston and telephone interviews conducted on March 31, 2020, and December 14, 2020.

2. Danné E. Davis, "Their American Dream," *Genealogy* 4:2 (2020): 1–12, https://doi.org/10.3390/genealogy4020045.

3. Davis, "Their American Dream."

4. Davis, "Their American Dream."

5. US Bureau of the Census, "A Half-Century of Learning: Historical Census Statistics on Educational Attainment in the United States, 1940 to 2000," April 2006, https://www.census.gov/library/publications/2010/demo/educational-attainment-1940-2000.html.

6. Davis, "Their American Dream."

7. Davis, "Their American Dream."

8. Marquis Davis (son of Elizabeth Hall Davis), telephone interview by the author, April 14, 2020.

9. Marquis Davis, telephone interview.

10. Uncle Dudley, "Key to the Deadlock," *Boston Globe*, August 15, 1963, 16.

11. Davis, "Their American Dream."

12. Marquis Davis, telephone interview.

13. Steven J. L. Taylor, *Desegregation in Boston and Buffalo: The Influence of Local Leaders* (Albany: State University of New York Press, 1998), 53.

14. Jim Vrabel, *A People's History of the New Boston* (Amherst: University of Massachusetts Press, 2014), 60.

15. Jonathan Kozol, *Death at an Early Age: The Destruction of the Hearts and Minds of Negro Children in the Boston Public Schools* (1967; repr., New York: Bantam, 1968).

16. Davis, "Their American Dream."

17. Boston Planning & Development Agency, *Historical Boston in Context: Neighborhood Comparisons by Decade, 1950–2015* (Boston, 2017).

18. Ronald Formisano, *Boston against Busing: Race, Class, and Ethnicity in the 1960s and 1970s* (Chapel Hill: University of North Carolina Press, 1991), 37–38; "METCO's History," Metropolitan Council for Educational Opportunity website, accessed July 27, 2022, https://metcoinc.org.

19. Danné Davis (daughter of Elizabeth Hall Davis), telephone interview, April 13, 2020.

Chapter 7

1. All information in this chapter, except where noted, is based on an interview conducted by the author with Willie Pittman on December 1, 2015, in Brockton, Massachusetts, a telephone interview with Pittman conducted on July 16, 2016, and a telephone interview conducted with Laniel Pittman, Willie Pittman's brother, on April 2, 2020.

2. US Bureau of the Census, *Census of Population: 1960*, vol. 1, *Characteristics of the Population* (Washington, DC: Government Printing Office, 1963).

3. John Lewis with Michael D'Orso, *Walking with the Wind: A Memory of the Movement* (New York: Simon and Schuster, 1998), 35–37.

4. Earnest Green (minister, Boughoma Missionary Baptist Church, and member of the Pike County Board of Education), telephone conversation with the author, March 3, 2021.

5. Lewis, *Walking with the Wind*, 10.

6. Lewis, *Walking with the Wind*, 37.

7. Robert B. Hanron, "State Launches Job-Equality Plan," *Boston Globe*, November 30, 1963, 2; Ian Menzies, "A Quiet Plan to Aid Negroes," *Boston Globe*, July 14, 1964, 21; "Freedom House Recruiters," *Boston Globe*, December 10, 1964; John B. Value, "Hub Firms Open 'Freedom House' Recruitment," *Boston Globe*, December 15, 1964, 27; John B. Value, "170 Firms Study Negro Unemployment," *Boston Globe*, June 19, 1965, 5; "Companies Note Job Increases for Negroes," *Boston Globe*, December 12, 1966, 25.

8. US Bureau of the Census, *Sixteenth Census of the United States: 1940*, vol. 2, *Population: Characteristics of the Population* (Washington, DC: Government Printing Office, 1943); US Bureau of the Census, *1970 Census of the Population*, vol. 1, *Characteristics of the Population* (Washington: GPO, 1973).

9. Ronald Formisano, *Boston against Busing: Race, Class, and Ethnicity in the 1960s and 1970s* (Chapel Hill: University of North Carolina Press, 1991), 37–38; "METCO's History," Metropolitan Council for Educational Opportunity website, accessed July 27, 2022, https://metcoinc.org.

10. Formisano, *Boston against Busing*, 75–86.

11. John R. Logan and Brian Stults, *The Persistence of Segregation in the Metropolis: New Findings from the 2010 Census*, census brief prepared for Project US2010, March 2011, http://www.s4.brown.edu/us2010.

12. Boston Planning & Development Agency, *Historical Boston in Context: Neighborhood Comparisons by Decade, 1950–2015* (Boston, 2017).

13. US Bureau of the Census, American Community Survey, 2019 American Community Survey 1-Year Estimates, accessed March 14, 2021, https://data.census.gov/cedsci/?.

Chapter 8

1. All information in this chapter, except where noted, is based on an interview conducted by the author with Geraldine Walker on January 5, 2016, in Boston and telephone interviews conducted on April 8, 2020; December 10, 2020; March 6, 2021; and March 13, 2021.

2. Nicholas Lemann, *The Promised Land: The Great Black Migration and How It Changed America* (New York: Alfred A. Knopf, 1991), 18–21; Charles S. Aiken, *The Cotton Plantation South since the Civil War* (Baltimore: Johns Hopkins University Press, 1998), 32.

3. US Bureau of the Census, *Census of Population: 1960*, vol. 1, *Characteristics of the Population* (Washington, DC: Government Printing Office, 1963).

4. Elizabeth Clark-Lewis, *Living In, Living Out: African American Domestics in Washington, D.C., 1910–1940* (Washington, DC: Smithsonian Institution Press, 1994), 48, 215.

5. Darlene Clark Hine and Kathleen Thompson, *A Shining Thread of Hope: The History of Black Women in America* (New York: Broadway Books, 1998), 215; Danielle L. McGuire, *At the Dark End of the Street: Black Women, Rape, and Resistance—a New History of the Civil Rights Movement from Rosa Parks to the Rise of Black Power* (New York: Alfred A. Knopf, 2010), xix.

6. US Bureau of the Census, *Census of Population: 1960*.

7. Bonnie Hurd Smith, "Melnea A. Cass (1896–1978)," Boston Women's Heritage Trail, accessed March 14, 2021, https://bwht.org/melnea-cass/.

8. F. B. Taylor Jr., "The Last Three Days in Boston," *Boston Globe*, April 7, 1968, 1; Donald Johnson, "Afro-American Flag Raised," *Boston Globe*, April 9, 1968, 13.

9. Michael S. Weaver, "Makers and Redeemers: The Theatricality of the Black Church," *Black American Literature Forum* 25:1 (Spring 1991): 54.

10. Alan Lupo, "The Blue Hill Avenue Story," *Boston Sunday Globe Magazine*, May 4, 1969, 36–47; *1974–75 Boston (Suffolk County) City Directory* (Boston: R. L. Polk Co., 1974?).

11. David Buse, "Home-Style Homecoming: Rebuilt Grove Hall Restaurant Back in Business after Serious Flood Damage," *Boston Globe*, August 28, 1993, 15.

12. "Sit-In Escalates into Riot," *Boston Globe*, June 3, 1967, 1; William J. Fripp, "From Quiet Vigil to Melee," *Boston Globe*, June 3, 1967, 4; Jeremiah V. Murphy, "Shooting of Firemen Disrupts Efforts to Ease Boston Tension," *Boston Globe*, June 4, 1967, 1; Robert L. Turner, "How the Tension Grew," *Boston Globe*, June 4, 1967, 1; Robert J. Anglin, "Rioting Hits for 3d Night," *Boston Globe*, June 5, 1967, 1; Robert B. Kenney, "Roxbury Simmers Down," *Boston Globe*, June 6, 1967, 1; Akilah Johnson, "The Forgotten Riot That Sparked Boston's Racial Unrest," *Boston Globe*, June 1, 2017, https://www.bostonglobe.com/metro/2017/06/01/the-forgotten-protest-that-sparked-city-racial-unrest/0ry39I37z87TwdBfrqUnTP/story.html.

13. John Daniels, *In Freedom's Birthplace* (Boston: Houghton Mifflin, 1914), 143–46.

14. Boston Landmarks Commission, *The South End: District Study Committee Report* (Boston, 1963), 6–13.

15. Jim Vrabel, *A People's History of the New Boston* (Amherst: University of Massachusetts Press, 2014), 110; Boston Planning & Development Agency, *Historical Boston in Context: Neighborhood Comparisons by Decade, 1950 to 2015* (Boston, 2017).

16. Boston Redevelopment Authority, *Boston in Context: Neighborhoods*, August 2015, http://www.bostonplans.org/getattachment/290cae05-72b0-47ba-a214-4a6645d43b01.

17. US Bureau of the Census, American Community Survey, 2019 American Community Survey 1-Year Estimates, accessed March 14, 2021, https://data.census.gov/cedsci/?; Natasha S. Alford, "Why Some Black Puerto Ricans Choose 'White' on the Census," *New York Times*, February 9, 2020, https://www.nytimes.com/2020/02/09/us/puerto-rico-census-black-race.html.

18. Marilynn S. Johnson, "Immigrant Religion and Boston's 'Quiet Revival,'" in *The New Bostonians: How Immigrants Have Transformed the Metro Area since the 1960s* (Amherst: University of Massachusetts Press, 2015), 151–90.

19. Boston Police Department, "2009 Boston Police Department Annual Crime Summary Report" (Boston, 2010), 4; Boston Police Department, "Part One Crime Reported by the Boston Police Department," 2019–20 (Boston Regional Intelligence Center, 2021); Boston Indicators Project, *A Great Reckoning: Healing a Growing Divide; A Summary of the Boston Indicators Report, 2009* (Boston: Boston Foundation, 2009), 39.

Chapter 9

1. All information in this chapter, except where noted, is based on an interview conducted by the author with Barbra Hicks on December 3, 2015, in Boston and a telephone interview conducted on April 29, 2020.

2. Robert H. Woodrum, *"Everybody Was Black Down There": Race and Industrial Change in the Alabama Coalfields* (Athens: University of Georgia Press, 2007); Robert Woodrum (assistant professor of history and political science, Georgia State University), email to the author, April 22, 2020.

3. Photo of employees at the Bradford mine, Alabama By-Products Corporation, 1939, Alabama Department of Archives and History, accessed July 27, 2022, https://digital. archives.alabama.gov/digital/collection/photo/id/19693/.

4. Charles M. Whitson, *Alabama Mine Map Repository* (Birmingham: Alabama Department of Labor, 2013), 39; US Bureau of the Census, *Census of Population: 1960*, vol. 1, *Characteristics of the Population* (Washington, DC: Government Printing Office, 1963).

5. Bryan Marquard, "Peter Fuller, Ran Auto Dealerships; Owned Horse Stripped of Derby Crown," *Boston Globe*, May 14, 2012; Douglas Martin, "Peter D. Fuller Dies at 89; Had to Return Derby Purse," *New York Times*, May 19, 2012; "Bank Officer New Head of NAACP Program Unit," *Boston Evening Globe*, January 22, 1970, 11; "Fuller Gives $62,000 to Dr. King's Widow," *Boston Globe*, April 8, 1968, 30.

6. US Bureau of the Census, *Sixteenth Census of the Population: 1940*, vol. 3, *Population: The Labor Force* (Washington, DC: Government Printing Office, 1963); US Bureau of the Census, *Census of Population: 1960*, vol. 1, *Characteristics of the Population* (Washington, DC: US Government Printing Office, 1963).

7. Brian Ballou, "Dorchester Auto Body Shop Is Beacon of Good Will," *Boston Globe*, April 2, 2012; "About," Hicks Auto Body, Boston, website, accessed April 5, 2021, http:// hicksautobodyinc.com/about.

8. Matt Gelb, "Ex-Quarterback Hicks an Athlete Who Cares," *The Heights* (Boston College), October 3, 1994, 26, "Willie Hicks: Class of 1987," Concord-Carlisle High School Hall of Fame, accessed April 5, 2021, http://www.cchshalloffame.org/ hicks.html.

9. Rick Smith, "Whatever Happened to: Willie Hicks, Concord-Carlisle/Boston College," *MetroWest Daily News*, September 21, 2008.

Chapter 10

1. All information in this chapter, except where noted, is based on an interview conducted by the author with Al Kinnitt on June 21, 2016, in Boston and a telephone interview with his first wife, Shirley Dean Coley, and his daughter, Stephanie Denise Castro, conducted on April 14, 2020.

2. Rev. Gregory Groover (pastor, Charles Street African Methodist Episcopal Church, Boston), telephone interview by the author, April 14, 2020.

3. Larry Hobbs, "Selden Park Once the Pulse of Local African American Community," *Brunswick News*, August 17, 2019; "Selden Park: History," Friends of Selden Park website, accessed April 5, 2021, http://friendsofseldenpark.weebly.com/history.html.

4. The documentary can viewed on Vimeo: https://vimeo.com/120902771.

5. M. S. Handler, "Brunswick, Ga., Fighting to Integrate," *New York Times*, September 1, 1963, 42; Orlando Montoya, "50 Years Later: The 'Quiet Conflict,'" Georgia Public Broadcasting website, August 23, 2013; Larry Hobbs, "Local Civil Rights Struggle One of 'Quiet Conflict,'" *Brunswick News*, February 24, 2018.

6. Richard Fausset, "Two Weapons, a Chase, a Killing and No Charges," *New York Times*, April 26, 2020, https://www.nytimes.com/2020/04/26/us/ahmed-arbery-shooting-georgia.html.
7. Alfreda Harris (longtime leader in Boston's Black community, longest serving member of the Boston School Committee, and Kinnitt's former supervisor), telephone interview by the author, April 14, 2020.
8. Harris, telephone interview.
9. Charles P. Pierce, "Hockey Town," *Boston Globe*, March 8, 2009.
10. Karl Hobbs (associate head basketball coach, Rutgers University), telephone interview by the author, April 15, 2020.
11. Stephanie Denise Castro (daughter of Al Kinnitt Jr.), text message to the author, March 6, 2021; Stephanie Denise Castro (daughter of Al Kinnitt Jr.), email to the author, August 31, 2022.
12. Tom Sullivan, "Park League Playoffs," *Boston Herald American*, November 16, 1979, C2.

Chapter 11

1. All information in this chapter, except where noted, is based on an interview conducted by the author with Elta Garrett on January 5, 2016, in Boston and telephone interviews with her conducted on June 7, 2016; December 14, 2020; January 22, 2021; and April 5, 2021.
2. US Bureau of the Census, *Census of Population: 1960*, vol. 1, *Characteristics of the Population* (Washington, DC: Government Printing Office, 1963); Tammany Family, "History of Sun," August 2018, https://tammanyfamily.blogspot.com/2018/08/the-history-of-sun.html.
3. Tammany Family, "History of Sun."
4. National Trust for Historic Preservation, "Rosenwald Schools," accessed March 22, 2021, https://savingplaces.org/places/rosenwald-schools#; Fisk University, Rosenwald Fund Card File Database, accessed March 22, 2021, http://rosenwald.fisk.edu/. See also Mary S. Hoffschwelle, *The Rosenwald Schools of the American South* (Gainesville: University Press of Florida, 2006).
5. Amy Rhiannon Sumter, "Environment, Labor, and Race: An Historical Geography of St. Tammany Parish, Louisiana, 1878–1956," PhD dissertation, Louisiana State University, 2008, https://digitalcommons.lsu.edu/gradschool_dissertations/3784.
6. *Smith v. St. Tammany Parish School Board*, 302 F. Supp. 106 (E.D. La 1969).
7. "Covington High School History: Across the Decades," accessed April 10, 2021, http://covingtonhigh.stpsb.org/parents/CHS_History/Regular/1968-74_2.html.
8. "Covington High School History"; Nick Reimann, "'I Woke Up . . . Shaking with Fear over Going to School'; St. Tammany Looks Back at 50 Years since School Desegregation," *New Orleans Advocate*, December 30, 2017.

9. Alexander Auerbach, "Four Young Teachers Quit Hub School Posts," *Boston Globe*, June 29, 1969, 69.

10. Michael Rezendes, "Mayor Gives Recognition to 11 Black Achievers," *Boston Globe*, February 28, 1994, 24; "Spirited Away," *Boston Sunday Globe*, February 19, 2006.

11. Hamilton-Garrett Center for Music and Arts website, accessed April 10, 2021, https://www.hamiltongarrett.org/.

12. Bernadette Horgan (director of public relations, Boston Symphony Orchestra, email to the author, April 1, 2021.

Chapter 12

1. Geraldine Walker, interview by the author, Boston, January 5, 2016; Ollie Sumrall Jr.; eight telephone interviews by the author, June 1–11, 2020; Lucy Parham, interview by the author, Boston, January 19, 2016; Elta Garrett, interview by the author, Boston, January 5, 2016; Willie Pittman, interview by the author, Brockton, Massachusetts, December 1, 2015; Charles Gordon, interview by the author, Boston, November 19, 2015.

2. Walker, interview; Sumrall, telephone interviews; Thomas Lindsay, telephone interviews by the author, April 20–22, 2020.

3. Garrett, interview.

4. Parham, interview; Sumrall, telephone interviews; Pittman, interview.

5. Lindsay, telephone interviews; Elizabeth Hall Davis, interview by the author, Boston, November 19, 2015; Pittman, interview; Parham, interview; Walker, interview.

6. Parham, interview; Pittman, interview; Sumrall, telephone interviews.

7. Parham, interview; Pittman, interview; Al Kinnitt Jr., interview by the author, Boston, June 21, 2016; Sumrall, telephone interviews.

8. John R. Logan and Brian Stults, *The Persistence of Segregation in the Metropolis: New Findings from the 2010 Census*, census brief prepared for Project US2010, March 2011, http://www.s4.brown.edu/us2010; Boston Planning & Development Agency, *Historical Boston in Context: Neighborhood Comparisons by Decade, 1950 to 2015* (Boston, 2017).

9. Besheer Mohamed, Kiana Cox, Jeff Diamant, and Claire Gecewicz, "Faith among Black Americans," Pew Research Center, February 16, 2021, https://www.pewforum.org/2021/02/16/faith-among-black-americans/.

10. Lindsay, telephone interviews.

11. Sumrall, telephone interviews; Pittman, interview.

12. For a discussion of one definition of an ethnic group, see Stephan Thernstrom, Ann Orlov, and Oscar Handlin, "Introduction," in *Harvard Encyclopedia of American Ethnic Groups*, ed. Stephan Thernstrom (Cambridge, MA: Harvard University Press, 1980), v–vi.

13. Thomas C. Holt, "African Americans," in *Harvard Encyclopedia of American Ethnic Groups*, ed. Stephan Thernstrom (Cambridge, MA: Harvard University Press, 1980),

5–23; Thomas C. Holt, "Black Life," in *Encyclopedia of Southern Culture*, ed. Charles Reagan Wilson and William Ferris (Chapel Hill: University of North Carolina Press, 1989), 137.

14. William H. Frey, "The New Great Migration: Black Americans' Return to the South, 1965–2000" (Washington, DC: Brookings Institution, 2004).

15. Parham, interview.

16. Steven Ruggles, Sarah Flood, Ronald Goeken, Josiah Grover, Erin Meyer, Jose Pacas and Matthew Sobek, IPUMS USA: Version 10.0 [(dataset) (Minneapolis, MN: IPUMS, 2020), https://doi.org/10.18128/D010.V10.0.

17. US Bureau of the Census, *Characteristics of the Population: Detailed Population Characteristics, Massachusetts* (Washington, DC, 1983).

18. T. J. Matthew and Brade E. Hamilton, "Total Fertility Rates by State and Race and Hispanic Origin: United States, 2017," *National Vital Statistics Reports* 68:1 (January 10, 2019): 6. Black women in Massachusetts had an average of 1.89 children.

19. US Bureau of the Census, American Community Survey, Five-Year Estimates, 2015–19, accessed March 28, 2021, https://data.census.gov/cedsci/.

20. See, for example, Thomas H. O'Connor, *The Boston Irish: A Political History* (Boston: Back Bay Books, 1997); Jonathan D. Sarna, Ellen Smith and Scott-Martin Kosofsky, eds., *The Jews of Boston* (New Haven: Yale University Press, 2005); Michael Liu, *Forever Struggle: Activism, Identity, and Survival in Boston's Chinatown, 1880–2018* (Amherst: University of Massachusetts Press, 2020); Peggy Levitt, *The Transnational Villagers* (Berkeley: University of California Press, 2001); Mario Luis Small, *Villa Victoria: The Transformation of Social Capital in a Boston Barrio* (Chicago: University of Chicago Press, 2004); Karin Aguilar-San Juan, *Little Saigons: Staying Vietnamese in America* (Minneapolis: University of Minnesota Press, 2009).

21. Federal Reserve Bank of Boston, *The Color of Wealth in Boston*, March 25, 2015, https://www.bostonfed.org/publications/one-time-pubs/color-of-wealth.aspx; Danny McDonald, "As Acting Boston Mayor, Kim Janey Appeared to Have a Leg Up in the Race. So How Did She Lose?," *Boston Globe*, September 21, 2021, https://www.bostonglobe.com/2021/09/21/metro/acting-mayor-kim-janey-appeared-have-leg-up-race-so-how-did-she-lose/; Deanna Pan and Dasia Moore, "A New Survey Says White Support for Black Lives Matter Has Slipped; Some Historians Say They're Not Surprised," *Boston Globe*, September 4, 2020, https://www.bostonglobe.com/2020/09/24/metro/new-survey-says-white-support-black-lives-matter-has-slipped-some-historians-say-theyre-not-surprised/.

Additional Reading

The Great Migration

Abel, Emily K. and Margaret K. Nelson. *Limited Choices: Mable Jones, a Black Children's Nurse in a Northern White Household*. Charlottesville: University of Virginia Press, 2021.

Adelman, Robert and Stewart E. Tolnay. "Occupational Status of Immigrants and African Americans at the Beginning and End of the Great Migration." *Sociological Perspectives* 46 (2004): 179–206.

Adero, Malaika. *Up South: Stories, Studies and Letters of This Century's African-American Migrations*. New York: New Press, 1993.

Alexander, J. Trent. "The Great Migration in Comparative Perspective: Interpreting the Urban Origins of Southern Black Migrants to Depression-Era Pittsburgh." *Social Science History* 22:3 (August 1998): 349–76.

Alexander, J. Trent, Christine Leibbrand, Catherine G. Massey, and Stewart E. Tolnay. "Second-Generation Outcomes of the Great Migration." *Demography* 54:6 (2017): 2249–71.

Arnesen, Eric. *Black Protest and the Great Migration: A Brief History with Documents*. Boston: Bedford / St. Martin's, 2003.

Baldwin, Davarian L. *Chicago's New Negroes: Modernity, the Great Migration, and Black Urban Life*. Chapel Hill: University of North Carolina Press, 2007.

Barnes, L. Diane. "Great Migration." In *Encyclopedia of African American History, 1896 to the Present*, edited by Paul Finkelman, 326–29. Oxford: Oxford University Press, 2009.

Battat, Erin Royston. *Ain't Got No Home: America's Great Migrations and the Making of an Interracial Left*. Chapel Hill: University of North Carolina Press, 2014.

Berlin, Ira. *The Making of African America: The Four Great Migrations*. New York: Viking, 2010.

Black, Timuel D., Jr. *Bridges of Memory: Chicago's First Wave of Black Migration*. Evanston, IL: Northwestern University Press, 2003.

Blocker, Jack S., Jr. *A Little More Freedom: African Americans Enter the Urban Midwest, 1860–1930*. Columbus: Ohio State University Press, 2008.

Boehm, Lisa Krissoff. *Making a Way Out of No Way: African American Women and the Second Great Migration*. Jackson: University Press of Mississippi, 2010.

Bunch-Lyons, Beverly. *Contested Terrain: African American Women Migrate from the South to Cincinnati, Ohio, 1900–1950*. New York: Routledge, 2002.

Chatelain, Marcia. *South Side Girls: Growing Up in the Great Migration*. Durham, NC: Duke University Press, 2015.

Close, Stacey K. "Black Southern Migration and the Transformation of Connecticut." In *African American Connecticut Explored*, edited by Elizabeth J. Normen, 239–52. Middletown, CT: Wesleyan University Press, 2013.

Close, Stacey K. "Black Southern Migration, Black Immigrants, Garveyism, and the Transformation of Black Hartford, 1917–1922." *Griot* 22:1 (Spring 2003): 55–68.

Coles, Robert. *The South Goes North. Children of Crisis*, vol. 3. Boston: Atlantic Monthly Press, 1971.

Cressler, Matthew J. *Authentically Black and Truly Catholic: The Rise of Black Catholicism in the Great Migration*. New York: New York University Press, 2017.

Eichenlaub, Suzanne C., Stewart E. Tolnay, and J. Trent Alexander. "Moving Out but Not Up: Economic Outcomes in the Great Migration." *American Sociological Review* 75:1 (2010): 101–25.

Frey, William H. "The New Great Migration: Black Americans' Return to the South, 1965–2000." Washington, DC: Brookings Institution, 2004.

Gerardo, G. Mehera. "Great Migration, Second." In *Encyclopedia of African American History, 1896 to the Present*, edited by Paul Finkelman, 329–31. Oxford: Oxford University Press, 2009.

Goodwin, E. Marvin. *Black Migration in America from 1915 to 1960: An Uneasy Exodus*. Lewiston, NY: E. Mellen Press, 1990.

Gottlieb, Peter. *Making Their Own Way: Southern Blacks' Migration to Pittsburgh, 1916–1930*. Urbana: University of Illinois Press, 1987.

Grant, Keneshia Nicole. *The Great Migration and the Democratic Party: Black Voters and the Realignment of American Politics in the 20th Century*. Philadelphia: Temple University Press, 2020.

Greenwood, Janette Thomas. *First Fruits of Freedom: The Migration of Former Slaves and Their Search for Equality in Worcester, Massachusetts, 1862–1900*. Chapel Hill: University of North Carolina Press, 2009.

Gregory, James N. "The Second Great Migration: A Historical Overview." In *African American Urban History since World War II*, edited by Kenneth L. Kusmer and Joe W. Trotter, 19–38. Chicago: University of Chicago Press, 2009.

Gregory, James N. *The Southern Diaspora: How the Great Migrations of Black and White Southerners Transformed America*. Chapel Hill: University of North Carolina Press, 2005.

Griffin, Farah Jasmine. *"Who Set You Flowin'?": The African-American Migration Narrative*. New York: Oxford University Press, 1995.

Groh, George W. *The Black Migration: The Journey to Urban America*. New York: Weybright and Talley, 1972.

Grossman, James. *Land of Hope: Chicago, Black Southerners, and the Great Migration*. Chicago: University of Chicago Press, 1989.

Hamilton, Horace C. "The Negro Leaves the South." *Demography* 1 (1959): 273–95.

Hamilton, Tullia Brown. *Up from Canaan: The African American Journey from Mound Bayou to St. Louis*. St. Louis: PenUltimate Press, 2011.

Harris, Laurie Lanzen. *The Great Migration North, 1910–1970*. Detroit: Omnigraphics, 2011.

Harrison, Alferdteen, editor. *Black Exodus: The Great Migration from the American South*. Jackson: University Press of Mississippi, 1991.

Hartman, Ian C. and David Reamer "A 'Far North Dixie Land': Black Settlement, Discrimination, and Community in Urban Alaska." *Western Historical Quarterly* 51:1 (Spring 2020): 29–48.

Henri, Florette. *Black Migration: The Movement North, 1900–1920*. Garden City, NY: Anchor Press / Doubleday, 1975.

Hunt, Matthew O., Larry L. Hunt, and William W. Falk. "Twenty-First-Century Trends in Black Migration to the U.S. South: Demographic and Subjective Predictors." *Social Science Quarterly* 94 (2013): 1398–413.

Jerkins, Morgan. *Wandering in Strange Lands: A Daughter of the Great Migration Reclaims Her Roots*. New York: Harper, 2020.

Johnson, Daniel M. and Rex R. Campbell. *Black Migration in America: A Social Demographic History*. Durham, NC: Duke University Press, 1981.

Jones, Tom. *On a Burning Deck: The Road to Akron. An Oral History of the Great Migration*. Columbia, SC: CreateSpace, 2017.

Kiser, Clyde Vernon. *Sea Island to City: A Study of St. Helena Islanders in Harlem and Other Urban Centers*. New York: Atheneum, 1969.

Leavell, R. H., T. R. Snavely, T. J. Woofter Jr., and W. T. B Williams. *Negro Migration in 1916–17*. US Department of Labor, Division of Negro Economics. Washington, DC: Government Printing Office, 1919.

Leibbrand, Christine, Catherine Massey, J. Trent Alexander, Katie R. Genadek, and Stewart Tolnay. "The Great Migration and Residential Segregation in American Cities during the Twentieth Century." *Social Science History* 44:1 (2020): 19–55.

Lemak, Jennifer A. *Southern Life, Northern City: The History of Albany's Rapp Road Community*. Albany: State University of New York Press, 2008.

Lemann, Nicholas. *The Promised Land: The Great Black Migration and How It Changed America*. New York: Alfred A. Knopf, 1991.

Logan, John R., Weiwei Zhang, Richard Turner, and Allison Shertzer. "Creating the Black Ghetto: Black Residential Patterns before and during the Great Migration." *Annals of the American Academy of Political and Social Science* 660:1 (2015): 18–35.

Marks, Carole. *Farewell, We're Good and Gone: The Great Black Migration*. Bloomington: Indiana University Press, 1989.

McCammack, Brian. *Landscapes of Hope: Nature and the Great Migration in Chicago*. Cambridge, MA: Harvard University Press, 2017.

Muller, Christopher. "Northward Migration and the Rise of Racial Disparity in American Incarceration, 1880–1950." *American Journal of Sociology* 118:2 (2012): 281–326.

Murch, Donna Jean. *Living for the City: Migration, Education, and the Rise of the Black Panther Party in Oakland, California*. Chapel Hill: University of North Carolina Press, 2010.

Painter, Nell Irvin. *Exodusters: Black Migration to Kansas after Reconstruction*. New York: Knopf, 1976.

Phillips, Kimberley L. *Alabama North: African-American Migrants, Community, and Working-Class Activism in Cleveland, 1915–45*. Urbana: University of Illinois Press, 1999.

Phillips, Kimberley L. "'But It Is a Fine Place to Make Money': Migration and African-American Families in Cleveland." *Journal of Social History* 30:2 (1996): 393–413.

Reed, Christopher Robert. *Knock at the Door of Opportunity: Black Migration to Chicago, 1900–1919*. Carbondale: Southern Illinois University Press, 2014.

Reich, Steven A. *The Great Black Migration: A Historical Encyclopedia of the American Mosaic*. Santa Barbara, CA: ABC-CLIO, 2014.

Rodgers, Lawrence R. *Canaan Bound: The African-American Great Migration Novel*. Urbana: University of Illinois Press, 1997.

Rutkoff, Peter M. and William B. Scott. *Fly Away: The Great African American Cultural Migrations*. Baltimore: Johns Hopkins University Press, 2015.

Schlichting, Kurt, Peter Tuckel, and Richard Maisel. "Great Migration of African Americans to Hartford, Connecticut, 1910–1930: A GIS Analysis at the Neighborhood and Street Level." *Social Science History* 39:2 (2015): 287–310.

Schlichting, Kurt, Peter Tuckel, and Richard Maisel. "Residential Segregation and the Beginning of the Great Migration of African Americans to Hartford, Connecticut: A GIS-Based Analysis." *Historical Methods* 39:3 (Summer 2006): 132–42.

Scott, Emmett J. *Negro Migration during the War.* Carnegie Endowment for International Peace, Preliminary Economic Studies of the War 16. New York: Oxford University Press, 1920.

Sernett, Milton C. *Bound for the Promised Land: African American Religion and the Great Migration.* Durham, NC: Duke University Press, 1997.

Shannon, Sandra G. "A Transplant That Did Not Take: August Wilson's Views on the Great Migration." *African American Review* 50:4 (2017): 979–86.

Tolnay, Stewart E. "The African American 'Great Migration' and Beyond." *Annual Review of Sociology* 29 (2003): 209–33.

Tolnay, Stewart E. "Educational Selection in the Migration of Southern Blacks, 1880–1990." *Social Forces* 77 (December 1998): 487–514.

Tolnay, Stewart E. "The Great Migration and Changes in the Northern Black Family, 1940 to 1990." *Social Forces* 75:4 (1997): 1213–38.

Trotter, Joe William, Jr., editor. *The Great Migration in Historical Perspective: New Dimensions of Race, Class, and Gender.* Bloomington: Indiana University Press, 1991.

Tuckel, Peter, Kurt Schlichting, and Richard Maisel. "Social, Economic, and Residential Diversity within Hartford's African American Community at the Beginning of the Great Migration." *Journal of Black Studies* 37:5 (May 2007): 710–36.

Weisenfeld, Judith. *A New World A-Coming: Black Religion and Racial Identity during the Great Migration.* New York: New York University Press, 2016.

Wilkerson, Isabel. *The Warmth of Other Suns: The Epic Story of America's Great Migration.* New York: Random House, 2010.

Williams, Lasvon Stennis. *The Second Great Migration.* N.p.: Two Bee Publishing, 2021.

Wright, R. R. "The Migration of Negroes to the North." *Annals of the American Academy of Political and Social Science* 27 (May 1906): 97–116.

Black Boston

Bailey, Ronald. *Lower Roxbury: A Community of Treasures in the City of Boston.* Boston: Lower Roxbury Community Corp. / Afro Scholar Press, 1993.

Ballou, Richard Alan. "Even in 'Freedom's Birthplace': The Development of Boston's Back Ghetto, 1900–1940." PhD diss., University of Michigan, 1984.

Bergeson-Lockwood, Millington W. *Race over Party: Black Politics and Partisanship in Late Nineteenth-Century Boston.* Chapel Hill: University of North Carolina Press, 2018.

Carden, Lance. *Witness: An Oral History of Black Politics in Boston, 1920–1960.* Boston: Boston College, 1989.

Clay, Phillip and James Edward Blackwell, editors. *The Emerging Black Community of Boston.* Boston: Institute for the Study of Black Culture, University of Massachusetts, Boston, 1985.

Cromwell, Adelaide M. *The Other Brahmins: Boston's Black Upper Class, 1750–1950.* Fayetteville: University of Arkansas Press, 1994.

Cruz, Tatiana Maria Fernández. "Boston's Struggle in Black and Brown: Racial Politics, Community Development, and Grassroots Organizing, 1960–1985." PhD diss, University of Michigan, 2017.

Daniels, John. *In Freedom's Birthplace*. Boston: Houghton Mifflin, 1914.

Du Bois, W. E. Burghardt. *The Black North in 1901: A Social Study*. New York: Arno Press, 1969.

Edwards, Rheable M. and Laura B. Morris. *The Negro in Boston*. Boston: Action for Boston Community Development, 1961.

Formisano, Ronald. *Boston against Busing: Race, Class, and Ethnicity in the 1960s and 1970s*. Chapel Hill: University of North Carolina Press, 1991.

Gamm, Gerald. *Urban Exodus: Why the Jews Left Boston and the Catholics Stayed*. Cambridge, MA: Harvard University Press, 1999.

Gibau, Gina Sanchez. "Diasporic Identity Formation among Cape Verdeans in Boston." *Western Journal of Black Studies* 29:2 (2005): 532–39.

Greene, Lorenzo Johnston. *The Negro in Colonial New England*. New York: Atheneum, 1971.

Greenidge, Kerri K. *Black Radical: The Life and Times of William Monroe Trotter*. New York: Liveright Publishing, 2020.

Grover, Kathryn and Janine V. da Silva. *Historic Resource Study: Boston African American National Historic Site*. Boston: National Park Service, 2002.

Hancock, Scott. "The Elusive Boundaries of Blackness: Identity Formation in Antebellum Boston." *Journal of Negro History* 84:2 (March 1999): 115–29.

Handlin, Oscar. *Boston's Immigrants, 1790–1880: A Study in Acculturation*. Rev. ed. Cambridge, MA: Belknap Press of Harvard University Press, 1991.

Hayden, Robert C. *African-Americans in Boston: More Than 350 Years*. Boston: Trustees of the Public Library of the City of Boston, 1991.

Hayden, Robert C. *Faith, Culture, and Leadership: A History of the Black Church in Boston*. Boston: Boston Branch, NAACP, 1983.

Hayden, Robert C. "A Historical Overview of Poverty among Blacks in Boston, 1950–1990." *Trotter Review* 17:1 (2007): 135–38.

Hock, Jennifer. "Bulldozers, Busing, and Boycotts: Urban Renewal and the Integrationist Project." *Journal of Urban History* 39:3 (2013): 433–53.

Horton, James Oliver and Louis E. Horton. *Black Bostonians: Family Life and Community Struggle in the Antebellum North*. Rev. ed. New York: Holmes and Meier, 1979.

Jackson, Regine O. "Beyond Social Distancing: Intermarriage and Ethnic Boundaries among Black Americans in Boston." In *The Other African Americans: Contemporary African and Caribbean Immigrants in the United States*, edited by Yoku Shaw-Taylor and Steven A. Tuch, 217–53. Lanham, MD: Rowman & Littlefield, 2007.

Jackson, Regine O. "The Uses of Diaspora among Haitians in Boston." In *Geographies of the Haitian Diaspora*, edited by Regine O. Jackson, 135–62. New York: Routledge, 2011.

Jacobs, Donald M. "The Nineteenth-Century Struggle of Segregated Education in Boston Schools." *Journal of Negro Education* 39 (1970): 76–85.

Jacobs, Donald M. *While the Cabots Talked to God: Racial Conflict in Antebellum Boston. The Black Struggle, 1825–1861*. Boston: Peter Lang, 1991.

Jennings, James and Mel King. *From Access to Power: Black Politics in Boston*. Boston: Schenkman Books, 1986.

Johnson, Akilah et al. "Boston. Racism. Image. Reality." *Boston Globe*, seven-part series, December 10–16, 2017.

Johnson, Marilynn, *The New Bostonians: How Immigrants Have Transformed the Metro Region since the 1960s*. Amherst: University of Massachusetts Press, 2015.

Johnson, Violet Showers. *The Other Black Bostonians: West Indians in Boston, 1900–1950*. Bloomington: Indiana University Press, 2006.

Kantrowitz, Nathan. "Racial and Ethnic Residential Segregation in Boston, 1830–1970." *Annals of the American Academy of Political and Social Science* 441 (January 1979): 41–54.

Kantrowitz, Stephen. *More Than Freedom: Fighting for Black Citizenship in a White Republic, 1829–1889*. New York: Penguin, 2012.

King, Mel. *Chain of Change: Struggles for Boston Community Development*. Boston: South End Press, 1981.

Kozol, Jonathan, *Death at an Early Age: The Destruction of the Hearts and Minds of Negro Children in the Boston Public Schools*. Boston: Houghton Mifflin, 1967.

Levitt, Peggy. *The Transnational Villagers*. Berkeley: University of California Press, 2001.

Mabee, Carlton. "A Negro Boycott to Integrate Boston Schools." *New England Quarterly* 41 (September 1968): 341–61.

McLarin, Kim. "The Great Migration and Me." *Boston Globe Magazine*, October 31, 2010, 6.

McRoberts, Omar M. *Streets of Glory: Church and Community in a Black Urban Neighborhood*. Chicago: University of Chicago Press, 2003.

Miletsky, Zebulon Vance. *Before Busing: A History of Boston's Long Black Freedom Struggle*. Chapel Hill: University of North Carolina Press, 2022.

Miller, Eben Simmons. "'A New Day Is Here': The Shooting of George Borden and 1930s Civil Rights Activism in Boston." *New England Quarterly* 73:1 (2000): 3–31.

Miller, Melvin B., editor. *Boston's Banner Years: 1965–2015. A Saga of Black Success*. Bloomington, IN: Archway Publishing, 2018.

Overbea, Luix. *Black Bostonia*. Boston 200 Neighborhood History Series. Boston: Boston 200 Corp., 1976.

Piersen, William D. *Black Yankees: The Development of an Afro-American Subculture in Eighteenth Century New England*. Amherst: University of Massachusetts Press, 1988.

Pleck, Elizabeth Hafkin. *Black Migration and Poverty: Boston, 1865–1900*. New York: Academic Press, 1979.

Roberts, Jennifer J. "One of Us." *Boston*, October 2014, https://www.bostonmagazine.com/news/2014/10/28/jennifer-roberts-irish-black-race-southie/

Roses, Lorraine Elena. *Black Bostonians and the Politics of Culture, 1920–1940*. Amherst: University of Massachusetts Press, 2017.

Schneider, Mark R. *Boston Confronts Jim Crow, 1890–1920*. Boston: Northeastern University Press, 1997.

Schwartz, Harold. "Fugitive Slave Days in Boston." *New England Quarterly* 27 (June 1954): 191–212.

Taylor, Steven J. L. *Desegregation in Boston and Buffalo: The Influence of Local Leaders*. Albany: State University of New York Press, 1998.

Theoharis, Jeanne F. "'We Saved the City': Black Struggles for Educational Equality in Boston, 1960–1976." *Radical History Review* 81 (Fall 2001): 61–93.

Thernstrom, Stephan. *The Other Bostonians: Poverty and Progress in the American Metropolis, 1880–1970*. Cambridge, MA: Harvard University Press, 1973.

Vrabel, Jim. *A People's History of the New Boston*. Amherst: University of Massachusetts Press, 2014.

Index